African American Families Today

African American Families Today

Myths and Realities

Angela J. Hattery and Earl Smith

ROWMAN & LITTLEFIELD PUBLISHERS, INC.
Lanham • Boulder • New York • Toronto • Plymouth, UK

Published by Rowman & Littlefield Publishers, Inc.
A wholly owned subsidiary of The Rowman & Littlefield Publishing Group, Inc.
4501 Forbes Boulevard, Suite 200, Lanham, Maryland 20706
www.rowman.com

10 Thornbury Road, Plymouth PL6 7PP, United Kingdom

British Library Cataloguing in Publication Information Available

Library of Congress Cataloging-in-Publication Data

Hattery, Angela J., 1966–
  African American families today : myths and realities / Earl Smith and Angela Hattery
    p. cm.
  Includes bibliographical references.
  ISBN 978-1-4422-1396-8 (cloth : alk. paper) — ISBN 978-1-4422-1398-2 (ebook)
  1. African American families. 2. African Americans—Social conditions—1975–
  3. United States—Race relations. I. Smith, Earl. II. Title.
  E185.86.S637 2012
  305.896'073—dc23

                                                                2012028669

∞™ The paper used in this publication meets the minimum requirements of American National Standard for Information Sciences—Permanence of Paper for Printed Library Materials, ANSI/NISO Z39.48-1992.

Printed in the United States of America

Contents

Acknowledgments

The United States enters the twenty-first century with regards to politics, the banking crisis, family formation—especially for gay and lesbian partners—to the ongoing debates on the election of Barack Obama as the first African American in the White House, and each issue proves to be fascinating.

Among others, we highlight some of the key issues leading into the 2012 presidential election. The debate around marriage equality; several states have passed legislation in favor of same-sex marriage, and others, most recently North Carolina voted to affirm and limit marriage to a contract between one man and one woman. Also are the debates over high unemployment and the widening wealth gap between whites and nonwhites.

As any author knows, finding ways to create even-handed discussions and debates on these issues in the framework of a book—and especially a book built around hot button topics—requires help.

In this acknowledgment we thank all of the thinkers, debaters, authors, friends, research assistants, and each other as we traveled the road of thinking about, researching, writing (and rewriting) *African American Families Today: Myths and Realities.*

Without colleagues and friends, who we read, discuss ideas with, agree with and at times disagree with, the ideas set forth here would not have been written. Listing the names of some and not others would be a tragedy so we will just say *thank you.*

To Angela—another project, another book. This book is different by entering the fray of "public sociology" where plain language and telling it like it is, helps us to understand the contemporary US political economy that impacts the life chances of all citizens (and others). The way we did this also allows us to examine specifically the issues and controversies that affect African Americans' life chances on a daily basis. Thanks for partnering in this adventure!

To Earl—In many ways this book feels like the compilation and refining of the issues we talk about and debate during our daily, early morning walks. What fun it has been to be able to take issues that seem either really simple or overly complex and work through them to expose what lies beneath. The claim that women will soon dominate the labor market is one of those issues that is more complex and the mass incarceration is one of those issues that is far both more complex and more nuanced. What a privilege to share our daily conversations with a wider reading audience. Thanks for always pushing me to think outside the box! Our partnership is a true pleasure and privilege.

Introduction

Was "slavery" an idyllic world of stable families headed by married parents? The recent controversy over "The Marriage Vow," a document endorsed by the 2012 Republican presidential candidates Michele Bachmann and Rick Santorum, might seem like just another example of how racial politics and historical ignorance are perennial features of the election cycle. The vow, which included the assertion that "a child born into slavery in 1860 was more likely to be raised by his mother and father in a two-parent household than was an African American baby born after the election of the USA's first African American President," was amended after the outrage it stirred. However, this was not a harmless gaffe.[1]

African American Families Today examines the myths and realities of African American family life and provides the reader with a critical examination of contemporary life chances for African Americans. It is essential in that we ask hard questions and examine facts rather than rely simply on perceptions to interrogate the often-heard assertion that the election of the first African American president of the United States has dramatically improved the lives of African Americans and their families.

We begin, in the introduction, by outlining the structure of the book, which we have chosen as a deliberate mechanism designed to impart a sociological analysis of the current state of African American families in a manner that is accessible to the nonsociologically trained student of the question. In short, our analytical strategy is to begin each chapter with a popularly held myth about an aspect of African American families. We then devote the bulk of the chapter to debunking the myth, using scientifically derived evidence that is presented in a way that is easily accessible. We provide the sources of these data not only to satisfy our critics, but because our greater aim is to distill the mystery of much of the sociological research and jargon so that the interested reader can go directly to the source and decide for him- or herself whether the myth is grounded in reality or not. As far as our credentials for writing this book and offering this challenge to readers, both the authors hold doctorates in sociology and have authored seven other books together, another four or five books between them, and dozens of peer-reviewed articles and book chapters.

Next we provide a brief overview and examination of the state of African American families today, during the term of the first African American president of the United States. Along the way we introduce the concept of a "postracial" society as well as discuss the ways in which scientific knowledge is generated and evaluated and how it will be used in this book.

THE CONCEPT OF A POSTRACIAL AMERICA

A great deal of scholarship as well as political rhetoric focused on the effects of the election of Barack Obama on our country, on African Americans in our country, and on whites and other racial or ethnic groups. The assumption is typically that Obama's election is indicative of such a deep transformation that it signals or allows for a boundary crossing, passing out of the painful history of slavery and Jim Crow segregation into what many term a postracial America. And, though this debate is not the central focus of our book, it *is the framework* that shapes both the book but also many of the myths that we use to investigate the state of African American families, and thus it is critical to engage this concept briefly here and throughout the text.

Specifically, as part of our in-depth exploration of the state of African Americans and their families in the period after the election of the first African American president we will interrogate the notion that the election of Barack Obama has heralded in or at the very least signaled this so-called postracial America; an America where race no longer matters, where we are all one big happy family wearing our color-blind glasses. We will argue definitively throughout that the election of Barack Obama symbolizes neither; that in fact we still live in a society that is characterized as much by racial discord as by notions of "the land of the free and the home of the brave"; a land in which the opportunity to go to college instead of prison remains shaped by race and social class. And, a nation in which life chances for all Americans lie at the intersections of race and social class.

This is a bold claim, and though we will devote eleven chapters to making our argument, we share an anecdote from the writing process. We were working on the book manuscript on the tenth "anniversary" of the bombing of the World Trade Center Twin Towers on September 11, 2001. Like many Americans we spent many hours that day watching various aspects of the televised memorial. We witnessed numerous survivors recount the last communication they had with their loved ones inside the towers or on airplanes headed toward destruction. During the broadcast, we were struck by the diversity of those murdered: men, women, children, Americans of every race, ethnicity, and national origin. It felt like watching the patchwork quilt that we were raised to believe characterizes our country. Around the same time, the commemorative issue of *Time* magazine, entitled "Beyond 9/11: Portraits of Resilience,"[2] arrived in our mailbox. Inside the pages of the photo-rich commemorative edition dedicated to the tenth anniversary of the September 11, 2001, terrorist attacks, *no African Americans are pictured in its sixty-four pages.*

We know from our research that African Americans were not only killed in the 9/11 attacks but also died attempting to search for and rescue those trapped in the towers. African Americans searched in their professional capacity as firefighters, police officers, and first responders, as well as regular, run-of-the-mill heroes who were simply responding to the crisis. These gross omissions—emblematic of the myriad of ways in which race is very much still at the core of life in the United States—remind us of Ralph Ellison's profound literary meditation on American citizenship in his novel, *The Invisible Man*, which he opens by saying: "I am an invisible man . . . simply because people refuse to see me."[3]

Written in 1953 Ellison captured the invisibility that we see again as African Americans struggle to gain a foothold on their contemporary life chances.

STRUCTURE OF THE BOOK

The book is organized in three key ways: (1) around issues, (2) by exploring the ways in which myths are used to perpetuate misunderstandings about African Americans and their families, and (3) by including compelling stories that debunk myths and commonly held beliefs. In terms of issues, we will devote a chapter to discussing each of the following concerns plaguing African Americans and their families: marriage and divorce, childrearing practices, teen childbearing, intimate partner violence, the role of athletics in the African American community, education, poverty and wealth, incarceration, and politics. We will begin each chapter by providing a brief summary of the issue; answering the questions: (1) what is it? (2) who does it impact? (3) why does it matter? Rather than simply assembling facts to address the status of African Americans and their families with regards to each issue, we will use commonly held myths or beliefs to engage the facts that pertain to each issue. Additionally, we will address the myths based on the typical perspectives of various relevant groups, for example, politicians, teachers, landlords, employers, and so forth. Lastly, we will provide compelling stories of individuals whose lives demonstrate the inaccuracies of myths and stereotypes as they are applied to real people. Stories may come from research—ours and that of others'—as well as from popular news sources, including the *New York Times.*

In the end we argue that despite the optimism associated with the election of the first African American president, that in fact, for a variety of reasons, the state of the African American community has not improved in any significant manner since his election. And, instead, a few years into the "postracial" society marked by the historic election finds more African Americans in poverty and in prison, more African American babies born to single mothers, and fewer African Americans graduating from high school than in any decade, including the height of Jim Crow segregation, that immediately preceded the civil rights movement.

OVERVIEW OF THE STATE OF AFRICAN AMERICAN FAMILIES IN THE FIRST DECADE OF THE TWENTY-FIRST CENTURY

Watching any news program or listening to talk radio in the months immediately following the election of Barack Obama, much of the rhetoric revolved around the degree to which the election meant that the United States had become a "post-racial" society.

What does it mean to live in a postracial society? The common understanding is that it means, quite simply, that race no longer matters.

Debaters on the TV and radio talk shows argued about whether the election of Barack Obama heralded in and signaled the fact that race no longer matters in the United States; something that would come as a welcome relief to victims of racism, especially African Americans whose entire existence on this continent has been shaped by race, as well as to liberal whites who are tired of apologizing for being "white" and are tired of feeling as if they have to take responsibility for a racist structure they don't believe they had any part in building. "I didn't own slaves so this is not my problem!"

As important, much debate in the public sphere, both during the months leading up to the 2008 presidential election and to those immediately following the inauguration of President Obama, focused on the ways in which the election of an African American president would change the lives of African Americans. We consider the concern, or hope—depending on whose perspective we are taking—that the election of Obama would translate into changes in the lives of everyday African Americans by using the rhetorical mechanism that we will utilize throughout each chapter: by examining a myth through the lens of theoretical or data-driven arguments.

Myth: White Americans expressed concerns that the election of an African American president would significantly shift resources and opportunities to African Americans and away from white Americans.

Reality: Interestingly, to hold this belief one must simultaneously hold the belief that white Americans received benefits simply for being white, and that these benefits were specifically tied to the person occupying the Oval Office, in this case, as it has always been, a white man. For members of white supremacy groups, this belief makes sense; they *do* believe in a racialized order. But, even most conservative white Americans would not admit to holding a belief that they personally benefited from being white, rather they tend to believe that they *earned* what they have achieved. This belief, in white achievement (and blacks' inability to achieve) raises two additional myths.

Myth: White people earn what they achieve.

In fact, data on wealth and poverty reveal that the vast majority of Americans—regardless of their race—stay in the same social class that they were born into; and among those who do move, most move down, not up.[4]

Thus, the myth that Americans—of any race—pull themselves up from their bootstraps is just that, a myth. The vast majority of wealthy Americans were born wealthy. And, contrary to popular belief, in fact, very few Americans who are born poor, white or African American, are ever able to achieve financial success. For example, data released in early 2012[5] revealed that despite this popular myth, nearly half of men who were born in the bottom 20 percent of families based on social class stayed there as adults; only 8 percent improved their social class standing. Conversely, nearly two-thirds of Americans born in the top 20 percent stay in the top 20 percent as adults. In other words, despite our ideology of class mobility in the United States, class is more likely to be determined by birth and passed on intergenerationally, a topic we will explore at much more length in this book.

Myth: African American people need to rely on "special treatment" to obtain success.

Belief in this myth is captured by examining attitudes toward affirmative action policies. Most Americans—white and African American—who oppose affirmative action essentially believe that these policies *give* people something they couldn't otherwise obtain because they are lazy or inferior; admission to college or a job offer under affirmative action are considered by critics to be a handout. In contrast, proponents of affirmative action argue that these policies are designed to address the cumulative advantages and disadvantages that accrued over the centuries of racial discrimination in the United States.

Not surprisingly, there is a huge racial divide in attitudes toward affirmative action. The vast majority of African Americans believe it is a policy that is necessary to "level the playing field" created by 200 plus years of slavery and 100 more years of Jim Crow segregation. Because the majority of whites believe that their own success is achieved from their own behavior, they assume that others, namely African Americans, could achieve more if they worked harder and focused more on upward mobility. They are, for the most part, resistant to affirmative action because it reinforces their beliefs that African Americans are unwilling to work for their successes and that most African Americans believe that they are entitled—as a "payback" for slavery—to a handout. As noted, this belief system ignores the fact that most white Americans who have "achieved" success were actually born into it!

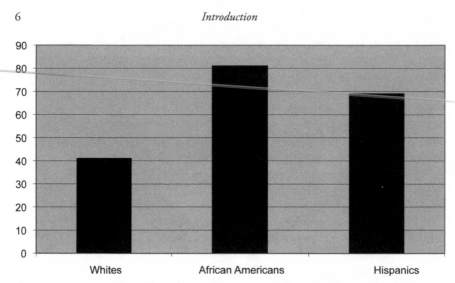

Figure I.1. Support for Affirmative Action (percent of people who support it) by race and ethnicity.

Some African Americans are also opposed to affirmative action as well, based on their belief that it undermines the abilities that African Americans have. In other words, opponents suggest that to support affirmative action policies is to believe that African Americans are *unable* to achieve on their own. It is important to note that much of the fiercest opposition to affirmative action policies by *African Americans* comes from those who personally benefited from affirmative action yet believe that their successes were entirely their own. Clarence Thomas is a case in point as he consistently has sought to weaken, if not abolish, affirmative action especially in the areas of schooling and work. Justice Thomas concurred with Chief Justice John Roberts in *Parents Involved in Community Schools v. Seattle School District No. 1*, where Roberts said "the way to stop discrimination on the basis of race is to stop discriminating on the basis of race." Thomas followed with this: "if our history has taught us anything, it has taught us to beware of elites bearing racial theories. . ." and "Our Constitution is color-blind."[6] And, yet, his biographers, especially Kevin Merida and Michael Fletcher, offer evidence that Thomas's admission to both Holy Cross and Yale Law School were a result of affirmative action.

Ironically, some African Americans who favor affirmative action policies, and understand the focus of these policies on structural disadvantages created by slavery and Jim Crow segregation, nevertheless may also believe somewhere deep in their hearts in the myth that opportunities are handed down to people who "look like" the president. For example, Tom Joyner, one of the few, and by far the most widely listened to African American radio talk show host, expressed expectations that an African American president would pay attention to the plight of African American people and provide opportunities for those who had been left on the outside of the institutions built and administered by whites. We should note that since the election he, along with public intellectual Tavis Smiley, has been one of the most vocal voices complaining that the election of Obama has done nothing for the African American community.

THE IMPACT OF AN AFRICAN AMERICAN PRESIDENT ON THE LIVES OF EVERYDAY AFRICAN AMERICANS

The fact is, that on virtually any measure of well-being or success, though a few African Americans have seen their lives improve and a few have had opportunities open up for them, the vast majority of African Americans are living *less well* than they did in the years leading up to the election of Barack Obama, and very few have seen new and better opportunities come their way since his election.

Now, three years after the inauguration of Barack Obama, at the beginning of 2012, African Americans are incarcerated at increasingly higher rates, high school dropout rates are higher than ever, fewer African Americans are enrolling in or graduating from college or earning advanced or professional degrees, more African Americans are living in poverty—the wealth gap between whites and African Americans has grown ever wider—and African Americans are more likely to die in their first year of life and they can expect to live shorter lives than white Americans. These measures of well-being are so disturbing and so important that discussions of each generate the key content of the book.

Clearly the recession that began prior to the 2010 presidential election set some of these processes in motion. For example, unemployment rates are at an all-time high—at rates not seen since the Great Depression—for all groups of Americans; the average continues to hover just below the double-digit mark. Yet, contrary to popular belief and perhaps expectations on the part of both white Americans and African Americans, when improvements in employment are seen, they tend to come from white Americans (and men) first, while African Americans continue to lag behind. For example, though the unemployment rate dipped slightly in early 2011, *unemployment rates for African Americans remain twice as high as those of white Americans.*

Of course, many whites and African Americans consider the enormous success of African Americans—including Barack Obama, Oprah Winfrey, and some professional athletes and celebrities like Michael Jordan, Tiger Woods, and Jay-Z—as evidence that inequities in employment, occupational opportunities, and pay have vanished. In fact these kinds of success have been achieved by *a very small number* of African Americans while the vast majority of African Americans are worse off than they were prior to Obama's election and they remain worse off than the average white American. How can these enormous successes be balanced against the data that demonstrate that African Americans are more likely to be unemployed, undereducated, and poor? We find Eugene Robinson's framework useful in explaining these competing observations.

Robinson argues that the historic *Brown v. The Topeka Board of Education* decision ushered in both the integration of social life and the often-invisible decimation of the African American community. The African American community was so severely fractured and divided that at the beginning of the third millennium, Robinson argues that there are at least four distinct African American communities. It is important to understand the process—which Robinson describes as "disintegration"—that led to the fracturing and reconfiguring of the African American community, and thus we briefly summarize Robinson's argument.

In short, Robinson argues that the severe restrictions of Jim Crow that required complete housing segregation, coupled with denying African Americans access to "whites-only" educational institutions, treatment in "whites-only" hospitals, opportunities to shop in "whites-only" department stores, and eat at "whites-only" restaurants led to the development of "exclusive" African American neighborhoods alongside the development of African American owned businesses and African American run institutions that serviced the African American community. As a result of both of these requirements of Jim Crow, namely housing segregation and the refusal of any service to African Americans, two important structures emerged: (1) diverse African American neighborhoods, and (2) diverse clients seeking services in African American owned businesses and African American run institutions, such as hospitals and universities.

Housing has been and remains one of the most segregated aspects of life in America. Prior to the civil rights movement, African Americans absolutely could not rent or buy homes in white neighborhoods. Most African Americans, regardless of their social class, lived in the same neighborhoods, which resulted in these neighborhoods being relatively diverse in terms of social class. And, even when they weren't totally integrated by social class, because whites relegated African Americans to living in less desirable and often smaller areas of the city, affluent, middle-class, and poor neighborhoods bordered each other in ways that created frequent contact among African Americans of differing social classes and occupations. So, for example, whereas poor, low-income, working-class, middle-class, professional and affluent whites lived in *separate neighborhoods*, it was very common in African American communities for plumbers, school teachers, and even doctors to all live in or on the edge of the same neighborhoods with the only exception being for the very affluent—like Alonzo Herndon of Atlanta or Frederick Douglass of Washington, D.C.—and the very, very poor. As a result, the African American *community* was diverse and yet had a shared interest: in this case safe and affordable housing and neighborhoods.

Similarly with regards to access to institutions, though there were variations in the prestige of universities, all African Americans who were college educated had to attend one of a very small number of black colleges. Thus, just like the neighborhood, networks that college educated African Americans carried into adulthood crossed over all kinds of professional and occupational lines. And, being a "Morehouse Man" or a "Spellman Woman"—the elite of the black colleges and universities—was likely more important than whether that education led to being a dentist or a second grade teacher. Furthermore, because few African Americans became dentists, for example, and because of strict codes of segregation, in any given community, it was typically the case that most African Americans went to the same dentist, attended the same schools and churches, and bought their produce from the same grocer. All of this, like neighborhood segregation, led to a shared sense of community and self-interest in spite of other distinctions. All African Americans, regardless of social class, could rally around the same demands, such as the right to vote, the right to move into any neighborhood, and school integration.

Along came integration and the unintended and unforeseen, as Robinson argues, disintegration of the African American community.[7] When the opportunity came for professional African Americans to attend elite white colleges or buy houses in elite white neighborhoods many chose to do so. And, when they did, not only did they have the opportunity to mix and mingle with white Americans, but the ties they once had with middle-class or working-class African Americans were broken.

Robinson argues that this disintegration—which is based on the fault lines of social class—fractured the African American community into four distinct and totally disconnected subcommunities. The effect of all of the issues we examine in this book on the so-called African American community depends significantly on the location of African American individuals and families in this fractured community. In other words, when we examine everything from marriage rates to educational attainment to unemployment and incarceration things look completely different for affluent and professional African Americans than for those who live at the bottom of the income distribution.

Robinson argues that as the fracturing and disintegration has taken place an unbridgeable gap has been created between the most affluent and the poorest African Americans and the two groups in between. Even though they share some interactions and interests with their "neighbors," the lack of shared space and interests has led to each of the four groups occupying distinct spheres within social life, the political world, and the economy. Robinson suggests that instead of one black America, now there are four:

1. a mainstream middle-class majority with a full ownership stake in American society
2. a large, abandoned minority with less hope of escaping poverty and dysfunction than at any time since Reconstruction's crushing end
3. a small transcendent elite with such enormous wealth, power, and influence that even white folks have to genuflect
4. two newly emergent groups—individuals of mixed-race heritage and communities of recent black immigrants—that make us wonder what "black" is even supposed to mean[8]

We find Robinson's argument not only useful but compelling, and as we move through the discussions in this book we will be mindful to point out to the reader the degree to which a phenomenon affects the entire African American community or if, as Robinson suggests, there really is no monolithic African American community, and thus the impact of any policy or phenomenon will be shaped by both race and also the social location of African Americans inside of this ever-widening, ever-complex entity we call the "African American community."

For example, across all sectors in the economy, African Americans are more likely than whites to be unemployed. Yet, when we look at the most disadvantaged of the unemployed—the long-term unemployed—the decision of the Obama administration to cut, rather than extend, benefits to the long-term unemployed affects the "abandoned" in ways that it does not affect the large middle-class, emergent community, or transcendents. Our discussions in the subsequent chapters will explore the complexities of this, and other issues, in much greater depth.

Similarly, with regards to the expectation—either hoped or feared—that an African American president would create opportunities disproportionately for "his own kind," we point out that the majority of appointments at the highest levels of government continue to accrue to white Americans, and disproportionately to white men. For example, the Obama appointments to secretary of state and secretary of defense both went to whites (albeit secretary of state went to a white woman) both of which had been held by African Americans in the Bush administration. The reader will recall that Colin Powell was secretary of defense and Condoleezza Rice was the national security advisor *at the same time*, which is all the more extraordinary given that these are undeniably two of the most important and influential positions in the US government.

Among the nominations that drew the most criticism were the two key appointments that Obama had the opportunity to make to the US Supreme Court. Prior to his election, the potential to nominate justices to the highest court in the land was among the most concerning to those who feared the election of an African American president or a Democrat of any race. As the reader will recall, Obama had the opportunity to nominate two justices in his first year in office. And, though his nomination of Sonia Sotomayor put the first Hispanic American on the bench, and her nomination along with that of Elena Kegan, extended the presence of women on the bench, Clarence Thomas remains the only African American on the bench. The reader will recall that Thomas is only the second African American to serve on the Supreme Court—being appointed after the retirement of Thurgood Marshall—and perhaps most striking in Obama's nominations was the clear absence of the opportunity being extended to an African American woman.

Now that the reader has a flavor of the journey we will take in this book, we turn now to an examination of the marriage, divorce, and family structure in the African American community.

1

Marriage and Divorce

Why Are All the Black Men Marrying White Women?

His story is the American story—values from the heartland, a middle-class upbringing in a strong family, hard work and education as the means of getting ahead, and the conviction that a life so blessed should be lived in service to others.

He was raised with help from his grandfather, who served in Patton's army, and his grandmother, who worked her way up from the secretarial pool to middle management at a bank.

After working his way through college with the help of scholarships and student loans, he moved to Chicago, where he worked with a group of churches to help rebuild communities devastated by the closure of local steel plants.

He went on to attend law school, where he served as the president of the *Harvard Law Review*. Upon graduation, he returned to Chicago to help lead a voter registration drive and teach constitutional law at the University of Chicago.

She grew up in a brick bungalow on the South Side of Chicago. Her father was a pump operator for the Chicago Water Department, and despite being diagnosed with multiple sclerosis at a young age, he hardly ever missed a day of work. Her mother stayed home to raise her and her older brother, skillfully managing a busy household filled with love, laughter, and important life lessons.

A product of Chicago public schools, she studied sociology and African American studies at Princeton University. After graduating from Harvard Law School in 1988, she joined the Chicago law firm Sidley and Austin, where she later met the man who would become the love of her life.

In 1996, she joined the University of Chicago with a vision of bringing campus and community together. As Associate Dean of Student Services, she developed the university's first community service program, and under her leadership as Vice President of Community and External Affairs for the University of Chicago Medical Center, volunteerism skyrocketed.[1]

The couple married in October 1992. They are raising two daughters.

Who is this mystery family? This description was written based on the official White House biographies for Barack and Michelle Obama. When you read the description did you automatically assume the family was white? If so, why? Because they attended Ivy League universities? Because they held prestigious jobs? Because they are married?

This chapter will address the myth that African Americans don't marry anyone and especially not each other. We will explore marriage and divorce patterns in African American families across the first decade of the twenty-first century. In addition to providing the facts on marriage and divorce rates, we will examine the myths and realities and consider the lives of well-known African Americans who have chosen to marry and stayed married despite the overall trends in lower rates of marriage in the United States overall, and among African Americans in particular.

Myth: African Americans don't marry because (1) slavery broke the African American family and it has never been repaired, and (2) they are of a lower moral character.

Reality: Though African Americans have the lowest rates of marriage of all racial or ethnic groups in the United States, half of all African Americans do marry, and because of the history of beliefs and laws that discouraged or prohibited interracial marriages involving African Americans, when they do marry, they are most likely to marry each other.

MARRIAGE AND SLAVERY

It is a commonly held belief that lower rates of marriage among African Americans can be traced directly to the experiences of slavery. Specifically the argument goes that because African Americans did not marry during slavery that they did not develop a strong sense of the sanctity of marriage as it is defined in Judeo-Christian traditions. Furthermore, this perception that African Americans have a lack of respect for marriage, deeply rooted in a religious understanding of the purposes and goals of marriage, expanded like a helium balloon into a deeper and more damaging myth that African Americans did not marry—or do many other things—because they were less morally developed than white Americans.

In 1787, while serving as an ambassador in France and just a few years before he was to begin his term as secretary of state, Thomas Jefferson wrote of enslaved African Americans:

> In general their existence appears to participate more of sensation than reflection. . . . [I]n memory they are equal to whites, in reason much inferior. . . . [and]in imagination they are dull, tasteless, and anomalous. . . . I advance it therefore . . . that the blacks, whether originally a different race, or made distinct by time and circumstances, are inferior to whites. . . . Will not a lover of natural history, then, one who views the grada-

tions in all the animals with the eye of philosophy, excuse an effort to keep those in the department of Man (sic) as distinct as nature has formed them.[2]

In fact, though slavery did disrupt the families of those who were captured in Africa and enslaved in the colonies and early United States, *there is no evidence that it led to a decline in the moral character of either slaves or their descendants.* Much like the debate over gay marriage in the first decade of the twenty-first century, the primary causes of the disruption of slave marriages and families were institutional: (1) slaves were legally prohibited from marrying, and (2) members of slave families were bought and sold at the will of the plantation owner and as a result they were often separated despite their desire to live together.

There are many reasons why slaves were not allowed to enter either legal or religious marriages: they were considered to be less than fully human or as Jefferson notes; they were of limited intellectual capacity; and, they were prohibited from entering religious marriages, which rely on the individuals' abilities to comprehend the covenant they are making with God and with each other. Legally, their status as 3/5ths of a human (as laid out in the Dred Scot decision of 1849) and the patronizing mentality of planters—including Jefferson—which led to the perception that the enslaved were childlike, with limited intellectual capacity, prevented them from meeting the requirements for entering into legal contracts. On these grounds they were denied the access to the legal institution of marriage, as well as any other contractual relationship, including landownership.

But, beyond all of these legal and religious justifications for preventing slave marriages, many plantation owners opposed slave marriages for practical reasons, namely they did not want to encourage the development of strong bonds that would lead to problems when slaves were sold, and they wanted to be able to control the breeding of slaves, both with each other and with the plantation owner himself. As one can imagine, no plantation owner who is raping or engaging in nonconsensual sex with his female property, for the purposes of pleasure or reproduction, would want the drama that would ensue if she were married. Furthermore, plantation owners had to constantly manage the issue of security and the probability of slaves running away to reconstitute families after a sale substantially increased this risk.

All of this did not mean that enslaved Africans and their descendants did not enter into permanent unions and form marriages. Nor did it mean that Africans arrived, as many colonists and early Americans believed, to this continent without a concept of permanent relationships.

African Family Structure

As the reader is well aware, but it is worth a reminder, Africa is a continent that is both enormous and diverse. Ranking second in both landmass and population (Asia leads in both categories), Africa is comprised of fifty-three countries—the most of any continent—and like many colonized areas, the majority of countries include a variety of distinct ethnic populations. Thus, to speak of Africa as a monolithic place is to render invisible its diversity. That said, there are some features of Africa and West Africa in particular, where the majority of the people captured or sold into the colonial slave trade originated. Most notable for our discussion here is the fact that the vast majority of Africans during the seventeenth, eighteenth, and nineteenth centuries lived in subsistence or agricultural economies that did not lead to accumulation. This is important because economic systems structure family form. For example, families in subsistence and nonaccumulating agricultural economies tend to be large for two reasons: (1) the labor inputs necessary to hunt, gather, plant and harvest are enormous, and (2) mortality rates are high—both infant mortality and child mortality—and life expectancy is low, and thus people expect that more wives will have to be taken and more babies born in order to build a family with enough members to function and survive. All of this is to say that enslaved Africans, coming to what would become the United States, across nearly 200 years, did not come deft of morality or "family values"; rather they came with notions and beliefs about family that were functional and utilitarian for the economic system in which they lived. Once they were embedded into the plantation economy of the seventeenth, eighteenth, and nineteenth century US economy, which revolved centrally around accumulation, enslaved Africans and their descendants sought out family structures that were similar to those that the white Americans they were owned by and worked for held. Not, contrary to "popular" belief, because these family structures were superior, but because they were more utilitarian in an agricultural economy that was based on accumulation. And, not only the ability to accumulate bumper crops from year to year, but the ability to amass huge landholdings through a process of inheritance that depended upon having fewer, not more, family members to inherit the land and wealth and thus keep it relatively concentrated.[3] Despite the intent of enslaved Africans and their descendants to adopt the monogamous model of family that developed among western Europeans and the colonists they sent to the early United States, as noted, legal marriage was prohibited among slaves. They were, however, allowed to develop and engage in other symbolic rituals designed to recognize marriages.

> Though slaves could not marry legally, they were allowed to do so by custom with the permission of their owners—and most did. But the wedding vows they recited promised not "until death do us part," but "until distance"—or, as one black minister bluntly put it, "the white man"—"do us part." And couples were not entitled to live under the same roof, as each spouse could have a different owner, miles apart. All slaves dealt with the threat of forcible separation; untold numbers experienced it first-hand.[4]

Jumping the Broom and Other Rituals

Most notable in the previous quote is the fact that slaves recognized the structural limitations to marriage—that to get married required the master's permission and the marriage was not recognized legally—yet this did not deter them from engaging in a ritual that symbolized the commitment between two loving partners. We argue that the desire to engage in a symbolic marriage, despite its lack of legal support, demonstrates the depth of the belief that slaves had in marriage and commitment and signals their strong desire to pursue this family form despite the barriers and risks—namely the risk of separation—that it carried. That the lack of legal marriage has been interpreted by some white Americans as signaling a lack of moral commitment to marriage on the part of slaves, demonstrates the lack of knowledge and understanding many in the United States have about the history of slavery, economic systems, and family form. "Jumping the Broom" is one of the more well-known rituals that is associated with the public ritualizing of slave marriages. In 2011 a Hollywood film by the same name represented the controversy that the tradition has in many contemporary African American couples and their families as they design modern-day weddings. African American Roots, Inc.,[5] is a website that caters to couples who seek to incorporate various traditions associated with traditional slave weddings, including jumping the broom, into contemporary wedding ceremonies. Their website offers tips, accessories for purchase, and nearly all of the services any wedding site offers, including invitations, cake toppers, and flower girl dresses.

Search to Reconstitute Families

Another indicator of the value of family life to enslaved African Americans was the search for family members that had been separated, sold off, run away or fought in the Civil War. The story of Henry "Box" Brown provides an excellent illustration:

> Among the best-known of these stories is that of Henry "Box" Brown, who mailed himself from Richmond, Va., to Philadelphia in 1849 to escape slavery. "No slave husband has any certainty whatever of being able to retain his wife a single hour; neither has any wife any more certainty of her husband," Brown wrote in his narrative of his escape. "Their fondest affection may be utterly disregarded, and their devoted attachment cruelly ignored at any moment a brutal slave-holder may think fit."[6]

In the years immediately following the Civil War, there is evidence of thousands of ex-slaves going to incredible lengths to find "lost" family members. For example, the famed historian Herbert Gutman examined firsthand various slave registers and marriage records during Reconstruction and later census data, and based on these sources he was able to document that when they were allowed to form marriages, slaves did just that.

Gutman's most important contribution, based on his analysis of the records of the Freedman's Bureau in the National Archives, was the indisputable evidence that at the point of freedom, during and immediately after the Civil War, slaves—both those who escaped and those who were freed—journeyed north, west, and throughout the South in the desperate search for wives, husbands, children and loved ones.[7]

AFRICAN AMERICAN MARRIAGE
IN THE POST–CIVIL WAR ERA

It has been well documented by historians, including both Gutman and Tara Hunter[8] that marriage rates among African Americans increased immediately after the Civil War. In short, once they were legally allowed to marry, African Americans did. We should note that this pattern is similar to and predates the sharp rise in interracial marriages after the historic US Supreme Court decision *Loving v. Virginia*, which in 1967 made it illegal to prohibit marriages between blacks and whites, as well as the rush to marry by gay and lesbian couples that we see in each and every state that passes same-sex marriage laws. As Hunter's research demonstrates, and we will discuss in the next section, African Americans and whites had similar rates of marriage from the end of the Civil War until the height of the civil rights movement in the early 1960s.

AFRICAN AMERICAN MARRIAGE
IN THE TWENTIETH CENTURY

Prior to the 1960s, most Americans married and there were very few differences by race. As the data in Figure 1.1 reveal the marriage rates of whites and African Americans first begin to diverge in 1970, and just ten years later in 1980 there is a fifteen-percentage point difference.

Role of Welfare in the 1960s

Critical to understanding marriage in the African American community is to understand that prior to the 1970s, African Americans and whites married at extra-

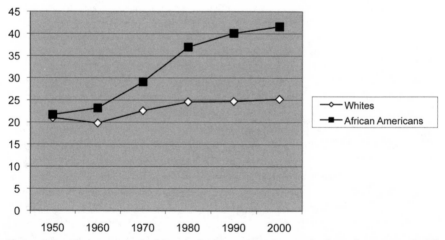

**Figure 1.1.   The percent of whites and African Americans who have "never married,"
1950–2000.**

ordinarily similar rates; indeed the rates of marriage in the 1950s and 1960s differed by only a few percentage points. So, what happens around 1970 that leads to the precipitous decline in marriage rates among African Americans? Some competing explanations include:

- African Americans no longer had an interest in marrying.
- African Americans lost their commitment to the institution of marriage.
- Marriage no longer served a function in the African American community; in other words, the needs of the family could be met without a legal marriage.
- Marriage became dysfunctional to African Americans; for example, being married prevented them from accessing other resources that they needed.

There is no research or other evidence to support the first two competing explanations. As we have demonstrated, African Americans had been legally marrying for the previous 100 years, ever since they were allowed to, and marrying at rates almost identical to whites. Based on research and polls on church attendance, beliefs in God, and other measures of religious commitment, African Americans consistently come out as more religiously committed, more likely to express a belief in God, and more likely to attend church regularly. Thus, there is no reason to assume that African Americans have lost their commitment to marriage. Finally, as all the data on poverty reveal, the best defense against being poor is not getting an education, it is getting married. In every configuration, from dual-earner households to two-parent families, when two adults are married and are present in a household the household is significantly less likely to be poor. In fact poverty rates for married-couple households are in many cases half of what they are for the majority of single-parent households and families, and this holds across all race and ethnic groups.[9]

With regards to the third explanation, that marriage is no longer functional, we note that by 1990 marriage rates had begun to decline in the white community as well. We will explore this trend in greater length later.

Thus, the conclusion we arrive at is that marriage must have become *dysfunctional* for some African American families. The answer as to why marriage became dysfunctional for African Americans in the late 1960s and early 1970s has everything to do with welfare reform.

The "War on Poverty" that President Johnson's administration launched in the 1960s included strict rules to qualify for Aid to Families with Dependent Children (AFDC). Among these was the requirement that there be only one parent present in the home. Thus, poor mothers with children would refuse to marry the fathers of these children because to do so would result in a denial of the much needed AFDC checks they received.[10] This practice was widespread among *low-income* African Americans and even had a name: "the man in the house rule."[11] As prohibitions against marriage became codified into welfare and public policy, norms around marriage, cohabitation, and nonresidential coparenting[12] evolved. We argue that as marriage became dysfunctional for low-income African Americans over time it also became normative. In other words, children who grew up under the "man in the house rule" were far less likely to marry themselves when they grew up. In just a few decades norms around expectations for marriage changed dramatically for African Americans, *especially those who are poor*. Much like the 200-year period of slavery, the African American community adapted or evolved toward a family structure that seemed to better serve its needs. Yet, it is critical to point out that this shift in the "marriage culture" is more or less confined to very poor African Americans, particularly those who were caught in the intergenerational cycle of welfare. In fact, in a recent study that created a firestorm of controversy, Charles Murray argues that though delayed, the same exact phenomenon is happening among low-income whites.[13] Middle-class, professional, and wealthy African Americans marry at rates that are distinct from poor African Americans and similar to white Americans.

Economic Differences

Using Robinson's framework, which is focused on highlighting the deep and growing chasm among African Americans of different social classes, it is worthwhile to examine the ways in which social class shape the likelihood of marrying among women of different racial groups. In other words, we ask the question, is Charles Murray right, that what started in the black community is now influencing Americans of other racial and ethnic identities as well? As the data in Figure 1.2 demonstrate, race, social class, and gender shape the likelihood of marrying by age thirty-five.

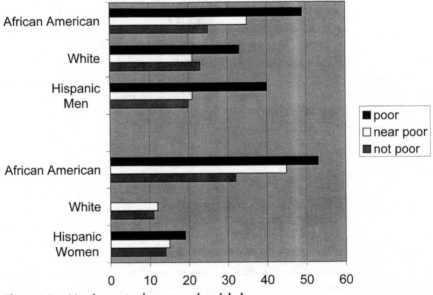

Figure 1.2.   Marriage rates by race and social class.

Drilling down into the table, several key findings emerge:

- Women are slightly more likely to be married by the time they are thirty-five than men, except for African Americans; African American women have the lowest rate of marriage (or conversely the highest rate of nonmarriage) by age thirty-five. For "not poor" African American women, the likelihood of marriage is ten percentage points lower than African American men who are "not poor."
- Whites, and white women in particular, are the most likely to marry by age thirty-five, even those who are "poor."
- Despite race and gender differences, the real story is about social class. The highest rates of nonmarriage are for those of any race who are "poor" and the rates of nonmarriage skyrocket for poor African Americans; nearly 50 percent of poor African American men have not married by age thirty-five and 55 percent of poor African American women have not married by age thirty-five.

The reader will recall that one popular rant among candidates during the 2012 Republican primary was the decline of the African American family and with it, the decline in valuing things like education and work. This data suggest, however, that politicians, family values proponents, and researchers at conservative "think tanks" and others who raise "concerns" about the decline of the African American family vis-à-vis the lack of marriage in the African American community, than have a much too simple understanding of the "problem." The "problem"—if there is one—is far more a story of poverty than of race, thus confirming our proposal that it was the welfare policies of the 1960s and 1970s that are to blame for the steep decline in marriage among African Americans. And, this reality confirms Robinson's contention that there are really four African American communities; in his vernacular, the transcendents and the middle class look far more like their white counterparts than the abandoned, who live so far on the margins that they are removed from major mainstream American institutions, such as marriage, and other institutions including education, work, and sports, as we will demonstrate later in the book. The only institution in which they are overrepresented is in prison.

Marriage versus Cohabitation

The real question we need to ask is, does the decline in marriage, for all Americans, but especially for poor African Americans, represent a shift from couples to single households or is it more accurately portrayed as a shift in the likelihood of entering a legal marriage? In other words, are couples continuing to form partnerships, live together, and raise children simply doing so without entering into legal marriages; is long-term cohabitation replacing marriage and, if so, is this change across the board or is it shaped by race or social class?

Beginning in 1970, there has been a very slow but steady increase in the number of adults who choose to cohabitate. Though some of these cohabitations lead even-

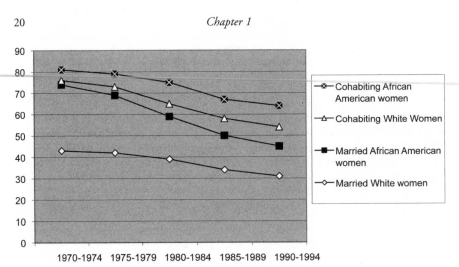

Figure 1.3. Trends in marriage and cohabition for white and African American women.

tually to marriage, other couples enter long-term cohabiting relationships never marry. Most scholars who study cohabitation and marriage are reluctant to claim that cohabitation will replace or is replacing marriage, but many suggest we are in a transition period in which either this trend will continue or rates of marriage and cohabitation will stabilize.

As with marriage rates, there are some interesting ways in which race, class, and gender shape cohabitation.

- Men are more likely to cohabit than women.[14]
- Younger people are more likely to cohabit than older people, though the highest rates of cohabitation are among the youngest and oldest groups in the population as cohabitation becomes more common among widows.[15]
- Though initially African Americans were more likely to cohabit than whites, the rates of cohabitation converged in the 1990s.[16]

But by far the greatest impact on the likelihood of cohabiting is social class. Low-income and poor people are significantly more likely to cohabit than any other social class group. And among women, cohabitation is a transition to marriage for middle-class women, but a substitute for poor women.[17]

This finding confirms that increases in the receipt of welfare, though they do not necessarily encourage marriage, may encourage cohabitation. For example, in the Fragile Families study, there is a correlation between a mother's receipt of welfare and the likelihood that she cohabits with the father of her children.[18] This finding suggests that researchers and policy makers may need to seriously consider the possibility that cohabitation has evolved as an alternative to legalized marriage for poor families, both African American and white, enabling them to continue to receive assistance (welfare, Medicaid, etc.) while retaining all of the same stability and advantages of marriage.

INTERRACIAL/INTRARACIAL UNIONS

Perhaps the second biggest myth about African Americans and marriage is the belief that African American women aren't marrying because all the African American men are marrying white women. Though it might be convenient to blame the low rates of marriage for African American women on white women, in fact, as shown above, social class is the biggest predictor of whether African American women will marry or not. Furthermore, as has always been the case in the United States, the vast majority of people who do marry, with few notable exceptions, marry people of their same race.

Attitudes toward Interracial Marriage

As recently as 2010, a study by the Pew Research Center[19] on attitudes toward interracial marriage revealed that despite the majority (80 percent) of Americans indicating that they would be supportive of a family member marrying outside of the race, the support differed significantly by the race of the intended partner. Eighty-one percent of those surveyed would support an interracial union involving a white partner, but only 66 percent indicated that they would support an interracial union involving an African American, with attitudes toward Hispanics and Asians falling in the middle, but both well above 70 percent. Thus the bias against incorporating African Americans into mainstream culture, something the researchers term "black exclusion," remains well entrenched.

Perhaps more disturbing, the Public Policy Polling published the results of a poll of registered Republicans taken in April 2011 that revealed that 46 percent of Republican voters believe that *interracial marriage should be legally banned*. Thus, it is clear that attitudes toward interracial marriage continue to vary by age and political affiliation and interracial marriage continues to be a highly polarizing issue in the American landscape.[20]

Actual Interracial Marriages

As we move deeper into the twenty-first century, the United States is becoming increasingly diverse in terms of race and ethnicity as well as the national origin of her population. Along with this increasing diversity comes growing rates of interracial relationships across virtually all lines of demarcation. An obvious outgrowth of this is the rise of children of interracial couples who increasingly desire to be identified as biracial or multiracial. The census, which is often slow to respond to social change, altered—for the 2000 tally—several categories such that now individuals can choose to identify with more than one race, cohabiting couples can be counted—both heterosexual and homosexual—and thus we have better estimates than ever before of the race or ethnic family composition of the US population.

The Pew Research Center has documented that one of the most powerful social changes that has affected the overall rise in interracial marriage is immigration; 25 percent of Hispanics and 30 percent of Asians are married to someone of another race, whereas only 8.9 percent of whites and 15.5 percent of African Americans are.

One of the assumptions that will be tested in this book is the degree to which the election of the first African American president, Barack Obama, is either a signal of or a precursor to a culture that can be characterized as "postracial." One of the most significant measures of postracial attitudes would be an increasing tolerance for interracial relationships and an increase in people marrying across racial boundaries. The decision to marry across racial boundaries and the increased acceptance of interracial unions is so significant a marker because marriage is the most intimate relationship any two people have. Furthermore, the history of the United States is marked by a deep resentment and fear of interracial unions, and the most policed boundary of all was that between whites and African Americans. In fact, marriages between whites and African Americans were so feared that they were illegal in most states such that the US Supreme Court ruling, *Loving v. Virginia*, that rendered unconstitutional the laws prohibiting interracial unions, was not handed down until 1967!

One myth or stereotype is that African American women cannot find partners because African American men are all marrying white women. Data from the Pew Report confirm that African American men and women have different rates of interracial marriage—with African American men being three times more likely to "marry out" than African American women. That said, white-black unions continue to constitute a tiny fraction of all marriages. Specifically, though interracial marriages are on the steady incline—14.6 percent of all new marriages in 2008 were interracial—marriages between African Americans and whites constituted only one in nine of all interracial unions. Other significant highlights from the report include:

- The most common interracial marriage (41 percent) involves a white partner and a Hispanic partner.
- Asian women are the most likely (40 percent) to marry out and their typical partner is a white man.
- The least common interracial unions involve whites and blacks—only 2 percent of all new marriages in 2008.
- African American women are the least likely to marry someone of another race.

SOLUTIONS

Concern about the plight of the African American family and the low rate of marriage among African American women in particular, has caused a variety of people to weigh in on the issue, including politicians like Newt Gingrich, scholars like Ralph Richard Banks who poses a provocative question in his new book, *Is Marriage for White People*, and writers for magazines targeting African American women, including *Essence*. Among the advice offered by Banks and many articles in magazines like *Essence* is that African American women should refocus and seriously consider pursuing white men as potential spouses.

One perspective, such as that offered by Harvard sociologist Orlando Patterson, notes that when black women enter into relationships with men of other races, especially white men, they gain access to valuable social networks (Patterson 1999), thus integrating them into the larger American society (Patterson 1999). For example, because white men own the majority of businesses, marriage to a white man would facilitate access to the ability to make money. Other perspectives, such as the challenge offered by Banks and writers in *Essence* take a more retaliatory approach; if African American men are not marrying African American women because they are marrying white women then African American women ought to do the same and pursue interracial marriages with whites as well.

All of that said, as noted earlier, there is still a high degree of uneasiness in the United States concerning unions between African Americans and whites, with white men holding the most conservative attitudes on this issue. Thus, practically speaking, we wonder where African American women might find willing partners?

CONCLUSIONS

When analyzing marriage patterns in the African American community we have to ask this question: does the election of the first African American president influence how African Americans participate in marriage, and in what way? In short, does this election signify that we have now entered a "postracial" America with regards to marriage or at least attitudes toward marriage and interracial marriage in particular, as actual changes in behavior—for example, marrying—will take longer to occur?

In this chapter we have examined the myth that African Americans don't marry. What the data have actually shown is that African Americans have always valued the institution of marriage and have entered into long-term committed relationships even when they were prohibited from legally marrying; and they continue to marry today. The data also show that rates of marriage have significantly declined since 1970, and that the decline has been substantially steeper for African Americans than for whites. Yet, when we examine the data more closely, we learn the real factor that is driving the decline in marriage is social class. Because African Americans are far more likely to be poor than their white counterparts, poverty, not race, seems to be the key contributor to declining marriage rates. We aptly demonstrated that poverty itself may not be the prohibiting factor as much as welfare policies that discouraged marriage. On the bright side, however, the data also suggest that while marriages are declining, cohabitation is on the rise, and for the poor, and especially for unmarried, poor mothers, long-term cohabitation may be replacing marriage. Thus, children being raised in these families seem to benefit from some of the advantages associated with two-parent households whether those parents are legally married or not.

Lastly, we examined interracial marriages as a symbol of an emerging postracial society. Though rates of interracial marriage increased substantially once interracial marriage was *legalized*, the rate has remained relatively steady since the 1970s, with the only exception being the tremendous rise in interracial unions for Hispanics and Asians, a trend that is likely fueled as much by immigration and growing populations inside the United States as by shifts in ideology. In short, though the story on marriage in the African American community is not as discouraging as many people believe, the election of the first African American president—who incidentally is the product of an interracial marriage—has in no way ushered in a postracial America where whites and African Americans no longer see "color" in their romantic relationships.

2

Childrearing Practices

Do Blacks Use Corporal Punishment More than Whites?

In May 2008, the South Carolina Supreme Court reversed a twenty-year prison sentence on a controversial drug charge. Regina McKnight, an indigent black woman, was sentenced for "homicide by child abuse" in 2003, and became the first woman to be prosecuted and convicted in the United States for giving birth to a stillborn baby. McKnight had no prior convictions, but her drug use during pregnancy violated a recently enacted South Carolina fetal drug law (FDL).

Prosecutors never proved that McKnight's drug use actually caused the miscarriage. In fact, she was arrested after seeking help at a local hospital. The state simply proved that she miscarried. South Carolina justified its interference with the pregnancy and subsequent prosecution based on an interest to protect fetuses from risks associated with drug exposure such as low birth weight.

Most states that pursue these types of prosecutions ignore the fact that miscarriages and stillbirths are caused by any number of factors ranging from assisted reproductive technology (ART) and alcohol abuse to obesity and secondhand smoke. Recent studies provide compelling evidence that even a father's age influences whether a baby might be born alive or dead.

By comparison, recent high-tech, high-publicity births, including that of Stacey Carey of Pennsylvania, who earlier this year gave birth to premature and severely underweight sextuplets with the aid of sixty hospital staff; Nadya Suleman, a California woman, who gave birth to eight babies; or the case of Brianna Morrison, a Minnesota woman who birthed six children in 2007 after using reproductive drugs, offer an interesting contrast. Some scholars suggest that it reveals how race and class still matter in the birthing.

The difference between McKnight's traumatic story and that of other moms like Morrison and Suleman, and so many others who used ART and birthed children at high-mortality risk, might seem obvious at a glance: one woman was arrested and incarcerated because she broke the law, while the other women were simply desperate to become mothers, and what's so bad about that?

Ideally, the maternity ward should be off-limits to the state. Compulsory sterilizations during the first half of the last century are a chilling reminder about too much

25

state interference. Nevertheless, there is a persistent question that arises from the juxtaposition of these stories, a question that relates to power, privilege, race, and class. If what states care about is ensuring the health of fetuses and promoting their development to birth, then why focus only on women like McKnight? Multiple birth ART babies are eight times more likely in McKnight's home state (South Carolina) to be born low birth weight, and low birth weight babies are forty times more likely to die during the first few months of life.

This report is edited based on the original story: *A Tale of Two Birth Wards* by Michele Goodwin (2011).

One interpretation of this story, or answer to the question it poses, is that we hold assumptions about childrearing and parental intentions that are shaped by race. Specifically, the policies and procedures that are invoked in cases of stillbirth or delivering a baby with certain complications rest on an assumption that African American women deliberately choose to put their unborn babies at risk—by making poor decisions—whereas white women's goal is to protect their unborn children even in the face of dangerous medical procedures. This and other assumptions about childrearing practices in the African American and white communities will be the subject of this chapter. We begin with the controversial practice of spanking.

Myth: African American parents are more likely to favor and use corporal punishment than white parents.

Reality: There are many factors that influence the likelihood that a parent will favor spanking, no spanking, or use other forms of corporal punishment. Though there is some evidence that African Americans are more likely to favor "a good spanking," many experts agree that this is simply a by-product of the fact that African Americans are more likely to be poor, young parents, live in the South, and hold conservative religious views, all of which are highly correlated with both attitudes toward spanking and the actual use of corporal punishment.

How we parent has historically been considered a private matter. Not surprising, as discussions of parenting practices have become more public, controversies over various practices have erupted. One example of this is spanking. In many circles, spanking is considered child abuse, whereas in others it is considered to be tough discipline that is necessary to raise children in the complex society in which we now live. To a large degree these circles are circumscribed by race; with the assumption being that African Americans are more likely to favor and use physical punishment, whereas whites are more likely to consider any physical discipline to be part of the slippery slope of child abuse. This chapter will explore childrearing practices—both attitudes and behaviors—in African American families. We will provide data that debunks the myth that childrearing practices are racialized and demonstrate, once again, that social class is a stronger predictor of the use of corporal punishment than race. Additionally, we will provide data that indicates that the reaction to corporal punishment is in fact the issue that varies by race: when white parents are investigated by child protective services (CPS) the matter remains in social services, but when African American parents are investigated by CPS the matter is often bumped up and becomes a criminal matter.

That said, we are very concerned about the use of physical discipline that is utilized by African American parents and because we conceptualize physical discipline as part of a slippery slope toward child abuse, we will end the chapter by exploring the risk factors that put African American children at higher risk for child abuse than white children. We begin with a discussion of one of the most controversial of all forms of discipline: spanking.

BELIEFS ABOUT SPANKING

As with many attitudes that Americans hold, certain factors influence the way people feel about spanking. The three most important factors that shape attitudes toward spanking are race, social class, and age. Overall, African Americans are more likely to believe that "a good, hard spanking" is sometimes necessary; poor people and young people are also more likely to believe that spanking is sometimes necessary. Specifically, nearly 80 percent of women under the age of twenty-four believe that "a good, hard spanking" is sometimes necessary whereas women over the age of twenty-five are ten points lower on this attitude at 70 percent support. Race is a much stronger predictor believing "a good, hard spanking" is sometimes necessary. Support for this attitude is 60 percent among white women; nearly all (91 percent) of African American women support this belief.

It is important to point out that there is not always a direct link between one's beliefs or attitudes and her behavior. Let's now consider the factors that shape the actual likelihood of spanking or using other forms of corporal punishment.

SPANKING AND THE USE OF CORPORAL PUNISHMENT

The *New York Times* ran a series on its opinion pages in the summer of 2011 in which they asked several "experts" to comment on the relationship between race and spanking or the use of corporal punishment. This fact alone is evidence of the controversial nature of spanking and the degree to which we attribute it to race.

Not surprising, not a single expert was willing to suggest that spanking is "racialized," or more specifically that African American parents are more likely to spank than their white counterparts. There are many ways in which to interpret this high level of agreement, which is rarely the case in the *New York Times* opinion pages!

- Perhaps the *New York Times*, which has a reputation for being "liberal," identified "experts" who would take a liberal approach to discussing spanking.

- Perhaps the experts felt pressure to be politically correct and not invoke a strong and negative racial stereotype that would paint African American parents as more violent and as terrible parents.
- Perhaps the scientific evidence simply doesn't support the myth that African American parents are more likely to engage in spanking and other corporal punishment even if they hold somewhat more "pro-spanking" beliefs.
- Or, perhaps the apparent link between race and spanking is actually reflective of the fact that African Americans are more likely to have other qualities and occupy other social spaces—religious views, being poor, being young, and so forth—that are correlated with spanking.

What Does the Research Say?

Elizabeth Thompson Gerhoff, a professor at Columbia University, conducted a meta-analysis of 300 studies on spanking and corporal punishment dating between 1938 and 2001. A meta-analysis is a study that examines dozens, or in this case hundreds, of scientific studies and analyzes them seeking to identify "universal" or generalizable trends. Gerhoff's study revealed inconsistent findings with regards to race and spanking or other forms of corporal punishment. Her research revealed that in some cases African American parents were more likely to spank or use other forms of corporal punishment, in other studies white parents were more likely to spank or use other forms of corporal punishment, and in many studies there were no differences. Perhaps most important is Gerhoff's finding that race disappeared as a predictor of spanking or using other forms of corporal punishment when the ways in which race overlaps with other key factors including age, region of the country, socioeconomic status, and religious views were considered.

Gerhoff's study demonstrated that the strongest predictors of spanking or using other forms of corporal punishment include:

- social class (low-income parents are more likely to use corporal punishment)
- education (both high and low education parents are less likely to use corporal punishment; those with only a high school education are the most likely to use corporal punishment)
- religion (the more conservative the religion) and the higher in religiosity (the more committed one feels toward their religion) are more likely to engage in corporal punishment
- geography; those living in the South are more likely to use corporal punishment than those living in other regions of the country

Thus, drilling down, it turns out that what appears to be attributable to race is in fact influenced by a series of factors—income, education, religion and religiosity, and region of the country—which shape the likelihood of spanking and using corporal punishment and which are highly correlated with race. This type of high correlation may attribute a relationship to race while masking the real factors that shape who spanks and who doesn't. In fact, one observation made by the panel of experts who discussed race and spanking in the *New York Times*[1] is that African Americans will stop spanking when their religious affiliations moderate, in other words, as they move away from the traditional, conservative African American protestant churches and identify more strongly with less conservative, *mainstream* churches.

Lastly, though there are individual factors that shape the likelihood that a parent will use corporal punishment, in fact, research on child abuse reveals that structural factors are much stronger predictors of the use of physically abusive behavior; and as with the factors we have just discussed, African Americans are more likely to occupy social spaces that predispose them to use physical punishment that can slide down the slippery slope and become what is legally considered to be child abuse.

CHILD ABUSE

Like many areas of life, the distinction between using corporal punishment, such as spanking, and physical child abuse, is blurry. That said, most experts who study and diagnose child abuse note that to constitute abuse, the physical punishment must meet at least one criterion:

1. It must be severe and beyond what most people would consider reasonable.
2. It must be ongoing.
3. It must result in detectable injuries.

In short, spanking, for example, may or may not constitute abuse, depending on a number of factors, including how often a child is spanked, how severe the spanking is, and the degree to which the spanking results in detectable injuries. Though there is no simple formula, one might argue that an occasional spanking that involves a parent spanking a child's clothed buttocks with an open hand does not constitute abuse, whereas daily spanking or spanking with a belt or rope or extension cord most certainly would, even if it occurred only once.

Our second concern, after attempting to identify which behaviors constitute abuse and which do not, is the likelihood that individual parents will become abusive and the likelihood that an individual child will be abused. Of particular importance as we consider the myth that African Americans are more likely to utilize physical discipline, is the question of whether they are more likely to engage in child abuse than white parents. Let's consider the risk factors for child abuse and determine the role that race plays.

Risk Factors

Research conducted by Office of Child Abuse and Neglect, part of the Department of Health and Human Services, identifies four domains of risk factors for child abuse and neglect: (1) parent or caregiver factors, (2) family factors, (3) child factors, and (4) environmental factors.[2] We will briefly discuss each risk factor and explore the ways in which it is shaped (or not) by race.

Parent or Caregiver Risk Factors

There is no research to suggest that there is any prototype of an abusive parent. That said, there are several parental qualities that predispose one to being abusive.

Experienced abuse as a child. One of the primary risk factors for engaging in abusive or neglectful behavior is having been the victim of abuse or neglect as a child or having been exposed to abuse in one's household while growing up. A couple of caveats. First, though the risk for perpetrating abuse or neglect is greater for those who were child victims—as many as one-third of all victims of child abuse grow up to perpetrate it—the *majority* of child victims do *not* grow up to be abusive parents. Second, the seemingly intergenerational transmission of abuse or what is often termed the "cycle of abuse" has little to do with genetics or biology and much to do with socialization and learned behavior. Parents who grew up without good parenting role models lack the information and modeling to be good parents themselves. Parents who grew up watching adults "solve" problems through violence, for example, may grow up without the appropriate tools for conflict resolution and may engage in violence to address their own problems. There is simply no question that one's childhood influences the "toolkit" one takes into parenthood.

Substance abuse and mental illness. A second risk factor that can affect child neglect is substance abuse and mental illness. Parents or primary caregivers who are substance abusers or addicts are at increased risk for engaging in physical abuse and neglect. One study reports that 40 percent of confirmed child abuse cases involved a parent with substance abuse or addiction problems.[3] The same is true for parents with mental illness. In both cases the parent may have compromised judgment and impaired decision-making skills that may lead to abuse or neglect. It is widely accepted that African American men and women suffer from higher rates of mental illness, even though they are often not diagnosed, simply as a result of the stresses they face having to deal with flat-out racism and discrimination as well as the stresses associated with poverty, blocked potential, and coping with other health issues.

Age. A third risk factor for engaging in child abuse or neglect is age. Younger parents, especially teenagers, are at a greater risk for engaging in physical child abuse and neglect than older parents. There are a multitude of reasons for this including the developmental stage of most teenagers, their limited ability to handle stress, their lack of realistic expectations for children's behavior—especially infants and toddlers—and their lack of knowledge about appropriate discipline. Additionally, teenage parents are far more likely to hold other risk statuses for abuse: the likelihood that they are single parents, that they are less likely to be employed, that they are more likely to be on welfare, and that they are less likely to have graduated from high school all contribute to the relationship between age and risk for perpetrating physical child abuse and neglect. African American girls have significantly higher rates of childbearing than white girls; African American girls have approximately three times the rate of teen pregnancy as white girls. Thus, as with so many other factors, what appears to be a race difference is actually a result of the significantly higher rate of childbearing by African American teens who, based on their age, are more likely to use physical discipline and engage in abusive or neglectful behavior.

Family Structure

Children growing up in single parent households are at a higher risk for all forms of child abuse and neglect. Indeed, the rate of child abuse for children growing up in single-parent households is double that of children living in two-parent households.[4] As with children of teenage parents, the sources of increased risk for physical abuse and neglect in single-parent households are similar: they are more likely to live in poverty, there is stress associated with being the sole caregiver, and so forth. In addition, children in *female-headed single-parent households* are at an increased risk for sexual abuse; stepfathers and mothers' boyfriends are by far the most likely individuals to perpetrate child sexual abuse.

Regardless of whether a child's parents are married or not, children who have a strong relationship with their father are at far less risk of all forms of child abuse and neglect. This finding confirms the argument that it is the *stresses* of single-parenting that increase a child's risk for being a victim of abuse or neglect *not the individual qualities of the single parent herself and certainly not her race.*

Another pathway by which single-parenting may be linked to greater rates of child abuse and neglect is the instability in the housing of single mothers.[5] Children whose mothers have chaotic or constantly shifting housing—often characterized by "doubling up"—sharing a home meant for one family with multiple relatives or friends—are at a higher risk for neglect simply because of the instability and the overcrowding of the household.

Based on a national study by the Department of Health and Human Services, Administration for Children and Families (ACF),[6] compared to children in two-parent households, children being raised by single parents had:

- 77 percent greater risk of being physically abused
- 87 percent greater risk of being harmed by physical neglect
- 165 percent greater risk of experiencing notable physical neglect
- 74 percent greater risk of suffering from emotional neglect
- 80 percent greater risk of suffering serious injury as a result of abuse
- 120 percent greater risk of experiencing some type of maltreatment overall

Given the fact that at the beginning of the twenty-first century, due to both increases in the divorce rate and the skyrocketing rate of births to single mothers, especially to African American mothers, we need to pay special attention to children living in single-parent households to be sure that they are safe and that their parent has adequate resources to provide for the needs of the child. Because African American children are more likely to be raised by single mothers, which puts them at a significantly greater risk for being abused or neglected, we need to be especially vigilant in educating single moms and detecting and interrupting child abuse when it occurs.

Child Factors

It is with caution that we write about "child factors" as this can easily be misinterpreted to suggest that certain children are to blame for being abused. Under no circumstances is a child responsible for being abused. Ever. That said, there are "qualities" of children that increase their risk for being victims of abuse, namely: age and disability.

Age

Though the relationship between age and the risk for abuse is not entirely clearcut, there are several trends that are worthy of exploration. First, the risk for serious physical abuse is highest for children between the ages of one and three, and after age three this risk begins to decline. In contrast, the risk for child neglect *increases* with the age of the child. These trends are best explained by considering the different needs of children. Infants and young children require the most intense and constant care and thus the increased risk for physical abuse may be driven by the stresses associated with parenting infants and toddlers. Infants between the ages of three and six months are at additional increased risk for injury for two reasons. First, because very young children are so small and fragile, it is "easier" for a parent or caregiver to significantly injure a child by simply shaking him. Second, infants at this age are at risk for being shaken because of a phenomenon termed "the period of purple crying." The period of purple crying refers to the fact that at this developmental stage infants cry more than at any other time in their lives. During this phase infants not only cry more, but they often seem inconsolable, there is often no apparent reason for the crying, they may appear to be in pain, and the crying may last for hours and commonly occur, at an already stressful time of day: late afternoon and early evening.

Though the risk for being neglected increases with age, infants are far more likely to die from neglect—a phenomenon termed "nonorganic failure to thrive"—than older children. Presumably this is because older children are more capable of obtaining food from other sources whereas infants are entirely dependent upon their parents or caregivers for their entire nutritional input.

Disabilities

Research and child prevention programs identify children with disabilities as particularly vulnerable to abuse; they are especially likely to experience *higher rates of maltreatment* than are other children. A national study, completed in 1993, found that children with disabilities were 1.7 times more likely to be maltreated than children without disabilities.[7]

As with age, one of the explanations for this relationship seems to be the additional stress that raising a child with disabilities may place on a parent. Additional sources of stress may come "from the child himself or herself" in the sense that many physical and cognitive disabilities require significantly greater caregiving needs, similar to the needs of infants and young children. Additionally, sources of stress may be compounded with certain communicative disorders such as autism in which the child may have such difficulty communicating that the parent or caregiver feels isolated and unsupported. Another source of stress that is rarely discussed is the economic stress associated with certain physical and cognitive or developmental disabilities. In cases of severe physical disability parents may face a host of financial burdens including operations to correct abnormalities, health aids—expensive wheelchairs, for example—and even modifications to the home. Rarely do people realize that the majority of these needs are not covered by any insurance and thus the financial strain may produce stress that is released in abusive or neglectful ways.

Similarly, having a child with a disability often puts tremendous strain on marital relationships, especially if the disability is the result of genetics in which case one parent may feel guilt associated with passing on a defective gene and the other may feel anger and resentment. All of these themes are explored in Jodi Picoult's novel *Handle with Care*, which we highly recommend. Picoult's novel follows the journey of a family raising a child with a disability, Osteogenesis Imperfecta (OI), or brittle bone disease. The novel depicts the toll that raising a special needs child has on all of the individual family members, including a sibling, on the parents' marriage, on their finances, and so forth.

The data on disabilities reveal that the rate of disability is 1.5 percentage points higher among African American children than among white children. Thus, yet another risk factor for abuse, disability, is correlated with race. Thus, differences in rates of child abuse and neglect that are initially attributed to race may actually be caused by racial differences in the risk factors for child abuse.

Environmental Factors

Researchers identify three environmental risk factors—qualities of the physical environment under which children and their families live—that contribute to an increased risk for child abuse and neglect: (1) poverty and unemployment, (2) social isolation and lack of social support, and (3) living in a violent community; *each of which are experienced more frequently by African Americans than by whites.*[8] Let's drill down to examine the complex relationships among race, environmental factors, and the risk for child abuse and neglect.

Poverty and Unemployment

There is strong, empirically verified, evidence that links poverty and unemployment to the likelihood of engaging in child abuse and neglect.

Children from families with annual incomes below $15,000 in 1993 were *more than 22 times more likely* to be harmed by child abuse and neglect as compared to children from families with annual incomes above $30,000.[9]

Scholars suggest four explanations for the relationship between poverty and an increased risk for child abuse and neglect.

1. Poverty leads to parental and familial stress, which increases the chances for abuse and especially neglect.
2. Poverty itself compromises the ability of a parent to provide adequate care and meet all of the needs of the child; at its most severe this will result in neglect.
3. There may be a relationship between parental poverty and the likelihood of parental substance abuse.
4. Finally, some scholars suggest that the risk for child abuse and neglect is not necessarily higher among low-income families, but rather that abuse and neglect are more likely to be *detected* in low-income families and ultimately referred to CPS. This may occur for a variety of reasons including the stereotypes that professionals such as teachers and healthcare providers may hold about the poor as well as a fear of reporting an affluent or well-known family in the community.

As every reader will no doubt acknowledge, African Americans have the highest rate of poverty in the United States. At the risk of seeming monotonous, *research suggests that it is poverty, and not race, that causes higher rates of child abuse among African American children.*

Social Isolation and Social Support

A series of studies suggest that parents who abuse or neglect their children report experiencing "greater isolation, more loneliness and less social support."[10] There are several reasons why African American mothers (and fathers) may feel a greater sense of isolation and a lack of social support. For example, the majority of the African American population lives in the South, and the South is one of the most rural, and most isolated regions of the country. Individuals living in the rural South may not have regular contact with a support system. Though more research needs to be done to determine whether isolation is a cause or result of abuse, the relationship between social isolation and child abuse is widely accepted by practitioners and thus many communities have programs designed to alleviate isolation.

Violent Communities

One of the greatest contributions sociologists make to understanding phenomenon such as child abuse is their focus on structural and institutional, rather than individual, causes. Beginning at the very end of the twentieth century, criminologists and sociologists whose research focused on poverty and race or ethnicity began to turn their attention to the role that the *environment* of a community may play in individual and family life. For example, noted sociologist William Julius Wilson asked the question: what role does a high level of unemployment in a neighborhood play in shaping individuals' attitudes toward work? (Wilson 1996). He argued, for example, that when children grow up in a neighborhood or community where the majority of adults they see regularly *do not go to work each day* they will not develop the same association between work and adulthood as children who regularly see the adults around them going off to work each day.[11] Following this approach, scholars interested in child welfare began to wonder about the role that violence in neighborhoods plays in shaping abuse in individual families. Scholars who focus on the ecology of child abuse and neglect note that:

> Children living in dangerous neighborhoods have been found to be at higher risk than children from safer neighborhoods for severe neglect and physical abuse, as well as child sexual victimization. Some risk may be associated with the poverty found in dangerous neighborhoods, however, concerns remain that violence may seem an acceptable response or behavior to individuals who witness it more frequently.[12]

Because we know that African American children are far more likely to live in public housing projects, rural ghettos, and violent communities, we suggest that this exposure to violence is an additional cause of the higher rates of abuse experienced by African American children as compared to children of other races and ethnicities.

Witnessing Violence

Relatively recently, scholars of child abuse and practitioners, especially social workers, have begun to recognize the impact that *witnessing violence*, especially domestic violence, has on young children. In particular, when boys witness domestic violence their risk for growing up to beat their own wives and girlfriends *triples*.[13] As a result of this devastating outcome scholars and practitioners have begun to formally identify children who witness domestic violence as *child abuse victims*. This label is important for many reasons: first and foremost, labeling the witnesses of domestic violence *as victims* entitles them to the types of social services that are generally restricted to victims. For example, children who witness domestic violence and live in counties where this is labeled as child abuse are entitled to counseling, intervention programs, and the development of family safety plans. Additionally, this identification as victims of child abuse renders them eligible for court interventions. For example, the repeated witnessing of domestic violence by a child may result in a hearing to determine whether the child should stay in the home or be removed temporarily or permanently. Though jurisdictions vary greatly in terms of their support for defining the witnessing of domestic violence as child abuse, one good example comes from the state of Minnesota where any child determined by the police officer who responds to a domestic dispute to have been "in sight or sound" of domestic violence is thereby considered a victim of child abuse and is referred to all of the relevant responders including CPS.

A child who is witnessing domestic violence in the home may exhibit many of the same symptoms of children who are experiencing emotional abuse, including low self-esteem, being withdrawn, and so forth. Unfortunately, the most significant indicator may not be visible for years, and that is the likelihood, especially for male victims, of becoming batterers. Because African American men are somewhat more likely to abuse their female partners, African American boys are more likely to grow up witnessing abuse and to ultimately grow up to batter their own partners, thus perpetuating an ugly cycle. Higher rates of domestic violence among African Americans, then, are not a result of race per se, but of the different rates of exposure young boys—white and African American—have to witnessing violence.

RACIAL DIFFERENCES IN CPS
AND FOSTER CARE PLACEMENT

We conclude the chapter by briefly examining the ways in which race shapes the likelihood that abuse will be identified and will produce an intervention. Clearly, we are very concerned about child abuse and neglect, and we believe that there are very few cases in which an intervention is not necessary. When we talk with adults who have experienced abuse as children, they often express the sentiment that they wish someone had paid attention, they wish that someone had cared enough to interrupt their pain. That said, when child abuse statistics are collected, they are typically based on calls to CPS or other organizations that intervene in child abuse rather than on surveys. Limiting child abuse statistics to that which is reported will lead to undercounting overall and especially in populations that are less likely to make a report or have a report filed on their behalf. We noted earlier that this practice leads to an underreporting of child abuse among the affluent and that leads to an artificial belief that child abuse is mostly about being poor. Because there are well-documented racial biases in the child abuse that gets reported, the statistics on the racialization of child abuse are in part artificial because they reflect the likelihood of *reporting* child abuse, not the likelihood of the abuse occurring to begin with. The story that opens this chapter is an illustration of this phenomenon.

One of the prevalent stereotypes of poor African American women—which is also invoked in the opening story to this chapter—is that they are addicted to both welfare and also to crack. Studies of differential treatment of pregnant women find that regardless of *similar* or *equal* levels of illicit drug use during pregnancy, African American women are *10 times* more likely than white women to be reported to child welfare agencies for prenatal drug use.[14] This racial disparity can only be explained by the power of racial ideologies in shaping perceptions. Simply put, when a pregnant African American woman is discovered using drugs, this confirms our stereotype of African American women as crackheads, and therefore she and her children are referred to child welfare agencies. In contrast, when a pregnant white woman is discovered using drugs this appears to be an isolated event, it doesn't match our stereotype, and interpreting her behavior as an isolated incident tends to reduce the likelihood that it will be reported to child welfare agencies. Similarly, when the abuse or neglect of an African American child is discovered—thus confirming our stereotype of African American parenting styles—it may be more likely to be reported to CPS than when the same is discovered of white children. Thus, the statistics on child abuse are, in part, a reflection of our beliefs about race and childrearing practices, rather than a simple reflection of actual rates of child abuse in American society.

INTERGENERATIONAL CHILDCARE PATTERNS

Lastly, it will come as no big surprise that there are generational differences in the use of corporal punishment. Public approval for and use of spanking and corporal punishment declined significantly across the twentieth century. This is important because African American children are vastly more likely to be raised by their grandmothers than children of any other racial or ethnic group. And, though this strategy, developed in large part to deal with high rates of childbearing among African American teens, has many benefits,[15] one disadvantage may be the greater use of spanking, corporal punishment, and activities that border on or become abusive by grandmothers who were raised as part of a generation that was more tolerant of and likely to use physical forms of discipline than contemporary generations. We will expand on this discussion in the next chapter as well.

CONCLUSIONS

When analyzing childrearing patterns in the African American community we have to ask this question: does the election of the first African American president impact African Americans' attitudes toward physical discipline or their use of it in their parenting practices, and in what way? In short, does this election signify that we have now entered a "postracial" America with regards to childrearing?

It is commonly believed that African American parents are more likely to support and engage in physical punishment, spanking, corporal punishment, and
even abusive behavior than members of other racial or ethnic groups. Yet, what we
have demonstrated in this chapter is that what appears to be a racial difference is,
in fact, often not. Dozens of scientific studies demonstrate that there is no clear
relationship between race and the likelihood that a child will experience physical
discipline or abuse. Instead, what appears to be a racial difference in rates of the use
of both physical discipline and child abuse is instead driven by the racialized nature
of a variety of structural causes of child abuse, including poverty, teen parenting,
single-parenting, a child's disability, and intergenerational childcare patterns.
When we control for all of these causes of child abuse and as well as the attitudes
that lead to the use of physical discipline, racial difference fade. In fact, African
American children are more likely to be the victims of physical punishment and
abuse simply because they are more likely to:

    . . . Be born of single mothers
    . . . Be raised by single parents
    . . . Live in poverty
    . . . Have disabilities
    . . . Be raised by grandmothers
    . . . Live in the South
    . . . Be raised by mothers who are committed to highly conservative, fundamental-
    ist religious beliefs
    . . . And, live in violent communities.

Because African Americans are far more likely to live in these circumstances, race
renders invisible the actual causes of child abuse.

    In terms of protecting our children, we are best served to consider structural fac-
tors, rather than focusing exclusively on race as the causes of child abuse. Additionally, we note that American society, in the wake of the election of the first African
American president, is likely to experience higher rates of child abuse; not because
African American people and "their values" have become dominant, but because the
rate of pregnancy, especially among African Americans, has risen, the rate of single
parenthood, especially among African Americans, has risen, as has the rate of poverty. Any rise in the rate of child abuse among African American children is likely a
result of changes in childbearing and the economy; *it is not caused exclusively by race.*
Lastly, it is critical to note that racial differences in the use of physical discipline and
child abuse will continue as long as African Americans are more likely to live in the
structural conditions—poverty, single-parent households, adhering to highly conservative beliefs—that create a greater likelihood of using physical forms of discipline
that can put one on the slippery slope toward child abuse.

3

Transition to Adulthood

Teen Childbearing

Kayla and her boyfriend, J.R., have been dating for six months and she's sure he's "the one." J.R. is already out of high school and Kayla has plans to go to nursing school once she graduates. Both Kayla and J.R.'s parents have been really support-ive, which is good since Kayla is pregnant.

J.R. works as a mechanic and also lives at home, but he hopes that he and Kayla can get their own place soon. Although Kayla knows she loves J.R., she's scared to move away from her mom since she feels she'll need the help once the baby comes. J.R. wants Kayla to depend on him rather than her mother.

Concerned about the couple's living situation, J.R.'s parents offer his grandpar-ents' old home for he and Kayla to live in, but only if they get married. While J.R. is happy with this option, Kayla thinks it's all moving too quickly and is unsure of what she wants to do. Kayla and her mom, Bev, talk about her worries and what she's getting into. Bev wants Kayla to realize what responsibilities come with being a wife and mother.

During a photo shoot that her mom arranges, J.R. proposes to Kayla and she accepts. They now have to figure out how they will have money to move out, take care of the baby, and pay for a wedding. However, before they even begin to worry about it, Kayla starts having contractions five weeks early.

Since baby Rylan came early, there was no time to work out the living situation so J.R. has to move in with Kayla's parents to help out. Bev agrees, as long as J.R. sleeps in the guest room, leaving Kayla getting up all night with Rylan. J.R. is anxious for them to have their own home, but Kayla is more hesitant than ever. She's scared to tackle motherhood alone without her mother nearby.

Kayla finally heads back to school and realizes quickly she and her friends have grown apart. While they're all looking forward to prom, all Kayla wants to do is spend time with Rylan. She finally talks with J.R. about her feelings on rushing into marriage and living together. Kayla knows without the support of her parents, she never would have been able to handle having a baby at seventeen. She's decided to take things one step at a time and make sure she's making the best decisions for Rylan and herself.

The story of Kayla was featured on MTV's show: *Sixteen and Pregnant*, Episode 217.

———————⊙⊙⊙⊙———————

Kayla's struggles—how to complete her education, how to stay connected to high school, whether to marry J.R., how to be a good parent—are no different than the millions of African American teenage girls who have babies each year. What's different about Kayla's story? Kayla and J.R. are white.

Myth: African American girls have looser sexual mores and that is the main reason why they have babies at significantly higher rates than white girls.

Reality: Certainly, for some African American girls, teen pregnancy is a choice. The choice to have a child may be based on the norms in her family and community or the glamorization of babies and the yearning for someone who will always love her. Yet, for many African American girls, their pathways into pregnancy are more complex; a very high percentage were initiated into sexual behavior in inappropriate ways and for others their access to birth control and abortion are severely limited, thus rendering the "choice" to have a child irrelevant. And for many, the choices they see in life are so limited that having a child seems to be the only pathway into adulthood and holds the only promise—which turns out frequently to be a lure—of a long-lasting romantic relationship.

In this chapter we will unpack the complex causes of teen childbearing among African American girls and explore the pathways to both sexual activity and having a baby. We will debunk the notion that teen childbearing in the African American community is the result of looser sexual mores with evidence demonstrating that, in addition to the fact that African American and white teens are having sexual intercourse at roughly the same rate, the factors contributing to different rates of teen childbearing are complex and structural more so than individual. As we discussed in the previous chapter, African American children are more likely to be the victims of child abuse than whites, and sexual abuse is no exception. Sexual abuse is unique because its outcomes are different than for the victims of physical abuse; specifically, victims of child sexual abuse are more likely to become sexually active at younger ages, they are more likely to become pregnant, and they are more likely to participate in other deviant behavior—drug abuse, prostitution—that leaves them more vulnerable to unwanted pregnancies. Therefore, we will expose the role that sexual abuse plays in teen childbearing. Additionally, we will consider the ways in which differences in family structure shape and in some cases create a preference for beginning one's childbearing as a teen. Lastly, we should point out that there are a small number of African American men who are raising their children as single parents. That said, our focus here remains on single mothers, and teenagers in particular, because of the special challenges that single teen mothers face and the additional risks their children face, particularly for infant mortality, birth defects, and all of the consequences associated with poverty. For those interested in reading more about single African American fathers—the overwhelming majority of whom are *not* teens—we provide a list of recommended readings.

SEXUAL ACTIVITY

The point of this chapter is to explore teen sexual behavior, pregnancy, and childbearing, and as we will confirm, rates of teen pregnancy vary significantly by race. Despite differences in teen childbearing, there is much less variation in sexual activity among teens. Obviously, to get pregnant, girls (and boys) must be sexually active. The average age of first intercourse, which has been steadily declining since 1990, has stabilized at age seventeen, with the average age of first intercourse for boys at 16.9 years whereas girls are, on average, 17.4 years of age when they first experience intercourse.[1] When we examine who is having sex, there are some differences by race and gender, but these are surprisingly small.

- Perhaps a bit surprising, among teenagers in ninth to twelfth grades, the *lowest rate* of sexual activity is reported by white boys, 29 percent report that they are sexually active.
- Consistent with popular stereotypes, the group most likely to report being sexually active are African American boys (50 percent).
- Teenage girls have a similar pattern; African American girls are more likely to report being sexually active (48 percent) than white girls (32 percent).[2]

When we look at the data within race, we see that boys and girls of the same race report a similar likelihood of being sexually active. This makes sense given our discussion in the previous chapter about interracial versus intraracial relationships.

TEEN PREGNANCY

According to the Guttmacher Institute, a national clearinghouse for teen sexual behavior, three-quarters of a million girls between the ages of fifteen and nineteen become pregnant each year. The vast majority of the pregnancies are unintended (82 percent), and a third end in abortion. Slightly more than half (57 percent) of all teenage girls carry their pregnancies to term and give birth; teen births account for 11 percent of all births in the United States. The "light" at the end of this tunnel is that teen pregnancy rates have been relatively stable over the last two decades, and the majority of teen pregnancies (two-thirds) are to girls who are eighteen or nineteen years old.[3]

As we noted previously, for girls the difference in the likelihood of being sexually active is only 10 percent higher for African Americans than for whites. Yet, despite these relatively similar rates of sexual activity, the racial differences in pregnancy are significant and disturbing. For every 1,000 girls aged fifteen to nineteen,

- 134 African American girls will get pregnant
- 131 Hispanic girls will get pregnant
- Only 48 white girls will get pregnant.[4]

If African American girls are only 10 percent more likely to be having sex than white girls, how can we explain the fact that their pregnancy rate is more than three times higher? Let's consider several possible explanations.

White girls are significantly less likely to become pregnant because:

- White girls have better access to contraception.
- The partners white girls choose are more willing to use contraception, or are less resistant to their partners' using it.
- White girls are less willing to have an abortion and this increases their use of contraceptives.
- White girls identify negative consequences with getting pregnant.

African American girls are significantly more likely to become pregnant because:

- African American girls are more open to having an abortion.
- The partners African American girls choose are more resistant to contraceptives or are more likely to desire to become fathers.
- African Americans girls are less likely to use contraception.
- African American girls have less access to contraception.
- African American girls identify fewer negative consequences to pregnancy; they may even desire to become pregnant.

There is no easy answer to this question, but we suggest several keys to understanding different pregnancy rates that we will shape our discussion throughout the remainder of the chapter.

First, there is some evidence to conclude that access to contraception is shaped by race; specifically contraceptives are expensive and the degree to which white girls have more options for purchasing contraceptives, including prescriptions they can get through their parents' medical insurance, likely shapes their likelihood of using contraception. Secondly, contraception is sometimes made available in schools through the guidance office or nurses' office. The ability to provide free condoms, for example, is directly related to the resources the school can devote to this; African

American girls are far more likely to attend under-resourced schools than white girls, and this may lessen the likelihood that they can obtain free condoms. Third, there are cultural differences, which will form the basis of our discussion hereafter, but the long and short of it is that there is a greater acceptance of and even an expressed preference for teen motherhood in the African American community. These attitudes likely influence both a girl's concerns about getting pregnant as well as her partner's preferences regarding contraception; many African American boys gain status by becoming fathers. This can also translate into less acceptance of abortion, though as we shall see attitudes toward abortion and the actual use of abortion are pretty far apart. Lastly, and on a much darker and more disturbing note, African American girls are very likely to experience sexual abuse; and though we cannot estimate the rate of pregnancy that arises from sexual abuse and rape, we can speculate that some portion of African American girls who find themselves pregnant not only didn't intend to become pregnant but didn't consent to the sex either.

TEEN CHILDBEARING

Despite extreme differences in teen pregnancy rates between African American and white girls, their rates of carrying the child to term and having the baby are more narrow. Though white girls only get pregnant at about one-third the rate of African American girls, African American girls are only slightly more than twice as likely to give birth.[5] We see that white girls who get pregnant have a better than fifty/fifty chance of having the baby (54 percent deliver), among African American girls who get pregnant, they have less than a 50 percent chance of having the baby (47 percent deliver).

According to the Guttmacher Institute only 15 percent of teen pregnancies end in a miscarriage, 57 percent are delivered, leaving 27 percent that end in abortion.[6] Based on the difference rate of teen childbearing compared to teen pregnancy, and assuming that miscarriage rates do not vary significantly by race, we can conclude that African American girls are more likely to end their pregnancies with an abortion than white girls are.

All of these numbers are a lot to take in. What's important to note is that despite the fact that African American teenage girls are far more likely to give birth than white girls, and this is indeed concerning for reasons we will consider in a moment, it is simply not the case that African American girls are getting pregnant and bringing babies into the world because they are more promiscuous than white girls. In fact, African American girls are only slightly more likely to be sexually active than white girls; they are, however, *much more likely to get pregnant* as a result of this sexual activity. Even though a baby born to a teen mom is more likely to be African American, when African American girls do get pregnant, they are somewhat less likely to have the child than white girls, most likely because they have an abortion.[7]

Of course, before we can consider the reasons why teens have babies, we must investigate another prevailing stereotype: that all African American mothers—and teen mothers in particular—are single mothers.

The Data on Marital Status and Teen Childbearing

Not all teen mothers are unwed mothers. That said, there are two disturbing trends associated with teen childbearing: (1) the number of teenage girls who are giving birth, and (2) the average age of the teen mother when she gives birth. First, we should note that teenagers have always had babies. In fact, at the turn of the twentieth century the average woman had her first child before she turned twenty. But, we should also point out that the average women who was born in the late 1800s did not finish high school, married before age eighteen, and died before age fifty. Today, that same teenager will graduate not only from high school but she will probably get some additional education after high school, if she marries at all she will not likely do so until her midtwenties, and she can expect to live until her early seventies. Therefore, teen childbearing today occurs in a different context and has very different consequences.

- Each year 750,000 teenagers become pregnant.
- Approximately half of these pregnancies go to term; more than 300,000 babies are born each year to teen mothers.
- One-third of all teenagers who become pregnant are seventeen or younger.
- Younger teens (under age fifteen) have the lowest rate of pregnancy, yet the 1 percent of all girls under the age of fifteen who will become pregnant is disturbing.
- Eighty-six percent of teen mothers are not married (compared to only 16 percent in 1960).
- In 1960 only 16 percent of teen births were to unwed mothers, but by 2003 this percentage had risen to 80 percent.[8]

At the end of the chapter we will explore the consequences of teen childbearing, but as a preview, it is not surprising to note that teens who give birth are less likely to finish high school, they are more likely to have a large number of children, they are less likely to marry, and most concerning of all, they are very likely to end up on welfare.

As we reconsider our previous discussion about *why* African American girls are more likely to get pregnant, we can conclude, at a minimum, that they are less likely to use contraception—and they have less access to it—and they are more willing to have an abortion, which may contribute to their reduced use of birth control, even if they are less likely to favor abortion in theory.

What emerges from all of this is a sense that "culture" or community norms must be important in producing such different rates of pregnancy, childbearing, and abortion in light of similar rates of sexual activity.

The Culture of Teen Pregnancy and Childbirth

It can be dangerous to invoke "culture" to explain racial differences in any type of behavior. Yet, it is reasonable to conclude, from the data we have presented in this discussion, that culture plays *some role* in explaining racial differences in teen pregnancy and childbearing. And, experts who study teen childbearing have come to some conclusions about differences in "culture" that may help us understand the choices girls make about getting pregnant and having babies.

Why Have a Baby?

As noted earlier, the majority of teens who get pregnant report that the pregnancy was unwanted, about half of these pregnancies end in abortion, so taken together, this begs the question: Why do unmarried teenage girls have babies? The answers to this question are complex and often unpopular. As sociologists we are concerned primarily with the structural rather than individual answers to this question. We will examine the roles of sexual activity, the opportunity structure, norms, and finally the impact of sexual abuse and premature sexuality as explanations for the question: why have a baby?

THE TRANSITION TO ADULTHOOD

One of the areas of interest to social scientists is "the transition to adulthood." Historically there have been certain "markers" of this transition, including finishing one's education, getting a full-time job, buying a home, marrying, and having children. In the last few years this issue of transitioning to adulthood has received a great deal of attention by both the popular press and scholars because the landscape into which this all-important transition is taking place has changed so dramatically. The popular film *Failure to Launch* features Matthew McConaughey trying to navigate a romantic relationship with Sarah Jessica Parker. The story revolves around his unwillingness to move out of his parents' house and her unwillingness to commit to a twentysomething who won't!

Perhaps some readers are struggling in their own families with these issues. Even if you are not, the issues are relatable to most of us. There are several important changes in our society that have led to this change in the transition to adulthood more broadly and some that are specific to the African American community. Over the last decade or so, one change that many argue has "extended adolescence" is the increased opportunity many young people have to continue to get educational credentials after high school. Not only are more Americans going to college than ever before, a trend that began in the 1960s, but more and more young adults are finding that they need even more education to compete in the job market. As a result, many young adults are not completing their education until their late twenties. And, in most cases this means they remain dependent upon their parents for financial support. This delay in completing one's education has a domino effect on the other markers of transition to adulthood; young adults are getting their first full-time jobs later, they are marrying later, and they are having children later. The current economic crisis has exacerbated this trend; as more and more young people graduate from college and can't find employment, they return to school hoping to both gain new credentials but also to delay their entry into the labor market with the hopes that things will improve with time.

The economic crisis has also created additional barriers to the transition to adulthood that are distinct, namely difficulties in find employment or being laid off have led to an increasing number of people going or returning to college. High school students who might otherwise have not been college bound and middle-aged adults who have been laid off are heading in droves to community colleges to gain the kinds of training they think will improve their chances for gainful employment. This phenomenon is distinct from the overall trend in delaying the transition to adulthood by going to college—which is primarily taking place in middle- and upper-middle-class families—because it is a result of individuals responding directly to the economic crisis rather than it being reflective of a shift in beliefs and norms among low-income youth. The housing crisis that is at the core of the economic crisis has also contributed to delaying the transition to adulthood for low-income young adults; basically it is far more difficult for young adults to move out at all, let alone buy their own homes. Again, though this affects all Americans, it is felt most severely by young adults who grew up in families with limited resources. In contrast, in middle- and upper-income families the delay is most likely limited to delaying the purchase of a home; young adults in these families are less likely to remain living at home and are more likely to require support from their parents to pay the exorbitant rents that characterize the markets where they find work and reside. This distinction is important because in lower-income families this means that young adults are still living at home whereas in middle- and upper-income families parents are able to reclaim their homes—the empty nest!

Returning to the framework provided by Robinson, we point out that the delays in transition to adulthood for African Americans will be shaped largely by their status in the African American community. Transcendents will likely find that their children follow the increasing trend among the professional and upper-income classes, they will earn advanced degrees, which will be the primary cause of their overall delay into adulthood. Furthermore, they will most likely experience a domino effect on the various markers, getting one's first job, buying one's first house, marrying, and having children will all follow after their education is completed.

For African Americans in the middle class, the trajectory will likely be related to the specific impact of the economic crisis on the transition to adulthood. Those who may not have been college bound may enroll in community college to better their employment options. Many will have to remain living at home because they cannot afford to pay their rent and their families cannot afford to supplement it. We can speculate that once the economic crisis ends middle-class African Americans will return to experiencing a more traditional transition to adulthood.

For many poor African Americans—the abandoned—the chances of achieving *any one of the markers for adulthood is low*. Though the economic crisis has some impact on the lives of the abandoned, the majority are already so marginalized from the mainstream economy that barriers to transitioning to adulthood are deeply entrenched, have existed for decades, and are not likely to recede once the recession is over. Thus, understanding how these barriers shape the decisions of the abandoned youth is critically important if we are concerned about their life chances.

The abandoned, as Robinson points out, live on the highly racially segregated margins where poverty is concentrated; in urban ghettos like Mott Haven, New York, or Oaklawn, Chicago, and in rural counties such as Tallahatchie, Mississippi. In these communities, fewer than half of all young people graduate from high school, fewer than 10 percent will go to college, unemployment is at least 20 percent, welfare dependency in some areas is as high as 50 percent or higher, and so on. When a young teenage girl learns that she is pregnant, she may realize that becoming a mother may be her only chance at achieving a marker of adulthood. Similarly, if she hadn't planned to graduate from high school or attend college, then the usual argument that motherhood will derail her from her goals—a major concern in more affluent families—is irrelevant. For a girl growing up in a middle- or upper-middle-class family having a baby will be interpreted as a major deterrent to achieving her goals—like going to college—or a "poor" decision. This decision may not seem so irrational for the poor teenage girl. Two sociologists who have studied this phenomenon, Kathryn Edin and Maria Kefalas, argue in the book *Promises I Can Keep: Why Poor Women Put Motherhood before Marriage*, provide a compelling rationale:

> The centrality of children in this lower-class worldview of what is important and meaningful in life stands in striking contrast to their low priority in the view of more affluent teens and twenty-something youth, who may want children at some point in the future, but only after an education, career, and other life goals have been achieved. Putting motherhood first makes sense in a social context where the achievements that middle-class youth see as their birthright are little more than pipe dreams: Children offer a tangible source of meaning, while other avenues for gaining social esteem and personal satisfaction appear vague and tenuous. (p. 49)

Though the focus in this chapter is on girls, who certainly don't get pregnant on their own, we pause for a brief discussion of African American boys and their transition to adulthood. African American boys growing up in the segregated and impoverished urban and rural ghettos also face blocked opportunities that derail their transition to adulthood. And, though becoming a father may be one marker they can achieve, the steep rise in incarceration, which we devote an entire chapter to, is coming to be seen by scholars who study mass incarceration, as the most important marker of adulthood among poor African American young men. This is important to note because it reinforces our argument that on the far away margins occupied by the abandoned, life is experienced differently and a culture has developed around blocked opportunity such that girls seek the transition through childbearing and boys through a trip to jail or the state penitentiary. Additionally, the high rate of incarceration of young, poor African American men may be another reason why the transition for girls—having a baby—may be a solo trip.

We began our quest to answer the question of why African American teenagers have babies so much more often than white teens by noting that culture must play a role. Clearly the structural circumstances experienced by those Robinson terms the abandoned who live on the margins have a direct impact on the choices many African American teens make to have a child. But, those choices, constrained as they are by structural barriers, shape cultural norms as well. And, if the norm becomes teenage childbearing then the choice to do so may be as much influenced by the structure as by the norms.

NORMS ENCOURAGING TEENAGE CHILDBEARING

Considering the earlier quote, we can predict that separate from the actual ability to achieve markers of adulthood, girls raised in communities that identify teen motherhood as something of value—as opposed to a deterrent on the road to achieving the American Dream—will encourage teen childbearing and provide the necessary social support for teen mothers. As a result, there will be a greater number of teens in these neighborhoods bearing and raising their children.

Linda Burton, a sociologist, set out to examine the role of culture in shaping the decisions teenage girls make to have their babies and become mothers. To answer the question, she interviewed dozens of African American teen mothers in a low-income community and asked them about their views on motherhood and the impact of motherhood on their lives. Their responses fell into four themes.

Theme One: Separation of Marriage and Childbearing

Teen mothers observed, accurately, that most women in their community did not get married. As we noted in the first chapter, social class is a major predictor of the likelihood of getting married and that marriage rates are especially low among poor African Americans. Many of the girls Burton interviewed said that they had already determined by their teen years that if they wanted to have children they would do so without husbands. Thus, when they found themselves pregnant they were more likely to go ahead and become mothers rather than delaying the inevitable: being a single mother.

Theme Two: Accelerated Family Timetables

African Americans have, and have always had, a shorter life expectancy than whites. As with most everything else we've talked about, this too is shaped by social class. Poor African Americans, who lack access to healthcare, nutritious food, a safe place to exercise, and so on, die earlier than more affluent African Americans and whites. Though this may not be articulated, it would clearly be apparent to most people. If African American women think of themselves as dying relatively young—most of the women in their lives have probably died by their sixties—then they will come to the conclusion that it is better to start childbearing earlier (rather than later) in life so as to be able to live long enough to raise their children and become a grandmother or even great-grandmother. This same reality existed across all of US history—until well into the twentieth century—when the average life expectancy finally rose. Until the mid-twentieth century most girls had their first child while still in their teens. Today we continue to see this pattern in the developing world where life expectancies are shorter. When and wherever life expectancy is short, teen childbearing is a common practice.

Theme Three: Compressed Generations

When teen childbearing occurs over several generations the outcome is called "compressed generations." To illustrate,

- If the average age at first birth is twenty-five (as it is in the United States today), then generations will be separated by twenty-five years or so. A child at age one will have a twenty-five-year-old mother, a fifty-year-old grandmother, and a seventy-five-year-old great-grandmother.
- If, as is the case in many poor African American communities, where teen childbearing has been the norm for many years, the generations are significantly closer together. A child at age one will have a mother who is fifteen, a thirty-year-old grandmother, a forty-five-year-old great-grandmother, a sixty-year-old great-great-grandmother.

Thus a ten-year age difference in one generation, when it is continued across many generations, increases exponentially the age differences in subsequent generations.

- The "mothers" are ten years apart (age fifteen versus age twenty-five).
- The "grandmothers" are twenty years apart in age (thirty years old versus fifty years old).
- The "great-grandmothers" are thirty years apart in age (age seventy-five versus age forty-five), and so on.

Both the girls and their mothers told Professor Burton that compressed generations were preferable because of life expectancy (accelerated family timetables) but also because the older women (the grandmothers and greatgrandmothers) wanted to be young enough to enjoy and keep up with their grandchildren and great-grandchildren.

Theme Four: Intergenerational Carecare Patterns

A common pattern in some segments of the African American community, especially among low-income and poor families, is the sharing caregiving across generations
of women. Grandmothers (who are in their thirties and early forties) often raise their
grandchildren, while their own daughters, who at fifteen or sixteen are considered too
young to raise children, care for their own grandmothers and great-grandmothers as
they age. The caregiving these teenage girls provide to their older relatives may involve
cooking, helping with chores around the house, and driving grandmothers and great-
grandmothers on errands, to appointments, and so on. Again, not only the daughters
but also the grandmothers and great grandmothers expressed a strong desire for teen
childbearing so that this caregiving pattern could be continued.

CHILD SEXUAL ABUSE AND TEENAGE MOTHERS

We conclude our discussion of the reasons why African American girls are more
likely to have babies than white girls by examining the relationship among race,
sexual abuse, and teen pregnancy.

One of the risk factors associated with teen childbearing is a history of physical or
sexual abuse in the life of the teen mother. For example, studies of Washington State
welfare recipients estimate that *half* of those women who give birth before age eighteen have been sexually abused and another 10 percent or more have been physically
abused.[9] Data from the National Survey of Children indicate that 20 percent of sexually active teenagers have had involuntary sex and *over half* of those who are sexually
active before age fifteen have experienced involuntary sex.[10] It should be obvious that
the relationship between child sexual abuse and becoming a teenage mother are complex. Part of the answer rests in the fact that child sexual abuse can lead to pregnancy
and the likelihood that it will is high because abusers rarely, if ever, are worried about or
use any form of contraception. And this problem is exacerbated by the fact that because
the sexual contact is abusive and nonconsensual the victim is rarely able to make any
demands on the interaction, including the demand for contraception. Lastly, we point
out that the data are clear that girls who are sexually abused in childhood or adolescence are far more likely to remain sexually active and they are significantly more likely
to engage in other behavior—drug abuse, prostitution—all of which exposes them to
the potential for pregnancy. Finally, we remind the reader that African American girls
are more likely to be the victims of child sexual abuse than white girls. Therefore, both
directly—from the abuse itself—or indirectly—from the consequences of the abuse—
it is likely that the racial difference in the likelihood of being abused contributes to the
racial difference in rates of teen pregnancy.

Returning to the question that we asked, and that is implied in the myth with which
we opened the chapter, why do African American teenage girls have babies more often
than white girls, we summarize the answer that we arrived at based on the data.

- African American girls are not having sex at dramatically different rates than white girls. Thus, the "loose morals" interpretation is not supported.
- African American girls are significantly more likely, however, to become pregnant as a result of this sexual activity. One likely cause is less access to contraception. Though the data on race and access to contraception are scanty, there are data that offer clues. For example, the states with the most restrictive access to contraceptives for teens are the same states with the highest rates of teen pregnancy. And, these states, primarily in the South, are also the states where African American teens are the most likely to live.
- Structural barriers for having a baby while still a teenager are more significant for white girls, which results in fewer white teens becoming mothers. Simultaneously, motherhood may be the only marker of adulthood that is available to African American girls, especially those who are poor, which would increase their propensity for choosing motherhood.
- Supports, both in terms of family support and norms, for teen childbearing are quite strong in the African American community, and especially among low-income African Americans, which undoubtedly leads to African American girls seeking motherhood, which would help explain their higher rates of pregnancy despite relatively similar rates of sexual activity.
- African American girls are more likely to be the victims of child sexual abuse which increases—both directly and indirectly—their risk for becoming pregnant.

So, why does all of this matter? We conclude the chapter by outlining the outcomes of teen childbearing on young women and consider how this will shape the options they will have as adults.

OUTCOMES OF TEEN CHILDBEARING

There are many risks and negative consequences for mother, child, and community that are associated with teen childbearing. For the mother, she is likely to get less education, to have higher levels of poverty, to have long-term dependency on welfare, and to have higher overall fertility. She is also unlikely to get married, which makes staying financially afloat a greater challenge. For the child of a teen mother, he is obviously more likely to live in poverty, he is more likely to experience abuse and neglect, and for daughters, she is more likely to become a teen mother herself.

- *Marrying the father of her child.* According to the Congressional Budget Office, only 20–30 percent of the fathers of teen mothers marry the mother of their child and only 20 percent of unmarried mothers received child support orders for the fathers of their children. This lack of support contributes to higher rates of poverty and reliance on welfare.

- *Higher fertility.* Primarily because they become sexually active early, they are not good users of contraception, and they have many sex partners, their exposure to getting pregnant is high. Higher fertility translates into larger family size, which makes it more difficult to provide adequately for all of her children, thus increasing her chances of relying on welfare.
- *Child abuse.* Teen mothers are at an increased risk for abusing and neglecting their children. One cause of higher rates of child abuse among teen parents is their age; they are not developmentally prepared to take care of a child all day long. As noted in the previous chapter, teen mothers are also at an increased risk for abusing and neglecting their children because of other risk factors for child abuse that are significantly associated with teen parenting, including poverty, being a single parent, having less of education, and having a larger number of children.
- *Education.* Just over half of teen moms complete high school during adolescence or early adulthood and those who do often complete the general equivalency degree (GED), which only guarantees that they have the most basic of skills. As most scholars of poverty have noted, the lack of skills those with only a high school degree have makes it significantly more likely that they will be underemployed or unemployed, living in poverty, and reliant on welfare.
- *Poverty.* More than 40 percent of teenage moms reported living in poverty in their twenties, and the rates are highest among African American and Hispanic teen moms.
- *Welfare.* Most of teenage mothers (and their children) end up on welfare (84 percent) with most remaining on welfare for long periods of time, for more than five of the ten years following the birth of their first child.

Because reliance on welfare is such a common experience for teen moms we decided to include a personal story gleaned from our years of teaching to personalize the struggles that teen moms face, Tammy's story.

Thus, the problem of teen mothers completing their education, a difficult task under the circumstances, becomes nearly impossible because of the welfare reform of 1996. Teen mothers, who are more than twice as likely to be African American, will find it virtually impossible to attend college and earn the credential that will ultimately lift them out of poverty and allow them to leave the welfare system.

CONCLUSIONS

When analyzing teen childbearing patterns in the African American community we have to ask this question: does the election of the first African American president affect how African American teens make decisions about childbearing, and in what way? In short, does this election signify that we have now entered a postracial

TAMMY'S STORY

The welfare reform bill signed into law under the Clinton administration (1996) was heralded as major progress for the poor and for society. It was designed to reduce the development of long-term, debilitating dependence on welfare. It was also designed to break the cycle of welfare families. The new welfare system, Temporary Aid to Needy Families (TANF), has had both positive and negative outcomes. Among the positive outcomes was the fact that welfare was no longer tied to either women or single-parenthood. Low-income single fathers can now receive welfare benefits and two-parent low-income families can as well (thus negating the "man in the house rule" discussed in the first chapter). However, it has also had some very problematic outcomes, particularly for teen mothers. The "cap baby" rule is particularly problematic given the higher rates of fertility associated with teen childbearing. Essentially, the "cap baby" stipulation was designed to prevent women who were currently receiving welfare from having more children. Though on the face of it this might seem like a good idea, in the end the person who is hurt is the baby. A cap baby—born while her mother is already receiving welfare benefits—is not eligible for any TANF programs. In other words, her mother will not receive additional cash support or food stamps once the new baby arrives. This means that the family will have to feed one more mouth with no additional funds. The baby is not eligible for Medicaid benefits either. We will discuss this issue at length in chapter 7, which focuses on poverty and wealth, but we note it here because it signals a policy that may have had good intentions but has serious, negative, perhaps unintended consequences.

The second policy that Tammy's story illustrates is the strict time limits that are now imposed on welfare receipt. Families are now limited to twenty-four months of continuous welfare and a lifetime cap of five years of total welfare receipt.

One of the authors saw firsthand the highly problematic outcome of this time limit through the eyes of a student on welfare. Her story serves to illustrate the effects not only on single mothers.

I met Tammy when I was teaching at a large, state institution, she was just beginning her senior year, it was August 1996. Tammy was enrolled in my sociology of gender course and once she became comfortable, she began to share with me, and subsequently with the class, her struggles as a single mother. She was raising two young children and going to school. Her dream: to get a good job and make a better life for her son and daughter. In August of 1996 Tammy was on "welfare." She received Section 8 housing, a voucher that allowed her to live in an apartment that rented for $500 per month (she paid only $125 of the monthly rent and the voucher paid the remainder). She received a childcare subsidy that allowed her to put her two children into a high quality daycare while she attended classes and studied. Like the housing voucher, she paid only a small portion of the daycare tuition. She also received food stamps and a monthly cash payment, what was referred to at the time as AFDC (Aid to Families with Dependent Children). She was to graduate with a B.A. in sociology in May 1997.

In early November 1996, as the cold weather settled in, Tammy arrived in my office one morning in a panic. Following the passing of the 1996 welfare reform legislation just the month before, Tammy had been called in by her caseworker to discuss the implementation of the new welfare policies (TANF). Because of the rule that limited continuous receipt of welfare to *2 years*, the state in which we lived had passed a law that prohibited full-time students pursuing degrees in *four-year colleges* from receiving any welfare. Why? The logic of the lawmakers was that a student who began a four-year degree program while on welfare would need twice the limit (4 years rather than 2) of welfare support in order to complete the degree. Cutting students off after 2 years (of both welfare and college) would leave students without any credentials. Thus, they allowed welfare recipients to enroll in technical schools and two-year colleges (that result in an Associates Degree-AA) but prohibited their enrollment in 4-year degree programs.

Despite the fact that Tammy had less than 7 months until she graduated with a 4-year degree and would presumably be able to move off of welfare and into work, the welfare office offered her a choice: she could either stay enrolled and graduate in May but lose her welfare, or she could keep her welfare and enroll in a 2-year degree program or a technical school. She put it to me this way: "They'll let me keep my welfare if I enroll in cosmetology school, but if I stay here at XY University, I will lose my welfare!"

America with regard to transitions to adulthood and specifically teen childbearing in the African American community?

Clearly, as all of the data we have presented here indicate, the crisis of teen pregnancy in the African American community is not a result of differences in morality or attitudes toward sex. In fact, the differences between the sexual activity of African American teen girls and white girls are relatively small in comparison to teen pregnancy rates. Rather, the incredibly perplexing rate of teen pregnancy among African American girls (and boys, though seldom does anyone talk about the boys in the equation), is actually a difference in getting pregnant. Though there is no single cause of the pregnancy difference in light of similar rates of sexual activity, a variety of studies suggest that there are differences in terms of contraceptive use—white girls are more likely to use contraceptives—which may also be a signal of differential access to contraception—and quite simply they do not get pregnant as often. Based on the difference in carrying the child to term, it also seems clear that when she finds herself pregnant, a white girl is less likely to terminate the pregnancy than an African American girl, which may reflect differences in attitudes toward abortion, but does not negate a greater emphasis of the importance and value of children in the African American community, and we argue most notably a lack of other opportunities to mark the transition to adulthood.

What, if any, impact did the election of the first African American president have on racial differences in teen pregnancy? Though one might expect that the "role models" provided by Michelle Obama and her daughters, Sasha and Malia, might offer another vision for life that might lead to a reduction in teen pregnancy, in fact, the factors that lead to higher rates of teen pregnancy among African American girls, because they are driven by cultural values and limited opportunities to achieve adulthood, are unlikely to be affected by the role models in the White House.

Teen childbearing is a complex phenomenon and there is no one silver bullet to reduce it. That said, we believe that one of the major factors in the high rates of teen pregnancy and childbearing among African American girls as compared to white girls, is culture and most importantly a cultural context in which other avenues that signal the transition to adulthood are blocked: educational attainment, buying one's own home, even marriage. That said, this culture of blocked opportunity and the preference for teen childbearing exists primarily among the poor, the abandoned. Thus, the role modeling that the first lady and her daughters provide is most relevant to African American girls who are of the same social class: those in professional families and the daughters of the transcendents. If anything, it is they who might raise their expectations based on seeing a woman who looks like them occupying the White House; not by changing rates of teen pregnancy, as these are already very low among this group, but by striving to become public servants themselves. After, of course, they graduate from top colleges and earn professional degrees.

Put as plainly as possible, the typical African American girl who gets pregnant as a teen may be a victim of sexual abuse, may live in a household that values teen childbearing, and she may face a lifetime of blocked opportunities. She will recognize that the opportunities that wait for Sasha and Malia, who attend school at Sidwell Friends and travel abroad, are not waiting for her.

The single pathway to adulthood that they can see and in light of a low probability that they will marry, the only way they see of tethering themselves irrevocably to a man will be through pregnancy. Thus, it is unlikely that teen pregnancy rates in the African American community will decline any time soon. Only when African American teens define the negative consequences of having children before they are "adults" as "negative" and not in their best interest will the rate of teen pregnancy and teen childbearing decline.

4

Intimate Partner Violence

The Dirty Little Secret

If Chris Brown did indeed hit Rihanna early Sunday morning, it may not have been the first time. According to TMZ.com, the pop star told cops that her R&B singer boyfriend had a history of abusing her before a weekend attack that reportedly left her bruised and bloodied, and the violence was getting progressively worse.

Us Weekly magazine also quoted unnamed sources close to Rihanna who claim this isn't the first time Brown's beaten and bruised her.

While representatives for Brown and Rihanna refuse to release details about the alleged altercation that reportedly landed her in the hospital and earned him a felony domestic abuse charge, rumors are swirling about what could have precipitated the fight.

One of the latest: Brown, nineteen, was flirting with British singer Leona Lewis, and Rihanna, twenty, flew into a rage.

According to the British paper the *Daily Mirror*, Brown was speaking to Lewis at a pre-Grammy party in Los Angeles hours before the late-night attack. While the conversation was innocent, it "set Rihanna off," according to an anonymous source quoted by the paper.

Other reports claim Rihanna got upset over a text message.

"He got a booty call. He got a text," an unnamed source told the *New York Daily News*. "Rihanna saw it and she got upset. They started to argue. She got out of the car. He wanted her to get back in, so he grabbed her. She pulled away. That's when she's told people he hit her."

Sheila Marikar, "Rihanna Tells Cops Brown's Hit Her Before," February 12, 2009, http://abcnews.go.com/Entertainment/WinterConcert/story?id=6863344&page=1

Many wondered about the impact of this incident on Brown's career. And, initially much of the focus was on the possibility the experience would create two of the most visible advocates against domestic violence. Yet, as the reader is undoubtedly aware, Chris Brown performed at the January 2012 Grammys. And, in response hundreds of young women commented on Twitter that they would happily put up with Chris Brown hitting them in exchange for getting to be his girlfriend.

Myth: All women are equally likely to become the victims of domestic violence.

Reality: Domestic violence does occur in every single population, including race/ethnicity, social class, education, religion, region of the country, and sexuality. That said, for a variety of structural reasons, African American women are more likely to experience domestic violence, and especially lethal and near-lethal forms of domestic violence, than white women.

In this chapter we will explore the reasons why African American women are more likely to be victims of domestic violence than white women. The obvious explanation is that African American men are simply more violent. We will demonstrate that the causes of the higher rates of domestic violence for African American women are not individual—African American men are not more violent by nature nor are African American women more vulnerable. Rather, as with many other issues we have examined and will examine in this book, African American men and women are more likely to live with external and structural factors that shape rates of domestic violence. Specifically, African American men are more likely to be unemployed and to have been incarcerated, both of which lead to an increased risk for perpetrating domestic violence.

INTIMATE PARTNER VIOLENCE IN THE UNITED STATES

Intimate partner violence (IPV) refers to the physical, emotional, psychological, and sexual abuse that takes place between intimate partners. These partners may be married or in a long-term committed relationship, or they may be dating. They may be living together or not living together. They may be separated or even divorced. They may be heterosexual or homosexual. What distinguishes IPV from other forms of interpersonal violence is that it occurs between two people who claim, or claimed, to love each other.

In many cases, IPV involves the occasional slap or punch. But more often than any of us would like to acknowledge, many victims of IPV sustain broken bones, stab wounds, severe bruising, and lacerations as well as psychological abuse and even rape. We have conducted in-depth interviews with nearly 100 men and women who are living with IPV—as victims and as perpetrators. Additionally, after we discuss IPV in class or give a public lecture, we routinely have women and men who come up to us afterward and share, often in hushed tones, their own experiences with IPV. As such, we have met women who were repeatedly referred to as "bitches" or "cunts." We have met women who miscarried pregnancies when they were beaten, punched, and kicked. One woman we met was kicked so severely that the boot print her husband's kick left on her back was visible to the doctors and nurses in the emergency room. Another woman we met was punched so hard in the mouth that her teeth punched through her upper and lower lips. And, another woman, while her children cowered in the hallway, was beaten in the head with a ball peen hammer. IPV is one of the most perplexing phenomena we will write about in this book.

According to the Bureau of Justice Statistics, which counts only those crimes reported to the police, in 2009, a half a million acts of IPV were reported.[1] Statistics that are based on national samples of women report that approximately 25 percent of women report an act of violence in the previous twelve months and nearly half report at least one act of IPV in their lifetimes.[2]

Domestic violence homicide is the most dramatic outcome of IPV. Domestic violence homicide can be intentional or it can result from a severe beating that may take place in minutes or across hours, that leaves the victim dead. Approximately 1,500 women are murdered every year by their intimate and ex-intimate partners; and domestic violence homicide is the leading cause of female homicide, accounting for one-third (33 percent) of all female homicides. When the perpetrator is male, he often murders his wife or ex-wife or girlfriend in front of her children. It is not uncommon for him to attempt or commit suicide as well. The reader may recall the case of Josh Powell who in February 2012 murdered his sons, ages five and seven, and then burned them and himself up in a house fire he deliberately set. He had long been suspected of killing his wife several years earlier. He murdered his sons and took his own life after a series of court hearings that removed the children from his custody and severely limited his access to them.

Each year between 200 and 300 men are murdered by their spouses or ex-spouses.[3] As the research of Angela Browne reveals and the documentary film work on the Framingham Seven documents, the majority of male victims of domestic violence homicide are killed by wives and partners whom they have been abusing.[4] Often for decades.

The data are clear: IPV crosses all conceivable lines of demarcation; women of all race and ethnic groups are victims of IPV, being rich is not a blanket protection from becoming a victim of IPV, women of all ages are battered, religion (or no religious affiliation) is no protection from IPV, women are beaten in all regions of the country and in both rural and urban communities. That said, there are certain risk factors that make IPV more likely, including marrying young, being poor, having lots of children, and being African American.[5]

THE DIRTY LITTLE SECRET

We are not alone in referring to IPV in the African American community as the "dirty little secret"; IPV is considered by many African Americans to be something that, like dirty laundry, should not be aired to outsiders. Why? African Americans have many serious concerns about the attention that IPV, and higher rates of IPV in particular, brings to the African American community. For example, acknowledging that African American men beat their wives and girlfriends is to both acknowledge that African Americans can be violent—which reinforces one of the most powerful and damaging stereotypes—and it can mean turning yet another African American man over to a criminal justice system that has treated African American men in ways that are far less than fair and are often simply flat-out racist. Like many minority groups, there is a long history in the African American community of dealing with problems internally and not involving the dominant group—whites—who are perceived as being interested in policing problems in the African American community while ignoring problems in their own community. We completely understand these concerns.

Yet, of greater concern to us, is that by treating IPV as a "dirty little secret," African American women who are victims of IPV are denied the help they need and the men who beat them avoid accountability. Both of these outcomes lead to increased rates of IPV in the African American community; devastating the lives of women, their children, and even the men who batter them, and destroying what might have been healthy and supportive relationships.

For decades, including in our own earlier work, scholars and practitioners have always argued, perhaps because they were nervous about reinforcing stereotypes or about being politically correct or focusing too much on the differences rather than the universal experience of IPV, that rates of IPV are more or less the same across all racial and ethnic groups. And, though there are important reasons to highlight the fact that IPV is present in all racial and ethnic groups, at relatively similar rates, the latest data on IPV indicate that rates of violence, and severe violence in particular, are in fact slightly lower among white families and higher in both African American and Native American families. After Native Americans, African Americans experience the highest rates of IPV. Perhaps more perplexing is the fact that even our own analysis of national data indicate that African American women are more likely to experience what we term "lethal and near-lethal" forms of IPV; they are more likely to be beaten, stabbed, assaulted with a gun and kicked compared to white women. The most recent reports indicate that the gap in rates of IPV between whites and African Americans has grown, rather than narrowed, in the last few years.

As we will discuss, one question that emerges about these new data is the cause of the increasing gap between the violence perpetrated in white and African American homes. Of special concern is the fact that rates of IPV have remained relatively stable in white families—in any case they haven't declined—but the rates have risen in African American families. Potential causes of a now detectable racial difference in IPV include:

1. Perhaps because IPV is the "dirty little secret" of the African American community—African American women have consistently, until recently, underreported their experiences with violence.

2. Perhaps rates were consistent across racial groups until recently and this is in fact a change in the phenomenon itself.
3. Perhaps changes in the economy, which are related to both IPV and have affected African American families sooner and more severely than white families have created an actual divergence in rates of IPV across different racial groups.

In the next section of the chapter we will explore the differences in experiences for African Americans and whites that put African American women at a higher risk for experiencing IPV. As a preview, African American women are at a higher risk for being the victims of IPV because their partners—who are most often African American men—face more significant risk factors that increase their likelihood of resorting to violence. These experiences include:

- High rates of unemployment
- An inability to earn a living wage and support their families as a result of under employment and wage discrimination
- High rates of incarceration, which contribute to unemployment as well as other stresses on intimate relationships and family

Let's dig in and examine the ways in which these experiences with work and incarceration specifically shape the likelihood of engaging in violence.

BREADWINNER AND UNEMPLOYMENT: SOCIAL CLASS AND MONEY

At the individual level, finances and money are strongly linked to IPV. A common belief about couples is that they fight about two things: money and children. There is no doubt that money is an important part of family life. Generally, couples argue about how to obtain money, how to spend money, how to manage money, and who should be earning the money and by what means it should be earned.

Regardless of how families actually arrange breadwinning, childcare, and cooking and cleaning, the long-held belief is that men are supposed to be the "breadwinners" for their families. Even if men can't be the sole providers for their families, the cultural belief is that men *should be* the *primary breadwinners*, they should, at a minimum, earn more than their wives. For African American families meeting this cultural requirement has always been a struggle. Unlike white men, who were, for the most part and until the latest recession, able to provide for their families—supporting a stay at home mom, a house with a couple of cars in the garage, and a college fund. African American men have seldom been able to serve as sole breadwinners for their families, not because they didn't want to be but because they face many forms of discrimination in the labor market. Specifically, African American men have always and continue to face discrimination in hiring and in earnings; and as a result, African American families have always relied on women's contributions to the household bank account as well as men's.

Despite differences in the structures of white and African American families, African American men are held to the breadwinner standard just as much as white men are. When they are not successful as breadwinners, African American men, like all men, often feel emasculated. One reaction to this feeling of emasculation can be violence. Many of the men we interviewed, both white and African American, reported that one of the key "triggers" they identified as leading to their use of violence against their female partners was a feeling of being emasculated because they were unemployed or employed but earning less than their wives and girlfriends thought they should be.

In many cases, the African American men we talked to also noted that though they were comfortable with their financial contributions to the household, it was their wives and girlfriends who made them feel inadequate. Men reported that they felt nagged, which they considered behavior that escalated their arguments toward violence. They also felt that their wives and girlfriends expected them to provide for all of their needs and whims, and they felt they were often compared—negatively—to the husbands of their wives' friends who earned more. For example, Eddie said the following:

> Small stuff, you know. She's always complaining about that I don't treat her like a wife, because I don't buy her what she wants, things like I can't afford, she always throw up in my face like what her friend's husband, what kind of car he bought her and what kind of gifts he bought her. Of course he can buy her a brand new car when he's the assistant chief executive at Wachovia. And uh, she a RN, got a master's degree at Wake Forest, you know, and she complain about, oh and he just bought this $160,000 house and you know you married me and you supposed to do this for me and my children, well what you, what you gonna do for yourself, and she always just nick nagging at me.—Eddie, thirtysomething African American man, North Carolina

This type of nagging and unfair comparisons often developed into arguments and these men admitted that situations like these often escalated and turned violent. We should note, of course, that though the men focused on the nagging and the escalation, that in fact they were the ones who chose to engage in violence in response to what they perceived as a threat to their masculine identities.

We will devote an entire chapter to poverty and inside of that will be a lengthy discussion of unemployment. For our purposes here, it is important to make the connection between breadwinning and IPV. Though many men worry about their ability to provide for their families, and though finances are by far one of the most common reasons couples fight and these fights sometimes escalate and men resort to violence, this scenario is far more common among African American families because of the greater difficulties African American men face in providing for their families—as a result of extremely high rates of unemployment, underemployment, and wage discrimination—and is a clear contributor of higher rates of violence in African American homes.

INCARCERATION

We will devote a whole chapter to incarceration. What is germane to our argument here is the fact that incarceration, like unemployment, can precipitate IPV. There are three specific ways in which the high rates of incarcerating African American men can lead to violence in their homes. The first is that time in prison can quite simply socialize men to be more violent and most importantly to solve conflict with violence. Learning to fight in prison teaches both violence as a conflict resolution strategy and it reinforces the idea that one's identity as a "real" man, in essence what it means to be masculine, can be demonstrated through violence.

Second, as most readers are well aware and as we will discuss in our chapter on incarceration, men (and women) exiting prison face huge barriers to employment. Because it is legal for employers to ask about felonies and about periods of incarceration, and because they can legally refuse to hire people with a felony, and often do, it is very difficult for men coming out of prison to find stable employment. When they can't, they fail as breadwinners—or even as basic contributors—and as noted earlier, this can lead to violence in their relationships and homes.

Third, and perhaps less obvious, is the fact that incarceration puts strains on intimate relationships. Men who are locked up have hours and hours each day to think and one of the things they worry about is whether their wives and girlfriends are waiting for them and being faithful to them. Similarly, as committed as wives and girlfriends may be, depending on their circumstances and the length of the incarceration, they may move on with their lives. They may simply become interested in someone who is present! Or, often they need to find a partner with whom they can share the household expenses—they need a man to help provide for them—and this practical concern may lead to seeking and entering into new romantic relationships.

Whether real or imagined, the jealousy that can arise when men are incarcerated can come home with them. And, when it does, especially when there are signs that either his wife or girlfriend has started a new relationship or even just formed platonic friendships with other men, this can also be a "trigger" to violence. This was illustrated to us by Wanda and Chris, both of whom we interviewed. At the time we interviewed them, Chris was incarcerated for making violent threats against Wanda, his longtime, live-in girlfriend, and her children. In addition to making verbal threats, he was finally arrested when he took a gas can and poured gasoline around their home threatening to burn it down.

Chris had been in and out of jail and prison across their twenty-year relationship, mostly for drug convictions and felony assault; as a former boxer Chris often got into fights when he was drinking or using drugs. During his periods of incarceration, Wanda makes friends with other men who continue to call her and come by after Chris is released into the "free world." On a typical evening or weekend when Chris is "out," other men call and drop by "their" house to see Wanda. This was a major trigger for Chris. He was jealous. When he tried to physically assert what he saw as "his right to his woman," Wanda reminds Chris that because he was not the breadwinner in the household—based on his frequent incarcerations as well as a disability—and thus he had no claim to enforce the "rules."

> My house. I'm paying all the bills. I'm talking about rent, gas, light, phone, cable, everything. Everything. Everything. I even buy his deodorant, okay? So who are you? "I don't want nobody around my woman." All this and that, this and that. "What you want with my woman? Don't be calling my house!" But this is his house he say. I'm like, I said, "mother fucker, this ain't your damn house. This is my mother-fucking house! You can get the fuck out!" So now I'm mad. Now I'm like get the hell out.

The long and short, then, is that many of the problems that plague African American men—unemployment, wage discrimination, and incarceration to name a few—affect families in yet another way: increased rates of IPV. Thus, as we think about ways to reduce violence in African American families, we need to consider far more than electing an African American president, we need to identify these types of structural causes. Working, for example, to reduce unemployment or end wage discrimination will have the additional outcome, we imagine, of making African American households safer for all.

INDIVIDUAL CAUSES OF IPV

In earlier discussions we eluded to the fact that violence begets violence: Growing up in a violent household or growing up as a victim of sexual abuse tends to predict living with violence in adulthood. In this section we want to explore these relationships so that we have a better understanding of the processes and mechanisms that produce this unfortunate outcome. Let's start with a discussion of the impact on boys and young men.

THE IMPACT OF WITNESSING
DOMESTIC VIOLENCE IN CHILDHOOD

As we noted briefly in a previous chapter, in our discussion about corporal punishment and child abuse, we identified the fact that boys who grow up in homes where their fathers or stepfathers or mothers' boyfriends beat their mothers are three times more likely to grow up to be batterers themselves.

As always, we need to point out that growing up in a violent home is in no way a one-way ticket to becoming a batterer. Period. Yet, because witnessing violence raises one's risk so substantially, it is important for us to discuss the *process* by which this happens and offer reflections on prevention strategies.

We suppose it is somewhat comforting to think that violent behavior is passed on from father, or father figure, to son genetically. If this were the case, we could simply stop the cycle of violence by identifying batterers and putting their sons immediately into an intervention or prevention program. Yet, in talking with the batterers we interviewed and hearing them describe their own experiences, it becomes immediately apparent that the process of transmission is not quite so simple. Not only is it *not* biological, it is not even as straightforward as a simple process of socialization. Most of the men we interviewed, who had grown up witnessing extreme violence—including one who at age fourteen watched his mother shoot and kill his abusive father—insisted that they held themselves to a higher standard. They understood clearly, even better than some professionals who are reluctant to consider witnessing violence as a *standard form* of child abuse, the damage that witnessing the abuse had done to them. They had been hurt terribly by it, and they insisted that they would not grow up to abuse their partners and repeat the cycle. *As such, they did not set out to teach their sons to be violent.*

When we examine more carefully the cases of the men we interviewed, what emerges is a highly complex process. In fact, what we learned from these men who were reflecting on their own experiences as sons who witnessed violence and who grew up to be fathers who were abusive to their female partners is that what gets passed on in this intergenerational transmission are beliefs about men and women; beliefs about gender.

Most fathers, and certainly the men we interviewed, believe that boys need role models. One important aspect of this role modeling is explicitly to teach their sons how to be men, how to be masculine. Batterers are no exception. Though they may not teach their children explicitly that they should hit their romantic partners, they teach them how to be the man of the house, how to be in control, how to require certain behavior from their romantic partners. Furthermore, they teach their sons lessons about women. For example, they teach their sons about appropriate roles for women, about behaviors that they believe are common in women, and about the ways in which women will try to manipulate and control them. In essence, they need not teach their sons to hit women, because partner violence—especially verbal abuse—will be an almost inevitable outgrowth of their general lessons about the way women are, what it means to be a man, and the roles of men and women in relationship. If boys learn that they are the ones in charge, that women are out to manipulate them, and that real men keep their women in line, then it is quite favorable that these boys will grow up to be perpetrators of IPV, even if they are determined not to become batterers like their fathers. In Ward's words:

> As far as my son goes, I'm gonna teach him to stand up for himself, not to let anybody run over him. Just to really be cautious about who he deals with, um to really, really get to know the person, not just having sex with them and stuff like that, to really get to know someone before you get involved with them, cause there's so many diseases, it's uh, you have some . . . out there and so he just really needs to be aware of what that person likes and dislikes and see if it matches up with some of the stuff he likes and dislikes before he gets involved with her and makes a mistake.

A correlation between violence witnessed or experienced in childhood and violence in adulthood is not limited to boys who grow up to batter. Girls who experience abuse, especially sexual abuse, are at an increased risk to grow up to live with abusive partners.

HISTORY OF SEXUAL ABUSE

A disturbingly high percentage of women experience child sexual abuse; and rates are even higher in the African American community. The vast majority of African American girls we interviewed experienced some form of child sexual abuse, ranging from sexual initiation—their first sexual experience—as young teenagers with much older men, to incest and even childhood prostitution. Child sexual abuse tends to produce two different reactions that can leave women vulnerable to IPV: (1) marrying as a way to escape and (2) trading sex for protection. We should note that both of these behaviors can and often do coexist.

Sexual Abuse and a Drive to Escape

Among the women we interviewed, those who were victims of incest commonly moved out of the house and married early, during their adolescence—a practice that was encouraged by the mothers, often as a reaction to the jealousy they experienced when they learned that their husbands were having sex with their daughters. We personally find this to be a perplexing response, but it was incredibly common and thus it is important to unpack. Debbie, one of the women we interviewed, described to us the severe abuse—both physical and incest—that she had experienced as a child and her move to escape. She ran away from home at age seventeen. Homeless for a time she slept in an abandoned trailer at the local fairgrounds and there she met a young man. After a few weeks they had sex, and feeling guilty about it, they married. Debbie describes her decision to marry John.

> It was after three days we met that we kissed. And we never really discussed that kiss or nothing. We just liked each other right away. So he took me to a jewelry store and bought me an engagement ring and a wedding band. Then he had this necklace around his neck that said "I love you" that somebody gave to him. So he took it off and put it around my neck. Then I put the engagement ring and he asked me to go with him. And I said, "Sure." *I wanted to be free from my family. I thought if I get married, my name changes and I'm free from my family.*

Similar to the young women we described in the previous chapter who saw child-bearing as their only marker of adulthood, for many women like Debbie getting pregnant or married was perhaps the only route for escape that they could see from the incest. *All* of the women who acknowledged that they had been sexually abused or prostituted in childhood entered their first intimate, romantic sexual *relationships* before they were eighteen. Frequently these relationships involved living together (married or not) within weeks or months of the first date. Moving in with a male partner—even going so far as to legally marry him—seemed the most obvious escape route, one that *almost always* led to physical, emotional, and sometimes sexual abuse at the hands of their lovers. In their attempts to escape the sexual abuse they were experiencing at home these *girls* often left with the first man who would take them away (usually by marrying him) and within months it was clear to these women that they had traded one sort of violence and abuse for another. Debbie paints a graphic picture:

> I wanted to please him, [sexually] because my mom never talked to me or nothing. I had to figure out what I'm supposed to do. I knew you screwed, but I wanted more than that. So I looked at the videos. And when I did something on him that I learned from the video, he was like, "Oh, where did you learn to do that? You had to do it before somewhere else." But then he got sexually abusive. He wanted to like use objects on me and all kinds of stuff. When he did that, that's when I started hating him. And I wouldn't let him do it and he would get mad. And then he would tear my pictures up of my family and burned them. He tore up some of my clothes he bought me. One time he got so mad, we was going down the road and he ran his car into an overpass bridge. We were both in it, and he was going 80 miles per hour. He totaled the car, but we both walked out of it. [AH: Was he trying to kill you?] Yeah. He wanted to kill both of us.

The strategies Debbie employed, like those of so many other women we interviewed, extend a well-established finding by scholars who study child sexual abuse. Their research notes that child sexual abuse is a major pathway to careers in stripping and prostitution as well as juvenile delinquency.[6] We argue that seeking out sexual partners as a means of escape is similar to stripping and prostitution in that each involves trading sexual access for economic support. In contrast, when battered women we interviewed had *not* experienced child sexual abuse their pathway into the violent relationship less frequently resembled an escape. Furthermore, they were far more likely to leave violent relationships the *first time* they were hit. As a result they were seldom forced into the cycle of trading sexual access for the economic support of a man who would help them flee the current abuse.

Trading Sexual Access for Protection

Women who have been raped or sexually assaulted often view all men as dangerous. Living with the awareness that they can be victimized again, some women may put up with sexual and physical abuse by their intimate partners in exchange for the protection these men provide from the outside world. Victims of childhood sexual abuse entered their adult lives in a nearly *obsessive* search of exactly that kind of male protection.

Candy was molested at age fifteen by her mother's boyfriend. Like many of the other women's stories we heard, she sought adult, intimate partners who would protect her even while abusing her. Candy lived with Mark, a physically dominant man who is horribly abusive. Among many incidents, he choked her until she was unconscious, beat her against the stick shift of their car until her pelvis broke (causing her a few days later to miscarry their child), slapped her, pulled her hair, jumped on her and broke several ribs (almost causing an additional miscarriage and landing Candy in the hospital for two days), and bit her in the face at least ten times. At 5'9" and 120 pounds, Candy is extremely thin. At 300 pounds, even Mark's slaps are extremely dangerous. Candy also indicated that Mark had raped her "once or twice." When we met her she had been living with this violence for four to five years. However, Candy rationalizes that although Mark may beat her and abuse her emotionally, he doesn't allow anyone else to treat her this way.

Candy stays with him because he provides protection from the violence she fears she might otherwise experience at the hands of a stranger. The abuse she experiences with Mark is predictable, making it preferable to the unpredictable nature of sexual harassment and sexual and physical assault that women face in the workplace and outside world.

> When things were good, they were so good. Like I said, I was always secure with him. He might try to hit me and *he might try to kill me*, but nobody else was going to do it. Nobody else was going to talk bad to me or hurt me or talk bad about me. That just wasn't going to happen. I was secure in that sense with him. *He was going to protect me from everybody else.*

Candy's quote illustrates not only an extreme example of the types of violence these women live with, but it also demonstrates her cognizance and awareness of her situation. Many people believe that battered women have no agency or that they don't know how to make good choices. Candy's statement is clear: she understands very clearly the trade-off that she is making. And, though extreme, Candy's case illustrates the trade-off that many battered women make: choosing life-threatening violence that is predictable over the kind of random violence they perceive awaits them in the streets. And, because violence is a hallmark quality of low-income African American neighborhoods, this risk is higher for African American women and especially those who are poor than it is for middle- and upper-class African American women or white women of any social class. African American women are therefore more often forced to chose to live in violent relationships to protect themselves from the violence in their neighborhoods.

And, in cases like Candy's, this choice also puts her at risk of becoming one of the 1,500 women who are murdered by their partners and ex-partners each year. And, it illustrates, profoundly, the mistake US society makes in teaching women to fear strangers when in fact their greatest risk for violence is in their own homes.

CONCLUSIONS

When analyzing domestic violence we have to ask this question: does the election of the first African American president affect the likelihood that African American men will batter and that African American women will face an increased risk of being victimized by domestic violence, and in what way? In short, does this election signify that we have now entered a postracial America when it comes to IPV?

Perhaps the most disturbing aspect of intimate partner violence in the African American community is the fact that home becomes dangerous for folks who need it most. As we will discuss in subsequent chapters, African Americans, especially men, face the highest rate of homicide and physical assault of all Americans. They also face the highest rates of stress-induced diseases, including heart disease and diabetes. Along with stresses that go hand in hand with high rates of unemployment and poverty, many people talk about the hidden costs of being African American. The stress and violence in the outside world make the need for home to be a safe, comfortable place to land that much more important. When home is a place of violence—both for the victims and for the children who witness it—the impact of racism and discrimination in the "outside" world are magnified.

As we noted when we opened our discussion in this chapter, men in all social class groups batter; that said, poverty is a risk factor for violence, both because people fight about money and also because men feel a responsibility to provide for their families and when they cannot they may feel emasculated—or they may feel nagged—and they may resolve these feelings by beating up their wives and girlfriends. Thus, not only are poor and low-income African American men more liable to batter, we can anticipate that rates of battering in the African American community will likely *increase* in response to the recession. In fact, we can be relatively certain that not only will rates of violence increase in low-income and poor households, but also in middle-class households where men are facing increased unemployment and higher than usual levels of underemployment, the perfect storm for emasculation that produces violent reactions. In short, the election of an African American president, regardless of the model he and his family provide—a healthy relationship, characterized by a strong woman, a confident man, a true partnership—will have little impact on violence in African American families unless this administration can reenergize the economy and put African American men back to work.

Lastly, we want to point out that because of powerful cycles of violence—both of among boys who witness violence and girls who are sexually abused—one the most powerful tools we have at our disposal to reduce IPV is to interrupt the cycle of violence by treating child witnesses of IPV as victims and by recognizing that girls who are victim of incest, are sexually abused, and especially those who are lured into sexual activity when they are too young and their "partners" are too old, are wounded and vulnerable. Though we should design and implement effective interventions with all children, we need to specifically target boys and girls who are caught in the web of violence and who are thus at risk for continuing the cycle of violence. We have lost too many African American boys, girls, men, and women to violence in the streets and when we ignore the violence in the home we allow an even greater tragedy to continue.

5

Education

What about Affirmative Action? Where Are the Guaranteed Seats for White Students?

In New York City, at the time this book takes place in the late 1990s, spends about $8000 yearly on each student overall, including special education . . . but considerably less than this—about $5000—on each boy or girl like Elio or Ariel in ordinary classrooms in the South Bronx. . . If you had the power to lift up one of these children in your arms and plunk him down within one of the relatively wealthy districts of Westchester County, a suburban area that borders New York City to the north, he would suddenly be granted a public education worth at least $12,000 every year and would also have a teacher who is likely to be paid as much as $20,000 more than what a teacher can be paid in the South Bronx. If you could take a slightly longer ride and bring these children to an upper-middle-class school district such as Great Neck or Manhassett on Long Island, Elio and Ariel would be in schools where over $18,000 are invested, on the average, in a child's public education every year.

Despite the many ways in which this issue has been clouded, nonetheless, there are few areas in which the value we attribute to a child's life may be so clearly measured as in the decisions we make about the money we believe it's worth investing in the education of one person's child as opposed to that of someone else's child.

Excerpted from Jonathan Kozol's book, *Ordinary Resurrections*, 2000.

Myth: The racial gap in high school graduation and the extremely low rates of college attendance among African Americans are a result of individual choices. Black kids are perceived to be lazy and having no interest in education other than as a pathway, for boys, to the NBA and the NFL. This is bolstered by the widely held perceptions that blacks who do seek an education are "selling out" or "acting white." If blacks wanted to lift themselves out of poverty, they would learn to value education and make a commitment to it.

Reality: Despite the fact that Kozol's descriptions of public schools were published a decade ago, the facts remain more or less the same. The majority of African American kids attend schools that are like those Kozol described: they are (1) severely under-resourced, and (2) almost entirely segregated. Both conditions make getting an education that matters difficult if not nearly impossible. As damaging is the fact that African American children of professional parents and those in the "upper classes" that Eugene Robinson describes populate the same exclusive public and private schools that the children of professional and wealthy white parents attend, thus masking and rendering nearly invisible the realities of segregation that most African American children continue to live under more than fifty-five years after the historic *Brown v. the Board* decision that ended segregation in public places, including schools.

This chapter will focus on the resegregation of the American public school system and the ways in which this resegregation exacerbates the resource gap between "white" and "black" public schools in the United States. Many middle-class white Americans fear that they are "losing ground" to African Americans in terms of education. This misconception is based in part on the fact they are aware that the African American children of doctors and lawyers and college professors, children like Sasha and Malia Obama, attend the most exclusive public and private schools, alongside the children of professional and prominent whites. This leads to two important misconceptions: (1) that their own children, who do not attend these schools, are losing an advantage they once had, and (2) that schools are truly integrated. The truth is that schools are as segregated now as they were in the 1960s. This is problematic for a number of reasons, but among them is the role that segregation plays in resource allocation, high school dropout rates, and underachievement.

BROWN V. BOARD OF EDUCATION: THE HISTORY OF SCHOOL SEGREGATION IN THE UNITED STATES

Denying African Americans access to education has been a fundamental part of their experience for the 400 plus years they have been in the United States. One of the primary mechanisms for keeping slaves on the plantation and exploitable by whites was the prohibition against teaching African Americans to read.

Shortly after emancipation, freed blacks began setting up schools all over the South, transforming education in the southern region of the United States in many interesting and unexpected ways. In short, as a result of the need to maintain strict segregation, and the concomitant requirement on African Americans to establish their own schools if they wanted access to any education, a system of public education was never established in the South. Adding to the complexities was the fact that wealthy whites, long aware of the tradition of outstanding education provided by boarding schools in the Northeast, established a long-standing pattern of sending their children to these northeastern private schools to be educated. Slightly ahead of the game in the South, as African Americans had more quickly realized the need to set up their own schools, it wasn't long until many observers including Du Bois, noted that African American children were outpacing poor whites in terms of education. The response of whites was to establish a system of public education for poor whites, who could not afford to have their children educated in the private schools in the Northeast, so they would not fall behind African Americans. Of course this system of education was segregated. A system that would be challenged on a regular basis until the historic US Supreme Court case that is colloquially referred to as *Brown v. the Board.*[1] The challenges continue in various forms in many parts of the South even today.

Across the entire history of the United States, the majority of African Americans attended inferior grammar and secondary schools. Those seeking to attend white schools, including colleges and universities, were often denied access. Some schools in the North desegregated voluntarily and in some cases early in the twentieth century, but schools in the South resisted integration severely and systematically. In some cases movements to integrate even under court order erupted into violence. The integration of Central High School in Little Rock, Arkansas, was so contentious that President Eisenhower sent National Guard troops to protect the eight young men and women attempting to attend school there. Similarly, when James Meredith attempted to integrate the University of Mississippi a near war broke out forcing President Kennedy to send in armed troops. Governor Ross Barnett closed the Ole Miss campus in response—temporarily suspending instruction for the all-white student body rather than integrate.

The *Brown v. the Board* decision which guaranteed African Americans the right to attend any public school was intended to offer access to the institution of education to everyone—or at least every citizen—in the United States, a fact which is now being heavily debated as it relates to the children of undocumented immigrants. Yet, it has been only partially successful. First, the Supreme Court decision was resisted. It was intensely resisted in the Deep South so much so that many Southern school districts were not integrated until the early 1970s, nearly twenty years after the historic decision.[2] The most severe resistance to school integration was in Mississippi. The resistance movement resulted in the development of a set of private, often religiously affiliated, academies, colloquially referred to as "seg academies" to recognize that they were and continue to be entirely segregated. An important point to note is that because they figured out a way to operate without taking any public funds they are not required by the *Brown* decision to integrate. We should note that they are also not required to be accredited and in many poor "seg" academies the teachers have less experience and fewer credentials than teachers in the "black public schools," as they are referred to. Though it is a hard case to make that poor "seg" academies offer an inferior education to public schools serving poor black children, it is interesting to note that poor whites endorse or at least accept inferiority in their own schools as long as they can remain racially segregated.

THE RESEGREGATION MOVEMENT

By the mid-1970s, primarily as a simple result of court order, but also as a result of districts in the South like Charlotte-Mecklenburg recognizing that if they voluntarily "integrated," they would be left alone to design the shape this integration would take; the United States entered a twenty-year period of relative school integration. Following the period of real progress in school integration (1970s–1990s), over the last twenty years we have seen a serious reversal of that trend—a 13 percent decline in overall integration. In short, an African American child in school today is more likely to attend highly segregated schools than his parents did! For example, although minority enrollment in public schools is now nearly 40 percent nationwide, the *typical* white student attends a public school that is 80 percent white. Furthermore, in many districts, the majority of African American students attend schools that are 100 percent African American.[3] And, consistent with the US Supreme Court case in *Plessy v. Ferguson*, Jonathan Kozol has demonstrated repeatedly—as illustrated in the excerpt that opens this chapter—across the last two decades that separate education is never equal.

EDUCATIONAL ATTAINMENT

Given this long history of a struggle for equal education, it is not surprising that education remains a site of inequality for African Americans. The data on educational attainment for African Americans and whites are dismal.

At the most basic level, graduating from high school, only 61.5 percent of African American youth graduate from high school—a figure thirty points lower than for white youth. Not surprising is the fact that girls are far more likely to graduate from high school than boys. Continuing on, we find some disturbing trends: the gender gap is substantially greater for all minorities, and African Americans in particular. Whereas white girls graduate at a rate only 5 percentage points higher than boys, the difference is double that for African Americans; 59 percent of African American girls graduate, but only 48 percent of African American boys do. The African American community is in serious trouble, and long term, if *fewer than half of the young men are graduating from high school.* It's difficult to envision how the prosperity associated with education will ever be reached by sectors of the African American community.

Returning to the framework provided by Robinson, wherein he described an African American community highly divided along class lines, with enormous chasms between the haves and the have-nots, we can safely assume that the likelihood of dropping out of or graduating from high school is not evenly spread across the different groups within the African American community. We can assume that the dropout rate is highest among the "abandoned," while rates among the middle class and the "transcendents" remains similar to the rates in the white community—a fact that further exacerbates the growing chasm inside the African

American community as well as between poor African Americans and the mainstream experience of most whites.

These differences in high school graduation rate translate into a series of parallel problems. First, the high school degree or its equivalent remains a requirement for many jobs that pay above the minimum wage. Thus, not having a high school diploma means one will only be eligible for the lowest paying jobs in the service sector (fast food shops and discount retail stores). The authors of the Manhattan Institute study sum up the outcomes for those not graduating from high school.[4]

- High school dropouts, on average, earn $9,245 less per year than high school graduates.
- The poverty rate for families headed by high school dropouts is *more than twice* that for families headed by high school graduates.
- Dropouts are much more likely to be unemployed, less likely to vote, and more likely to be imprisoned than high school graduates. *And, this is particularly true for African American men.*

It goes beyond saying that the disadvantages to not having a high school diploma are exacerbated in the current recession where the very jobs—that allowed someone (usually a man) with only a high school diploma or even without one—to earn a decent living have disappeared, either having been exported abroad or discontinued entirely. And, clearly, high school graduation is a prerequisite for the next step: earning a college degree.

One way to "count" college graduation is to consider the percent of people in the US population who have a bachelor's degree. But, given that college attendance has risen dramatically across the second half of the twentieth century—beginning largely with the GI Bill that made college affordable and accessible to middle-class Americans—a more accurate gauge is to examine graduation rates based on students entering college during the first decade of the twenty-first century. For those entering college in 2003, graduation rates are discouraging for all racial and ethnic groups. But they are dismal for African Americans; only 16 percent of whom earned a four-year college degree (bachelors) in six years (by 2009), half the rate (36 percent) of whites. Looking closer, there are a number of contributing factors. First, we should emphasize that 16 percent of all African Americans earned a college degree by 2009, *but only 16 percent of those who entered college* successfully earned a degree within six years. Given that only 50 percent of African American young adults graduate from high school, even if all of them entered college, with a graduation rate of only 16 percent this would translate into an overall rate of earning a college degree at more like 8 percent for the entire population of college age African Americans. And, because we can safely assume that not all of the college-eligible young adults enter college, the college degree "yield," if you will, is probably closer to 5 percent. Again, it is important to note that the 5 percent of African Americans who do earn a college degree each year are not evenly spread across the population, thus adding

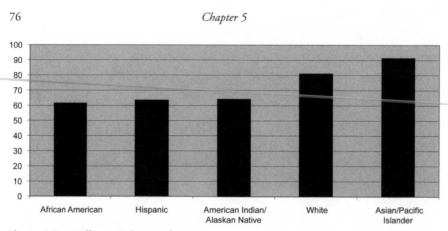

Figure 5.1.   College attainment by race.

another layer to the ever-widening gap among the subgroups in the African American community; in this case the college graduation rate likely separates further the middle-class black community from the "transcendent" in one direction and from the "abandoned" in the other.[5]

Despite all of the rhetoric colleges and universities engage in around diversity and the "competition" that many institutions seem to be engrossed in about whose entering freshman class is the most diverse, there is a persistent and disturbing racial gap in college graduation. What's most interesting to note is that the gap, though it exists at both public and private colleges, is substantially greater at private schools, where the graduation gap is 30 percentage points (whites graduate at 70 percent and African Americans at only 45 percent).[6] This suggests, among a number of other things, that social class differences persist even among African American and white families who believe they have the resources to send their kids to college. We will discuss this issue at much greater length in a subsequent chapter, but here we point out that among African Americans and whites who earn the same amount of money, there is a substantial gap in the wealth that each family holds. Because the majority of this wealth is likely invested in owning a home or in financial investments, and because these are the types of resources many families rely on to pay for their children's college education, we suspect that it is wealth differences, not "earnings" differences that contribute to the significant dropout rate among African American youth who enter private colleges. Our personal experience teaching at a private college for fifteen years is that private colleges are eager to admit a diverse incoming class, e.g., African American students. Except for the very well-endowed schools (Harvard, Yale, Princeton, Duke), these same colleges are rarely able to offer the level of financial support, especially non-loan support, that will allow these students to stay in college for four years and earn a degree.

Last, one of the most concerning problems facing African Americans and higher education is the state of the historically black colleges and universities (HBCUs). Like so many other institutions that were built by African Americans to serve the needs of their community during the hyper-segregation of Jim Crow, the HBCUs were once thriving institutions with important histories and missions, but they were devastated by integration. As colleges and universities began to open their doors to African Americans, many of those who could enter "white" institutions did so; in large part because "white" institutions, be they elite colleges or flagship state universities (e.g., University of North Carolina, University of Michigan), always have and continue to be ranked among the most competitive in the nation. Fair or not, there is not a single HBCU that ranks in the top 100 according to *US News and World Reports* annual college rankings. Morehouse College is the highest-ranked HBCU and it comes in at 127 among national liberal arts colleges.

Today, most HBCUs struggle with enrollment and all struggle with finances. Exacerbating their problems are their persistently low graduation rates. It is not uncommon for an HBCU to report a graduation rate lower than 25 percent. We have to ask the question, what African American parent would encourage their child to attend college at an HBCU with a lower graduation rate for African American students than the average public institution that graduates just under 50 percent of its entering African American students? The struggles of the HBCUs, which had already been considered inferior by whites, only serve to lessen the value of the degree earned.

When we evaluate even further and consider the low graduation rates at private colleges and universities, where incidentally, African American students are also grossly underrepresented, and couple that with the declining presence and prestige of even the top HBCUs, we see yet another layer of difference and inequality. Even among college graduates, African Americans are less likely to be able to seek high-powered careers in law, medicine, finance, banking, education, and so forth quite simply because their credentials are less likely to be from the leading institutions and more likely to be from lower-ranked colleges and universities. This alone creates barriers to access and inequalities in careers even among the highest achieving African Americans and whites. That the boardrooms of America are almost entirely white, and male, is an outcome of these many layers of inequality. Finally, the belief that African Americans need even better credentials than whites, creates a situation in which the very few African Americans who do graduate from Harvard Law School—as did President Barack Obama—may see extraordinary success, but these successes will be rare. Though whites who graduate from their local state university may be able to achieve similar results, as did Dick Cheney, alumnus of the University of Wyoming, this will be even more rare for African Americans.

ACCESS TO EDUCATION: LEGACY

One of the most interesting and least talked about forms of systematic or institutionalized discrimination is the use of "legacy" as a factor in making college admissions decisions. Though we imagine there is wide variation in the ways in which colleges might use "legacy" in making an admissions decision—from an automatic admission to a small point value assigned to an applicant for being a legacy—the bottom line is that colleges and universities do give some preference, regardless of its size or value, to the children of their alums. This creates one more layer of discrimination for African Americans.

We argue here that preference for legacies can be considered the ultimate in affirmative action, precisely because it gives preference based on "status" rather than qualifications. Furthermore, legacy is primarily a benefit that accrues to whites for two reasons: (1) historically higher rates of attending college, and (2) racial segregation. What is particularly insidious about legacy is that it is often associated with institutions that refused admission to African Americans until relatively recently, and thus African Americans *have been completely locked out of legacy preferences.*

For example, many Southern universities, both public and private, did not admit African American students until the early 1970s. As a result, when they include legacy status as part of their admissions decisions, it takes an entire generation *after* admitting the first African American students to have even the *potential* for extending legacy preferences to African American applicants. Simply put, a cohort of *children* of African American alumni, the potential beneficiaries of legacy preferences, didn't even exist until 1990 *at the earliest.* In contrast the children of white alumni have benefited from this practice for at least 150 years. Legacies are a great example of the ways in which policies and practices that may not seem discriminatory on the face of it, create incredible barriers for African Americans while simultaneously allowing whites to benefit from the vast majority of the advantages. Like so many forms of racism, policies like this do not require "racist" individuals; they work to allow whites to retain advantages regardless of the personal beliefs or politics of the person charged with implementing the policy, in this case the director of admissions, or the beneficiary, in this case the college applicant.

This example also makes it completely clear that regardless of intent or desire or individual effort, there are barriers to African Americans earning college degrees despite their best efforts. These barriers are far more powerful than the myths that many people hold that African Americans don't go to college because they are lazy or because they think going to college is "acting white" or because they don't know the value of a college education.

Of equal importance is the way in which these kinds of advantages are invisible to whites. First, many white people are ignorant of the role that legacy plays in college admissions. Second, even if they are aware of it, they are likely to attribute their own successes, in this case being admitted to a competitive college, as their own doing, rather than realizing that their status—as a legacy, or the advantage their ancestors had to be admitted while African Americans were systematically denied access that created the legacy to begin with—plays a substantial role in their admissions. As we noted, this is one of the most powerful and ignored forms of "affirmative action." The very same people who claim that affirmative action is reverse racism, likely are unaware or choose to ignore the many long-standing policies from which they benefit. Oftentimes the same beneficiaries of policies like legacies in college admissions are the ones most apt to scream about race-based affirmative action policies implemented by their very same alma maters.

WHAT DOES A COLLEGE EDUCATION GET YOU?

A study, completed in 2011, by Georgetown University researchers noted that a college education continues to "buy" the recipient goods in the labor market. College graduates earn, on average, 84 percent more than high school graduates, which translates into $2.3 million over the lifetime of the college-educated worker.[7] What is most perplexing about this research is the finding that a college education does little to close the wage gap between African Americans and whites. For example, African Americans with a master's degree earn the same amount as whites with only a bachelor's degree. There are many possible reasons for this that may have to do with the kinds of degrees that African Americans earn (sociology versus engineering), the status of the institutions from which they earn these degrees (as we noted earlier), and the types of jobs they seek. That said, findings like this, and we note the same applies to gender, are strong indicators of discrimination at work—in terms of hiring, pay, the ability to advance, and so forth.

Despite the fact that racial (and gender) earning gaps persist even among college-educated folks, it is clear that earning a college degree, as well as an advanced degree, is an individual approach and solution to many of the problems facing African Americans. We need to recognize that education is our most valuable asset and it is one of the few ways that any of us can improve our personal circumstances. (We will address the often relied upon strategy in the African American community of focusing on athletics as a way "out of the ghetto" in the next chapter.)

Yet, clearly, much of what we have talked about in this chapter, and what we have argued, is that most of the problems with education and the African American community are not about individual decisions or actions, but about structural causes and barriers.

A NOTE ABOUT FOR-PROFIT COLLEGES

One of the most controversial players in the American system of higher education is the proliferation of for-profit, mostly online, colleges and universities. These colleges and universities target populations of people who share a set of characteristics—minorities, college dropouts, the unemployed and underemployed, soldiers returning from war, felons about to exit prison, and middle-aged divorced women—who are vulnerable to their exploitive tactics. Specifically, they lure student "consumers" in by promising that student loans will pay for the entire cost of the degree, that they can earn a degree entirely online, and that this degree will translate into the high paying careers that have otherwise eluded them. In reality, most students who enter these types of programs never graduate, they wind up with tens of thousands of dollars in student loans, and they never achieve the careers they are looking for. Reasons for this are the positions they seek often require more training or different credentials and the jobs they promise waiting on the other end of the degree are extremely limited. As a result, many of these programs have faced lawsuits and government investigation for unethical behavior and fraud.

An example of the ways in which for-profit degree programs lure students, despite a lack of appropriate jobs postgraduation, is the relatively recent proliferation of culinary institutes and schools. The typical graduate spends nearly $50,000 for a nine-month degree program only to graduate and instead of finding a job as an executive chef, she finds that the only jobs available are as line cooks making $10 an hour. Additionally, these for-profit degree programs benefit from television; namely programs like Bravo's *Top Chef* that run during the day when many unemployed, or recently released inmates or service people are home watching television.

CONCLUSIONS

When analyzing education, does the election of the first African American president affect how African Americans access educational institutions, and in what way? In short, does this election signify that we have now entered a postracial America with regards to education?

In this chapter we have explored racial differences in educational attainment and the so-called achievement gap as well as the myth that the cause of this gap is something inherent in or unique to minorities and African Americans in particular. Discouraging as it is, more than fifty years after the historic *Brown v. Board of Education* decision that officially desegregated schools (and other public institutions), African American youth fall miles behind their white peers in terms of graduating from high school, earning a college degree, and virtually every single measure of educational attainment. That said, when we drill down two important phenomena emerge: (1) the primary causes of the racial differences in education and achievement are structural rather than individual, and (2) racial differences vary significantly by social class, and in many cases it is actually social class that is the horse driving the cart.

The predominant myth, in its many iterations, is that African Americans drop out of high school more often and graduate from college less often *for individual reasons.* The no-longer acceptable flat-out racist explanation—that African Americans are simply less intelligent—has been replaced by what race theorists like Eduardo Bonilla-Silva identify as the new face of racism, termed "symbolic racism." In short, Bonilla-Silva describes symbolic racism as a set of beliefs that many whites, especially liberal whites, hold including the belief that racial barriers have been erased, that the United States is now a "level playing field" and that they simply don't see race (they are "color-blind"). Because they truly believe, often deep in their hearts, that the structural barriers African

Americans faced historically have been destroyed and because they believe they would personally never discriminate, then the only reasonable remaining explanation for gaps in education is individual; African Americans are lazy, place a lower value on education, believe being educated is "selling out" or "acting white."

In fact, the biggest contributor to lower achievement among African Americans is quite simply that they continue to attend segregated and under-resourced elementary, middle and high schools. The issue of segregation and the use of affirmative action at all levels of education, from school redistricting to the use of race in college admissions is back on the docket of the US Supreme Court, as the justices may choose to revisit a case they decided in 2003 involving a white student who sued the University of Texas based on her denial of admission, *Fisher v. University of Texas*. In 2003 the US Supreme Court upheld the right of the University of Texas to consider race in admissions decisions. But, now, many years after the key decision at the University of Michigan (*Grutter v. Bollinger*) and with a new complexion among the justices, there is some concern that if they hear this case and rule in favor of the plaintiff that affirmative action policies in higher education will forever be dismantled.

The authors of the Georgetown study we referred to earlier noted that the racial gap in students' verbal skills actually increased the longer that children were in school; what begins as a small gap in vocabulary among entering kindergartners grows substantially by the time students enter middle school. If lack of parental involvement or interest in education were to blame, we would expect this gap to be greatest among younger, preschool children who are socialized primarily at home with their parents and to decline over time, as they proceed through school. Since the opposite occurs, the Georgetown researchers ask, what is wrong in schools?

As we reviewed a myriad of studies for this chapter, it also becomes clear quickly that there are important and substantial variations in education by social class. Though whites at all income levels are more likely to graduate from high school and attend college, there is far less of a racial gap among professionals, upper-income families, and the wealthy. Not only do the children of wealthy African Americans and whites achieve at similar levels, but African American youth who are raised in professional and upper-income families succeed perhaps because they are not subjected to the structural disadvantages that plague middle- and low-income African Americans; namely they attend the same public and private high schools as their white counterparts. This is important not only because it makes a strong case for the role that schooling plays in achievement, but also because the presence of these children in predominately "white" schools, renders invisible for white parents the continued presence of a segregated system. For professional and upper-income whites, who tend to be the most liberal on race issues, they pick up their children in the carpool lane or attend school plays and they see African American students alongside their own. They then come to the conclusion that schools must be integrated and any persistent problems that remain must not be the result of structural disadvantages, which is a part of the basis of the development of new forms of racism, including symbolic racism. They may also be lulled into thinking that any persistent problems are simply related to social class, or they may buy into the stereotypes we discussed earlier and therefore they may suggest that solutions must be individually based: we need to increase African American interest in education.

As should be clear, the election of the first African American president will in no way, by itself, change anything about the educational experiences of African Americans. Though we would like to think that as president he serves as a role model to young African American youth who might now aspire to a career in politics, the truth is that the vast majority of African Americans (save those in the professional and upper classes—and who will likely achieve success regardless of his presence as a role model in the White House) attend the types of schools that Jonathan Kozol describes and there is little hope that they will gain the educational skills necessary to pursue this dream. Without radical changes to the system of education: specifically adequate funding for all schools and true desegregation and integration, we have very little hope for the future of African American youth and our country in general.

Lastly, as Eugene Robinson's framework points out, the fact that social class strongly influences the educational experiences of African Americans which in turn significantly shapes their futures—they become the new generation of doctors and lawyers and college professors, so to speak or they face a lifetime of underemployment sprinkled with bouts of unemployment—contributes in important ways to the growing gap among the "haves and the have-nots" in the African American community: separating the transcendents and the mainstream middle class from the abandoned. In subsequent chapters we will expose the ways in which education attainment contributes to a life shaped by poverty or wealth.

6

Athletics

Ticket out of the Ghetto
(or, Straight Out of Compton)

The Robert Taylor Homes in south Chicago have been called the place where hope dies. I'm living proof that's not the case. . . . Robert Taylor is down the Dan Ryan Expressway about a mile south of Comisky Park. Twenty buildings along a two-mile stretch. Home to about twenty thousand people. The best overall description of the place is just one word. They were—and are—projects. And the Robert Taylor Homes in particular now have the reputation of being one of the worst inner-city projects in the entire country. The kids who grow up there tend to be written off as no good, and a lot of them are never expected to amount to anything by their parents, their friends, the press, or by anybody, really. . . . The standard line is that you may very well come out of the Robert Taylor Homes wearing a uniform with a number, but it's more likely to be issued by the state prison, not a baseball or basketball or football team.

Kirby Puckett's *I Love This Game! My Life and Baseball.* New York: Harper Paperbacks, 1994, 37–38.

Kirby Puckett was a highly successful baseball player who spent his entire career with the Minnesota Twins, led them to two World Series titles, went to many All-Star games, and received MVP awards, as well as other awards.

Myth: The clearest pathway to success for African American men is via sports simply because African Americans—both men and women—are naturally gifted as athletes.

Reality: As with educational underperformance, there is little evidence to conclude that athletic dominance in sports—which by the way is in many ways a misperception because African Americans only dominate in the higher profile American sports of football and basketball—is a result of individual gifts and talents. Rather, just as with educational achievements, there are strong structural forces that shape African American dominance on the US sports scene.

This chapter will take on the myth that sports is the best or perhaps the only route to the American dream for African Americans. We will begin by challenging the myth that African Americans are dominant in sports because they are imbued with natural talents and gifts: the myth of the natural black athlete. Next we will debunk the notion that sports is dominated by African Americans by revealing that this dominance is limited to only a few sports; though African Americans dominate as players on the fields of college and professional football and on the courts of college and professional basketball, they are woefully underrepresented in every other sport as well as in sports leadership of all sports, including football and basketball. Finally, our discussion will reveal that the most utilized pathways to success are actually *mainstream* routes—the professions. We will close the chapter by considering the role that African Americans' own beliefs about sports as the avenue to success plays in their singular pursuit of this pathway at the exclusion of others. As Jack Olsen, award-winning journalist, said in 1968: "The Negro has the keener desire to excel in sports because it is more mandatory for his future opportunities than it is for a white boy."

THE NATURAL BLACK ATHLETE

Both the general public as well as noted researchers continue to be fascinated by the possibility of the concept of the "natural black athlete." There are many reasons why both African Americans and whites are intrigued by this possibility.

- It "explains" the fact that the NBA has gone from nearly all white just fifty years ago to approximately 85 percent African American today thus allowing whites to feel "off the hook" for not producing the next "great white hope" for basketball.
- It offers a ray of hope to African Americans who see their options in other arenas—education, politics, business—either closing down or remaining narrow.
- It offers whites a way to feel good; despite the fact that every single business, including the business of sports, is dominated by whites. It produces the false sense that African Americans have a place they can dominate, too.

For what it's worth this last point probably provides a mechanism to assuage the guilt many white people carry about the lack of "progress" for African Americans in every other venue, similar to the way that the election of Barack Obama makes many whites feel better about themselves and restores their belief in the underlying values of American society.

The concept of the "natural black athlete" has a long and very controversial history. It has been used, primarily by white scholars, to attempt to explain the sudden rise in dominance by African Americans in various sports, but primarily track and field, football and basketball. As the reader is probably aware, these sports were transformed fairly radically and quickly, beginning in the 1950s, from entirely white, to a majority African American. The main question plaguing white scholars is the question: What happened to the white athlete?

Much of the focus of scholars who study the concept of the "natural black athlete" has been on track and field and specifically the sheer dominance of African Americans in the sprint events. Expanding beyond the United States, we see that the men's and women's 60-yard, 100-yard, and 200-yard races are dominated by people of African descent, primarily US runners and runners from the Caribbean. Indeed Usain Bolt, a Jamaican runner holds, the current title of "fastest man on the planet." In short, the belief is that speed is a "black" trait.

This notion that speed is a "black trait" is further reinforced by the dominance of Kenyans and Ethiopians in the middle- and long-distance events, ranging all the way from the 1,500-meter to the marathon. What perplexes scholars and sports commentators alike is the fact that the physical qualities—especially body type—that are believed to give black people the biological gift of speed vary tremendously based on the distance of the race. For example, the Kenyans and Ethiopian men and women who dominate the middle and very long distance races are typically short, very thin, and unusually long-legged. In contrast, the blacks who dominate the sprints are taller and more muscular. Both men and women often have unusually large thighs, buttocks, and shoulders while having very thin waists. The conundrum is how to explain the dominance of black runners while taking into account that the physical traits needed to dominate vary; in short, how can the gift be a "racial" trait, when the natural gifts that lead to the advantage vary so much. This conundrum has led scholars to hone in on some of the biological differences between East Africans—the Kenyans and Ethiopians—and West Africans who were the primary population captured into slavery in the "new world" and who are the ancestors of most "African Americans" as well as blacks throughout the Caribbean and Central and South America. One physical trait that has received much attention, and with which readers may be familiar, is "muscle twitch." The scientists who pay attention to the biological traits of the "natural black athlete" have identified two separate categories, "slow" and "fast" muscle twitch fiber. Their hypothesis is that East Africans have more "slow" muscle twitch fiber, which gives them the muscle endurance that is an advantage in running long distances whereas West Africans are noted for having a higher ratio of "fast" muscle twitch fiber, which allows for the more explosive ability that is an advantage in short distance races. Although everyone has muscle fiber, the need to explain the "natural black athlete" hypothesis has led to the belief that these traits are uniquely distributed across the African continent.

What often falls off the "radar screen" of those engrossed in this heated debate is the overlooked fact that "pure" West Africans *do not* dominate the sprints, instead it is "African Americans," many of whom are actually of some mixed race ancestry, who do. Furthermore, other racial groups that can be characterized as sharing the typical body build of East Africans—short in stature, very thin, very low body fat—namely populations in part of Asia, including South Asia, do not dominate to nearly the same degree in the longer distances. This should be our first clue that something besides "race" is at work.

Yet, these beliefs are widely held. Even the legendary Roger Bannister, the first human being to run a sub-five-minute mile, speaking before an audience at a meeting of the British Association for the Advancement of Science, espoused his belief in the racial distribution of athleticism:

> As a scientist rather than a sociologist, I am prepared to risk political incorrectness by drawing attention to the seemingly obvious but under stressed fact that African American sprinters and African American athletes in general all seem to have certain natural anatomical advantages.[1]

There are several problems with the arguments associated with the "natural black athlete." Briefly they fall into two areas: (1) the misappropriation of the racial category "black" as a biological category rather than a social construct, and (2) the tendency to ignore structural factors including environmental factors, cultural factors, and social class that contribute to athletic success and even dominance. We illustrate these problems with the case of two groups with extraordinary talents but also extraordinary circumstances: Kenyans and Sherpas.

Race and Biology

Let's consider the Kenyans, for example. In addition to being African, and "black," native Kenyans grow up and live their whole lives at high altitude. The advantage in lung capacity—which is a key component of long-distance running—that is gained by living for decades at high altitude is enhanced by the fact that they also train in this environment. Perhaps, then, the advantage has nothing to do with being "black" and has everything to do with living and training at high altitude. We are even willing to concede that this advantage becomes part of the genetic code and is passed down over generations. Thus, an advantage that accumulates over centuries is certainly biological. But this is different from a physical trait being "racial." We note that there are other examples of this kind of modern evolutionary process, including a change over the last several thousand years in the lactose tolerance of one Kenyan ethnic group, the Masai.

To test this hypothesis, we turn to an examination of another group, the Sherpas of Nepal, an ethnic group rarely if ever discussed in sports literature. Yet, the Sherpas, like the Kenyans, have amassed sport credentials at least as impressive. The Sherpas are a small ethnic group who have lived for centuries in the high altitude of the Himalayas. Living in isolation from the rest of the world, they were "discovered" in the 1950s when the British began their conquest of Mount Everest. Sir Edmund Hillary, the man who is credited with being the first person to summit Mount Everest, employed a Sherpa (the Sherpas are such a small ethnic group that "Sherpa" is the term for their ethnicity as well as the last name of all of the people in this group) to carry his pack to the summit. There is much controversy surrounding this summit as many now claim that the Sherpa actually reached the summit before Hillary. In any case, Sherpas have served as guides and "pack animals" for *every* attempted and completed summit of Everest. While Americans, Europeans, Asians, and others struggle—often aided by oxygen bottles—to drag their bodies, *once in their lifetimes*, to the summit, Sherpas carry the supplies of the climbers to the summit often *more than once a year*. In May 2004, Pemba Dorjie, a twenty-five-year-old Nepalese Sherpa guide, scaled Mount Everest in twelve hours and forty-five minutes, setting a new record for the fastest climb of the world's highest mountain. It should be noted that it takes the average climber *a month* from base camp to the summit (as they need time to acclimatize to the altitude) *and the final journey from camp four to the summit typically takes twelve to twenty-four hours*. Thus, his climb is more than extraordinary.

Not to offend the reader here, but the Sherpas are not "black" nor are they from Africa. In fact, they are Central Asian. They are cultural and geographic neighbors to Indians, Mongolians, and Pakistanis. Considering the case of the Kenyans and the Sherpas, we would argue that the primary physical advantage, exceptional lung capacity, is derived from generations, in fact centuries, of living a very difficult and physical life at an extremely high altitude, not from skin color or "race."

In short, everyone who studies elite athletes understands clearly that they are born with biological advantages—exceptional lung capacity, coordination, body type—including things like the ratio of arm length to leg length and torso, as many have noted of Olympic swimmer Michael Phelps whose body was featured on the cover of *Time* magazine. These biological advantages may in fact be inherited.

When we think about race, we think about it as something that is inherited. In fact, it is not race itself that is inherited; it is the set of traits that we associate with certain racial groups, including skin color, hair texture, facial features—nose width, eyelid shape—that are inherited. Anyone who has ever lived in a family (which presumably is everyone) is aware that the traits get passed differently to different family members. For example, in a family with a very tall parent and a very short parent, sometimes all of the children end up being the height that is their parents' average, sometimes only one trait is passed along—all of the children are tall—and sometimes the trait is passed on distinctly, with some children in the family being tall and others being short. With regards to race, inside families and across generations there are quite often differences in skin tone, hair color, eye color, facial features, and hair texture. Think, for example, about the Williams sisters—Venus and Serena. Though they share the exact same parents, yet they are far from being identical. It is very common in African American families, for example, for some members to be light enough in complexion and with Euro-like features, that they may be "misperceived" as white. Historically, many, many of these folks literally "passed" into the white community and obtained the official designation as "white." If a person can literally "change" her race simply by capitalizing on others' perception of these traits associated with race, then it is clear that race itself is not a biological construct. Rather, as sociologists and others argue, race is a social construct; something that can be manipulated by social forces. Similarly, as we noted in the first chapter of the book, an analysis of census categories reveals quite clearly that the official definitions of race in the United States have changed over time. In 1990 a person who emigrated from Mexico would be identified as Hispanic. Today, that same person must choose either "white" or "black" as his race and could designate "Hispanic" as an ethnic identity. Again, race itself is not passed on from generation to generation; it is a social construct that varies as a result of changes in the political and social landscape.

Previously we noted that although people of West African descent—African Americans and Caribbeaners—have dominated the sprints over the last decade, there has been no such dominance of people actually born and raised in West Africa. For example there are no world record holders from countries like Ghana, a country from which perhaps millions of people were captured into the North American slave trade. The descendants of West African slaves, African Americans and those living in the Caribbean, often have some white or Native American ancestry as well. How do we reconcile these competing facts—no world record holders from Ghana and many from the United States and the Caribbean—if we assume that race is the determinant factor in "speed?" We can easily reconcile these competing facts by recognizing that it is not "race" that is inherited, but rather a set of traits that may not or may be correlated with what amounts to a "loose" definition that prescribes who is "black" and who is "white." Additionally, there may be environmental factors—as we saw with the Kenyans and the Sherpas—as well as cultural factors that are also associated with racial categories, that move us closer to a clearer understanding of what amounts to the myth of the "natural black athlete."

THE MYTH OF THE DOMINANCE OF THE "BLACK" ATHLETE

It's interesting the degree to which the myth of the "natural black athlete" has been so easily adopted and widely accepted by both whites and African Americans. Clearly, whites have a vested interest in adhering to the myth of the "natural black athlete" for at least two reasons: (1) it allows them to explain the decline in the dominance of whites in many highly visible sports in the United States: football, basketball, and track and field; and (2) it allows them to accept the dominance of African Americans in one arena or institution—sports—while continuing to deny them access to the areas of true power: government, banking, the professions, and higher education. Because whites watch powerful African American men who play football and basketball, earning tens of millions of dollars, they can conclude that the playing field is level.

African Americans—save a few key critics—are also quick to embrace the myth of the "natural black athlete." Their self-interest in adhering to this myth seems to be the fact that it allows African Americans to claim dominance in *some* area, and a very popular and visible, if not powerful, arena. It's a way of feeling powerful and dominant in light of the reality that no other single arena or industry is dominated by African Americans. As we have noted in other chapters throughout this book, the election of Barack Obama certainly did not change that.

However, we see that in fact the myth of the "natural black athlete" is not the only myth swirling around the intersection of race and sport. Frankly, it is also a myth that African Americans dominate in sports. In fact, in the United States it is whites who actually dominate sports and globally it is Europeans and Hispanics. Really? Yes! In the United States alone, the *vast majority* of sports at the high school, college, and professional levels, are almost entirely played by white athletes—swimming, tennis, golf, hockey, lacrosse, volleyball, softball, and soccer. When we add baseball into the discussion we see that a league that Jackie Robinson worked so hard to integrate, has seen a steep decline in African American players such that today, after peaking in the late 1990s at 15 percent, major league baseball is slightly less than 8 percent African American. In the same decade of steep decline for African Americans, Hispanic presence in the league has risen to nearly 40 percent. Additionally, African Americans are nearly completely absent from the one US sport that puts more people in the seats every year than any other: NASCAR. Worldwide, the most popular sport of all, soccer, is dominated by Europeans and players from Latin America.

Perhaps we can make an argument that the qualities attributed to the "natural black athlete" are not translatable to sports like NASCAR. Okay perhaps they aren't. It's unclear to us how the argument could be made that the primary traits of the "natural black athlete," namely speed, strength, and agility would not translate to the host of sports that are dominated by white people (American or European) and Latin Americans: especially the internationally dominant sport of soccer, but also tennis, golf, swimming and softball. Of course two African Americans have very recently dominated the sports of tennis and golf—Serena Williams and Tiger Woods. Their enormous success, while important to the black community as well as to the sports themselves, has hardly translated into either sport becoming dominated by African Americans. Only a handful of black athletes play at the elite levels of either sport. Perhaps most discouraging is the fact that both Serena Williams' father, Richard, and Tiger Woods have worked tirelessly and invested large sums of money into opening up these country club sports to African American youth.

How then can we explain the dominance of African Americans in certain sports and their simultaneous near exclusion from the vast majority of sports? We will explore structural and cultural explanations that turn out to provide more powerful ways of understanding the world of sports other than the myth of the "natural black athlete."

STRUCTURAL EXPLANATIONS

The only place to start with this discussion is to consider the ways in which sports have been, in the United States, across the entire twentieth century, a site of incredible contestation. We don't mean the athletic contest. Rather, we mean the way in which sports represents, perhaps as strongly as schools, public restrooms, movie theaters, and lunch counters, a place in which race has been hotly contested. Of course, anybody who has even a remote knowledge of sports will know the names of pioneers like Jackie Robinson, Bill Russell, Arthur Ashe, and Althea Gibson, as they are the names and faces we associate with the integration of sports. Less well known is the story of an African American swimming coach, Jim Ellis, who revamped a decrepit community center swimming pool in inner-city Philadelphia. The subject of the Hollywood film *Pride*, starring Terrance Howard and Bernie Mac, exposes the structural barriers that limit the access African Americans have had to the sport of swimming.

Lest the reader be lulled into thinking that this is ancient history, in the summer of 2009 a private swim club, which had agreed to extend swimming privileges—once per week—to a local summer school program for disadvantaged minority youth, rescinded the contract after only one week. The swim club members were apparently concerned that the sixty-plus minority children would "change the complexion" of the club. This sounds eerily similar to the concerns that were raised across the twentieth century as communities in the South struggled with the potential desegregation of public swimming pools. We should note that many communities across the South handled this by building new swimming pools in the "black part of town," which essentially worked to keep the pools segregated by proximity rather than by law.

Perhaps less well known except by the greatest of sports enthusiasts or sports historians is the story of Willie O'Rea, the first African American to play in the National Hockey League. Despite his best efforts, hockey remains not only highly segregated but the culture of hockey remains racially charged. Just when we thought things might be getting better, in the spring of 2012 during the first round of the Stanley Cup playoffs, in a particularly tight and heated set of games between the Washington Capitols and the Boston Bruins, the ugliness of racism reemerged. During the last game of the series, which was tied, Washington Capitols' player, Joel Ward, who is black, scored the winning goal in overtime. His goal ended the season for the Bruins and allowed the Capitols to advance to the next round. We include here just a small sampling of the kinds of tweets that were made immediately upon the dramatic win:

- Can't believe Boston just let a sand nigger beat them #gobacktothejungle@ abrownn36
- stupid nigger go play basketball hockey is a white sport
- Of course it's the fucking nigger. White power!

Ward's experience is eerily similar to the treatment of another African American athlete, Georgetown University's basketball superstar, seven-foot center Patrick Ewing. Ewing not only endured similar assaults but in some arenas fans also held up posters that compared his image to that of a chimpanzee. Serena and Venus Williams endured verbal assaults in 2001 at Indian Wells and have vowed never to return to play at that tournament venue. Tiger Woods is only one of a handful of African Americans *ever* admitted to Augusta National, where the Master's tournament is played. Incidentally, it continues to refuse to extend memberships to women. As an interesting aside, the debate over women's membership at Augusta National revved up in 2012 when, for the first time, the tradition of extending an honorary membership to the CEO of the sponsoring company, IBM, was a woman. In the end, though given an opportunity to soften its history of exclusion—African Americans, Jews, and women have been barred—the board of Augusta National refused to extend an honorary membership to IBM CEO Virginia Rometty.

It seems clear then that African Americans don't play certain sports not because they aren't interested or because they don't have the appropriate skills, but because they are officially banned from the facilities in which these sports are played, or because there are no appropriate facilities near where they live, or because they face so much racism and so many hassles when they do enter these facilities that they understandably choose not to, as was the decision the Williams sisters made with regards to Indian Wells.

We suggest that it is not random that African Americans are not banned from football fields or basketball courts but that they are barred from country clubs and swimming pools. With regards to swimming pools, as noted previously, whites have historically been concerned about African Americans contaminating the pool. In the 1960s in Montgomery, Alabama, after several African American youth were caught swimming in the pool , the city fathers poured mercury in the public swimming pool to properly sanitize it.

We also speculate that another concern about integrated swimming pools is a concern about sexuality; namely that just like movie theaters, the swimming pool is a place where youth might become sexually attracted to one another. And, heaven forbid, white and African American youth might actually act on that attraction.

The story of the county clubs—where the access to sports like golf and tennis is the greatest—is the story of more than sexuality; it is the story of families and marriage. For generations the country club provided a place where a family could be sure that their sons and daughters could meet the "right" people and hopefully, if all went well, dating would follow and ultimately marriage between the "right kinds" of families, both racially and also in terms of social class. The more and more integrated schools became, the more important it was to restrict membership at country clubs. Whether intentional or not, the desire to restrict access to the social world of the country club also significantly limited the opportunities African Americans have had to play the "country club" sports of tennis and golf.

CULTURAL EXPLANATIONS

People are fond of so-called cultural explanations for virtually everything that has to do with race. In the previous chapter, for example, we explored the myth that

African Americans don't value education. This is an example of a "cultural explanation"; in this case for the racial gaps in achievement and education. It is tempting here to assume that African Americans simply do not enjoy or value certain sports. We would suggest that perhaps there are cultural preferences for sports. For example, when we examine the landscape of sports globally it is clear that everywhere but in the United States soccer is the national pastime and national soccer teams are an important part of national identity. But the cultural preferences for golf and tennis among whites and basketball and football among African Americans, to the degree that they exist, are best understood as the result of responses to the structural barriers we discussed previously.

There is certainly an argument to be made, as well, that all kinds of activities and material items become "race-ed"; in other words, there is a great deal of effort on the part of corporations and their advertisers to target certain audiences with certain products. This is nothing new, targeting certain demographic groups—women, youth, and African Americans—has been a dominant strategy for decades. For example, cars that are targeted to women include safety features and a "cuteness" factor—think of the VW bug and its flower holder and the palette of colors in which it is available. Perhaps in response to the recession and sluggish car sales, VW has since attempted to design the newest versions of the beetle to be more masculine.[2] Similarly, the case can be made that sports that are dominated by African Americans come to be imbued with cultural values that are both external and internal. Let's consider basketball for a moment, the sport that has more African American players than any other.

In NCAA Division I college basketball, more than 60 percent of the players are African American and this figure climbs to more than 80 percent when we examine the NBA. As a result, when a viewer turns on the television, he is likely to see that at any given time in the game at least eight, if not nine, or all ten, of the players on the court are African American. This can send the message, regardless of the race of the viewer, that this is a "black" sport. For an African American child or teenager the message may be interpreted as "this is something African American people do" and since I am African American, this is for me. Conversely, the opposite may occur when an African American teenager flips past a broadcast of NASCAR and doesn't see anyone who looks like him among the drivers, the pit crews, the owners, the announcers (except for Brad Dougherty), or even the tens of thousands of fans.

Internally, the complete dominance of basketball by African Americans, who come to the game with all of their beliefs and values and "culture," transform the image of the game as well. Today, the image of the typical basketball player is a man with tattoos covering much of his body, he wears flashy clothes, he wears expensive and highly visible jewelry—including huge diamond studs in his ears, watches covered in diamonds—he drives an expensive car, while several others sit idle in his multicar garage, and he lives in a huge McMansion. He is also likely to be photographed regularly by the paparazzi in the VIP lounges of the best clubs, surrounded by a stable of beautiful women of all races, ethnicities, and hues. He is also seen "hanging out" with African American entertainers and actors. Think of watching the New York Knicks and seeing Spike Lee, from his courtside season seats, jumping up and down as Carmelo Anthony makes a move into the lane and dunks the basketball. Taken all together, basketball comes to be seen as not only something that is for African Americans, but it becomes something that *is* African American. For the record, NASCAR can be analyzed in a similar way; it comes to represent and in fact be a part of the white community, and more specifically part of the rural, Southern white, male identity.

This transformation of the culture of basketball can have many outcomes, and most of them are not positive nor do they work to advance equality in the United States.

1. Whites also come to see basketball as a "black" sport. Interested and talented white youth may lose interest in or be encouraged out of playing basketball. The fear may be that to play basketball will require young white kids being exposed to African Americans and African American "culture," that they will be in the minority, and their parents may think it will expose them to "bad influences." This is too bad as basketball can be a wonderful game!
2. In the United States, football and basketball have by far the biggest television viewing audiences, though we should point out that NASCAR draws the largest crowds. Both sports are dominated by African Americans. Thus, after a fall Saturday filled with college football or a weekend in March with endless basketball games, whites may easily and understandably come to the conclusion that the playing field is finally level, that we have entered a postracial society. The danger is that this conclusion is simply and patently false.
3. African Americans who spend the same weekends watching college or professional sports may come to the same conclusion as whites: that certain sports are for them. The positive benefit to this is that African American boys and girls can see people who "look like them" and they can be inspired by and aspire to athletic success. There are at least two downsides to the stream of images coming across the television screen: (1) the perception that other sports are *not* for them (tennis, golf, NASCAR), and (2) the belief that athletics is the only place for them and, by extension, their only pathway to success. Both are tragic in their own right, but of significant concern is the latter, because it offers a false promise while simultaneously encouraging that all of one's eggs be put in the athletic basket while leaving baskets for education, in particular, empty.

PATHWAY TO SUCCESS OR THE DANGLING CARROT

Many important African American intellectuals have weighed in on this issue and we will summarize their arguments here. From Henry Louis Gates, Harvard professor, to Harry Edwards, University of California–Berkeley professor and advisor to the NFL, their concern is that the myopic focus that the African American community has placed on sports as the singular route to success, and for poor African Americans it is considered the *only way out of the ghetto*, is devastating to the African American community for several reasons.

First, because athletic success requires an extremely high level of commitment—time and money—it makes it very difficult to pursue anything else while one is pursuing the dream of becoming an elite athlete. This is true from the middle school level all the way through college. Thus, individuals and their families must make choices, and if the choice is to attempt success through sports, especially those most readily available to African Americans—football and basketball—then beginning at a very young age the child must devote the majority of his time to this pursuit and the family must invest most of its available resources into this pursuit. Practically, what this means is that practice is more important than studying. Families go to great lengths to get their children, mostly sons, into the best Amateur Athletic Union (AAU) programs or worse yet, one of the many high school sports factories. This may be costly to them, but it may also, if they are poor or have limited resources, make them vulnerable to coaches and agents who promise to make this happen. Every year, talented young men find themselves in violation of NCAA rules and thus ineligible to play or even enter college, because their families took "help" in getting them into the right high schools or into the best college programs. While he was in college, Reggie Bush's family lived in a house that a University of Southern California booster paid for. In exchange for this "help," Bush was forced to give back his Heisman Trophy and USC was forced to vacate wins, including a national championship, that accrued during the "Bush" era. Perhaps Bush's loss is not that devastating in the long run because his time at USC allowed him to become one of the top draft picks and he is playing with a lucrative contract in the NFL. There are countless other stories, mostly of high school boys, who won't ever go to college on an athletic scholarship because the coach paid their family's rent so that they could live in the neighborhood that was zoned for a high school sports factory.

Henry Louis Gates said twenty years ago:

> The blind pursuit of attainment in sports is having a devastating effect on our people. Imbued with a belief that our principal avenue to fame and profit is through sports and seduced by a win-at-any-cost system that corrupts even elementary school students, far too many black kids treat basketball and football fields as if they were classrooms in an alternative school system. OK, I flunked English, a young athlete will say. But I got an A plus in slam-dunking.[3]

Second, the vast majority of African American men who enter college to play football or basketball will *not* make it; either by graduating or playing professional sports.

If they make it to college, most arrive unprepared either because they attended an under-resourced school like those Jonathan Kozol describes, or because practice was more important than studying. When they get to college this will only get worse; the time demands on them, which we have observed across decades of teaching on Division I college campuses, are often upward of thirty to forty hours per week, making it extremely difficult for them to find time to study. If they come in underprepared, they will likely need *more time* than the average student needs to be successful academically. As a result of both a focus on their athletic development— and the hopes of a professional career—and their state of being underprepared, their hopes of graduating are significantly diminished. Despite all of the white-washing the NCAA does to graduation rates, the majority of successful football and basketball programs—from Alabama to Oklahoma to UCONN—graduate far fewer than 50 percent of their African American football or basketball players.[4]

> The worst victim is the African American athlete, and society's promise that sports will lift African American youth from poverty to riches and fame is a cruel illusion. Yet parents, coaches, and administrators buy into the media package and encourage the illusion; African American athletes themselves sacrifice educational opportunities to the glittering dream of the sporting arena. The dream goes like this: even if I don't make the pros, I'll at least get a college degree.[5]

They are also unlikely to have a career playing (or coaching) sports. As the NCAA is fond of pointing out in its public service announcements aired during football bowl games and March Madness, of the 400,000 student athletes, across the three divisions, competing on a field or court this year, "almost all" (indeed more than 90 percent) will make their living doing something *other* than sports. The invisible and ignored message embedded in these advertisements is that fewer than 10 percent of these athletes will have a professional career in sports, and among those few who are drafted, the average time they will spend in the league is well short of five years and most will never make more than the league minimum (anywhere from $80,000 to $450,000 a year). Though that seems like a lot of money to a twenty-year-old, sustaining these earnings for fewer than five years will result in lifetime earnings far below the typical college graduate. The question is: are you better off graduating from college or seeking a professional career in sports? The answer for the vast majority of college athletes is the former. But, as we know, by filling our television screens with men like LeBron James who can "take his talents" wherever he wants to or Michael Vick—an ex-felon—who can sign a contract worth $100 million, the illusion is that sports holds the best chance for an African American to make it. For the very few who do make it, they make it really, really big! Which only increases the lure.

ATHLETICS AS A WAY TO PAY FOR COLLEGE, OR WHAT DOES SOCIAL CLASS HAVE TO DO WITH IT?

Social class probably has very little to do with the attraction young people of all racial and ethnic identities have to sports. Athletes are powerful, many of them are attractive, they command big salaries—or so it appears on TV—they are recognizable. What kid doesn't want that type of success? Some African American teenagers growing up in professional or wealthy households, may indeed go to college on an athletic scholarship and pursue the dream. But, we would argue, that the difference is that these young people also have available to them a variety of role models of career success that are provided by their parents, neighbors, relatives, and so on. Their parents are more likely to know instinctively or anecdotally what the numbers confirm: that far fewer African American men make a living playing sports than the number who make a living in the professions. Thus, putting all of one's eggs into the athletic basket is short-sighted, especially if this means attending college but failing to earn a meaningful degree. Again, Henry Louis Gates puts it in perspective:

> Too many of our children have come to believe that it's easier to become a black professional athlete than a doctor or lawyer. Reality check: according to the 2000 census, there were more than 31,000 black physicians and surgeons, 33,000 black lawyers and 5,000 black dentists. Guess how many black athletes are playing professional basketball, football and baseball combined. About 1,400. In fact, there are more board-certified black cardiologists than there are black professional basketball players.[6]

In fact, African Americans are *seventy-five times more likely to become physicians than professional athletes*. A fact that is probably shocking to most readers.

But, the question lingers about the options for low-income and poor African American youth. In short, what are their odds of going to college without an athletic scholarship and even more profound, what are their odds of graduating from the types of high schools Jonathan Kozol describes and then attending the kind of college that can prepare her to gain admission to medical school and finally becoming a cardiologist or dentist?

Quite truthfully, the odds are probably lower that a young man from Compton or Pahokee, Florida (a noted hotbed for football) will grow up to become a dentist or a college professor than that he will have a career, however brief, in the NFL. Thus, we ask the difficult question, is it really a poor decision for the young African American man from Pahokee, who has some athletic ability, to put all of his eggs in the athletic basket? At the individual level, this may in fact be his best decision. But at the community level, these individual decisions end up to devastation.

Charles Barkley, former NBA all-star and now television commentator, a man who himself found his way out poverty through sports, notes:

> Sports are a detriment to blacks, not a positive. You have a society now where every black kid in the country thinks the only way he can be successful is through athletics. People look at athletes and entertainers as the sum total of black America. This is a terrible, terrible thing, because that ain't even one tenth of what we are.[7]

CONCLUSIONS

When analyzing the world of sports we have to ask this question: does the election of the first African American president affect how African Americans access

SportsWorld,[8] and in what way? In short, does this election signify that we have now entered a postracial America with regards to sports?

The central question that we have examined in this chapter is the myth of the "natural black athlete" and the consequent notion that the best pathway to success for African Americans is through athletics. We have argued vehemently that the myth of the "natural black athlete" is just that, a myth, and that the most probable route to success is not through sports. The numbers confirm that African Americans would be far better off investing their energies and talents into getting an education than into what is essentially a lottery for athletic success. Yet, we must address, realistically, the reasons for what appears to be poor decision making on the part of African Americans.

1. The media continues to perpetuate several important myths, including the belief that African Americans are "natural" athletes, that the playing field is level and that sports is a route to success.
2. Frankly, African American athletes are far more visible than African American professionals like Henry Louis Gates or even, we would argue, Barack Obama and thus they are not as powerful a role model as LeBron James or Michael Vick.
3. The majority of African American youth attend under-resourced, segregated schools and their chances for achieving success through routes that require a college education or beyond are, quite simply, unlikely.

As with all of the other issues we have addressed in this book, though most African American youth—and white youth, for that matter—are attracted to professional athletes and the perceived lifestyles they live, African Americans who live in professional families, and certainly those who could be identified using Robinson's term as "transcendents" have so many other opportunities available to them that they are unlikely to invest in the unreliability of sports as a route to success and they are more likely to participate in sports as they were meant to be: as leisure activities.

That said, children growing up in low-income and poor households are less likely to have professional role models readily available to them. Rather than growing up around doctors and lawyers and college professors, they see their options as low-wage or physically demanding work, which is certainly less attractive to them, or to anyone, than the images they see of professional athletes. Additionally, they are not likely to attend schools that prepare them adequately for college. Even if they do get accepted to college, how will they pay for it? For despite the rhetoric that there are scholarships and loans widely available for low-income college students, this is simply not the case. In fact, recent studies acknowledge that even with financial support, low-income students can expect to graduate from college with a minimum of $50,000 in student loans. A savvy teenager will worry how he will pay this back, especially given the jobs he sees in his community. Furthermore, as we learned while we were simultaneously revising this book and doing taxes, scholarships are considered taxable income by the federal government. So, the very student who needs a great deal of financial support—perhaps a "full ride" valued at $40,000 or $50,000—may be required to pay taxes on the very support that is critical to his pursuit of the American dream. The odds are simply not in favor of a poor, African American teenager realistically being able to pursue the American dream through a professional career.

In short, athletics will continue to be an empty promise until several structural changes are made:

- Equality in the public school system that allows *all* children to become prepared academically for college
- Affordable higher education
- More visibility of African American professionals—doctors, lawyers, college professors, business leaders, and politicians
- Aligning athletic salaries with those traditional professions

We conclude by acknowledging that one advantage for the white community of the dominance of athletics for African Americans is that it cordons them off into one area of life while preserving the areas of real wealth and power for whites. In short, being "cordoned-off" into one "zone," in this case athletics, restricts membership in the other zones—such as the professions that require educational credentials—where the odds of successfully accessing the American dream are seventy-five times greater. In other words, while the average college football player, if he is black, will neither make it to the NFL nor graduate, the average white male college student who majored in business and graduated will find doors of opportunity opened up for him in the most important sectors of the American economy. Because his African American counterpart "dropped out" of the academic race, the young white college graduate will find less competition for these lucrative and highly desirable positions.

What will be the impact of the election of Barack Obama on the aspirations of African American children? Despite the highly desirable possibility that his presence as the leader of the Free World and his occupancy of the White House will provide a role model for young African Americans, the truth is that as long as Michael Jordan and LeBron James are more recognizable than him, his presidency will have little impact; and his impact will be even less for poor African Americans, who not only face tremendous obstacles in education, housing, and employment opportunities, but for whom athletes are more likely to seem familiar, like the person next door, or their older brother, than the president seems.

7

Poverty and Wealth

Look at Oprah, Obama, and Jay-Z— The Playing Field Must Be Level

Each year for the past two decades, the U.S. Census Bureau has reported that over 30 million Americans were living in "poverty." In recent years, the Census has reported that one in seven Americans are poor. But what does it mean to be "poor" in America? How poor are America's poor?

For most Americans, the word "poverty" suggests destitution: an inability to provide a family with nutritious food, clothing, and reasonable shelter. For example, the Poverty Pulse poll taken by the Catholic Campaign for Human Development asked the general public: "How would you describe being poor in the U.S.?" The overwhelming majority of responses focused on homelessness, hunger or not being able to eat properly, and not being able to meet basic needs. That perception is bolstered by news stories about poverty that routinely feature homelessness and hunger.

Yet if poverty means lacking nutritious food, adequate warm housing, and clothing for a family, relatively few of the more than 30 million people identified as being "in poverty" by the Census Bureau could be characterized as poor. While material hardship definitely exists in the United States, it is restricted in scope and severity. The average poor person, as defined by the government, has a living standard far higher than the public imagines.

As scholar James Q. Wilson has stated, "The poorest Americans today live a better life than all but the richest persons a hundred years ago."

In 2005, the typical household defined as poor by the government had a car and air-conditioning. For entertainment, the household had two color televisions, cable or satellite TV, a DVD player, and a VCR. If there were children, especially boys, in the home, the family had a game system, such as an Xbox or a PlayStation. In the kitchen, the household had a refrigerator, an oven and stove, and a microwave. Other household conveniences included a clothes washer, clothes dryer, ceiling fans, a cordless phone, and a coffeemaker.

The home of the typical poor family was not overcrowded and was in good repair. In fact, the typical poor American had more living space than the average European. The typical poor American family was also able to obtain medical care when needed. By its own report, the typical family was not hungry and had sufficient funds during the past year to meet all essential needs.

Poor families certainly struggle to make ends meet, but in most cases, they are struggling to pay for air-conditioning and the cable TV bill as well as to put food on the table. Their living standards are far different from the images of dire deprivation promoted by activists and the mainstream media.

Regrettably, annual Census reports not only exaggerate current poverty, but also suggest that the number of poor persons and their living conditions have remained virtually unchanged for four decades or more. In reality, the living conditions of poor Americans have shown significant improvement over time.

Consumer items that were luxuries or significant purchases for the middle class a few decades ago have become commonplace in poor households. In part, this is caused by a normal downward trend in price following the introduction of a new product. Initially, new products tend to be expensive and available only to the affluent. Over time, prices fall sharply, and the product saturates the entire population, including poor households.

As a rule of thumb, poor households tend to obtain modern conveniences about a dozen years after the middle class. Today, most poor families have conveniences that were unaffordable to the middle class not too long ago.

Robert Rector and Rachel Sheffield, *Air Conditioning, Cable TV, and an Xbox: What Is Poverty in the United States Today?* The Heritage Foundation, July 19, 2011, www.heritage.org/research/reports/2011/07/what-is-poverty

Myth: African Americans are poor because they are lazy and because they are unable to defer gratification—rather than living frugally and saving to buy a house, they spend money on expensive jewelry, satellite dishes, and cars—and they never save up enough to buy things like a home or pay for their children to go to college. Their poverty is *not real* and it is their own fault.

Reality: The reality is that African Americans are less able to accumulate wealth for structural reasons, including working lower-wage jobs because they have less education, and they are subject to wage discrimination as well as discrimination in various aspects of banking, such as being vulnerable to subprime mortgages, that prevent them from accumulating wealth at the same rate as whites who have similar earnings. The presence of a few very wealthy or powerful African Americans—Oprah Winfrey, Barack Obama—creates the perceptions that the ability to achieve the American dream is equal for all racial groups and that the inability to reach those goals is thereby primarily individuals who are lazy or poor decision makers.

In this chapter we will examine two very different sides of the same coin: wealth and poverty. Wealth guarantees access to the American dream and reduces the risk of so many crises facing African Americans and their families. At its absolute extreme, the absence of wealth or access to it can result in families living on the outer margins of the economy: in poverty and reliant on welfare, as do the millions of African Americans Eugene Robinson refers to as the abandoned. We will analyze the degree to which African Americans and their families have access to the American dream (via wealth), and we will examine the experiences of those living on the margins, those unable to access the American dream and who must rely on welfare to raise their families. Additionally, we will explore the reasons why African Americans have less wealth and the reasons why they are more likely to be poor. Rather than conceptualizing poverty as a set of unfortunate circumstances and individual choices, we will focus on the structures—including differences in access to education, job discrimination, discrimination in lending, and housing segregation—that shape the likelihood that one will be rich or poor. We will conclude this chapter with some suggestions for reform that should reduce not only poverty but more importantly the gap in access to the American dream.

WORK THAT PRODUCES INCOME

After 250 years of slavery and another 100 of Jim Crow segregation, today African Americans work in all sectors of the US economy. This is the good news. In the American workplace you can find African Americans inside the post office, as well as delivering the mail, as secretaries, supervisors—including in the supervision of whites—as managers, architects, physicians, and lawyers. With the dismantling of segregation in schools around the country, African Americans work as schoolteachers and college professors. At the corporate level there are now six or seven African American CEOs of Fortune 500 companies and a handful of Division IA universities have presidents who are African American.

Despite being present in all of these various occupations and professions, despite working in all kinds of institutions and businesses, and despite the opportunity to lead organizations—in politics, higher education, sports, and business—opening to African Americans, very few African Americans actually work in these jobs or professions and even fewer have managed to rise to leadership positions.

This is problematic for three reasons:

1. Despite the gains made in the latter half of the twentieth century, for the most part, work is still highly segregated and African Americans are still most likely to work in occupations with the lowest prestige and the lowest pay.
2. The ability for a few, but only a very few, African Americans to achieve professional success and rise in even fewer cases to the top of organizations contributes to the split in the African American community that Robinson so aptly describes; a split that is devastating for those left behind.
3. Perhaps most problematic is the fact that the perception of whites, when they see an African American college president or head football coach or physician

or serving as US president is that the playing field is now level, that all of the doors that once restricted access to these areas to whites, have been flung open for all African Americans.

The logical conclusion that results is the belief that with all of these doors of opportunity opening up, African Americans who remain poor, working in low-income jobs, unable to amass enough in their savings accounts to buy a home or send a child to college are at fault for their own failure to succeed. Because look, Oprah did it, Barack Obama did it—what's wrong with the millions of African Americans who haven't? Or, as suggested by the researchers at the Heritage Foundation, poor African Americans are exaggerating what it means to be poor; things must not be that bad if they have a Wii or an iPhone.

INCOME DISPARITIES

Despite the fact that African Americans have made significant gains in terms of access to occupations, as a group they continue to fall significantly behind whites in average earnings. Based on data gathered by the US Census, in 2010 the median household income for all Americans was just over $49,445 per year, which is 7 percent below the figure in 1999, direct evidence of the impact of the recession on American families. Looking closer we see that the median household income for white families was nearly $52,000 per year. African American families lived on far less, $32,000 per year or $20,000 *less per year*. In short, African Americans earn only 61 percent of what whites earn.

Looking at another layer, a report released in October 2011 by the Congressional Budget Office revealed that income grew at significantly different rates based on the social class of the earner. In its report, the budget office found that from 1979 to 2007, average inflation-adjusted after-tax income grew by 275 percent for the 1 percent of the population with the highest income. For others, those earning in the top 20 percent of the income distribution, the average real, after-tax household income grew by 65 percent. By contrast, the budget office noted that, for the poorest fifth of the population, average real, after-tax household income rose by only 18 percent.[1]

Though the median income is an important statistic, and it is quite a good measure of disparity at the lower end of the income distribution, it suffers from a flaw based on the way income is distributed in the population that makes it less accurate at describing income at the high end of the distribution. A median is like a line that divides a population in half; half of the population falls below the line (or median) and half the population lies above the median. Because income has a fixed bottom—$0—but no fixed ceiling, the median income measure *masks* the incredible disparity at the *top* of the income distribution.

Taking just the highlights, for example, though 7.3 percent of the US households live on less than $10,000 per year, twice as many African American households (14.4

percent) live on this little. At the other end of the spectrum, very few American households, only 2 percent, live on more than $250,000 per year. Yet among these wealthiest of Americans, 2.1 percent of white households have this much income or more whereas only half a percent (0.6 percent) of African Americans do. But another way, white Americans are only half as likely as African Americans to be among the poorest households yet they are nearly 4 times more likely to be among the wealthiest.

POVERTY

Poverty in the United States, by all measures, is growing in both severity and frequency. It is no surprise that by every measure of poverty taken since the recession of 2007 hit, more Americans are living in poverty and the poverty they are experiencing is more severe.

People love to talk about poverty. Researchers talk about poverty, TV pundits talk about poverty, and politicians especially love to talk about poverty; how much there is or isn't, what it means to be poor, or as Clarence Thomas does regularly, describe their personal rise out of poverty. During the "debt ceiling debates" of the summer of 2011, Representative John Boehner was famous for sharing his personal experience climbing out of poverty. Most people believe they know what poverty is, but in fact, most people know nothing about the way that poverty is measured, yet knowing exactly how poverty is measured is necessary to have a better understanding of what poverty statistics actually mean.

The official poverty rate, as calculated by the US Department of Health and Human Services (HHS), is based on the number of Americans who live below the official poverty line. Because the definition of poverty rests on "a household or family's" needs, estimating the poverty rate requires the setting of minimum thresholds based on the *type* of family in which one lives.

In 2011, data from the US Census reported that 46.2 million Americans were poor for an overall poverty rate of just under 10 percent, which for a family of four—two adults and two children—was set at $22,113 per year. The reader will recall from the previous discussion that this figure is half of the median household income. This is important because it helps us to better see the actual distance at which the poor and marginalized—the "abandoned"—live from the middle class.

Table 7.1. Poverty Rate by Family Type

Single Individual	Under 65 years old	$11,344
	65 years or older	$10,458
Single Parent	One child	$15,030
	Two children	$17,538
Two adults	No children	$14,602
	One child	$17,522
	Two children	$22,113
	Three children	$26,023

It will come as no surprise to the reader that certain subgroups in the population are more likely to be poor, including nonwhites, women, the elderly, and children—whose likelihood of living in poverty is of course dictated by the likelihood that their parents live in poverty. In terms of race, in 2011, 9.4 percent of whites lived in poverty; African Americans were three times more likely to be poor (27.4 percent). Put another way, whereas one in six Americans live in poverty, more than one in four African Americans do. Not surprising, families headed by single black women are the most likely to be poor, 38 percent are. It is important to remember the children here, as the reader will recall from previous discussions, 75 percent of African American children are born to single mothers. We learn that almost 40 percent of African American children live in poverty. For a single mother raising two children, this amounts to living on less than $18,000 per year.

ARE AMERICANS REALLY POOR?

In October 2011, the Heritage Foundation, a conservative think tank, took on all of the leading research, by economists, sociologists, nonpartisan governmental organizations like the Census and the Congressional Budget Office, and proclaimed that all of this research was "bunk"; in short they argue that poverty is a relative term and that the number of Americans who are truly destitute is tiny. "The average poor person, as defined by the government, has a living standard far higher than the public imagines."[2] In short, the researchers from the Heritage Foundation argued that to be poor in America is to live at a standard above the average citizen in Europe or to live at or near the standard of the wealthy in developing nations like Kenya. For example, they argue that the poorest of American households had, on average, the following items that are considered to be luxuries in other countries: not one but two color TVs, game systems like an Xbox, a DVD player, and, yes, air-conditioning and indoor plumbing. They also claim that the fast food and cheap convenience foods that the poor routinely eat are far more nutritious than most of us acknowledge. We would never argue that poverty doesn't have a relative component, but to claim that the poor in this nation are "not that poor" because they have indoor plumbing is, frankly, ridiculous. Indoor plumbing is an important aspect of upholding the sanitation expectations of any postindustrial nation.

Unfortunately, the argument is powerful, even if misguided, because it reinforces two important myths: (1) that the poor aren't really as bad off as they claim to be, and (2) that the poor are poor because they make bad decisions. With regards to the first point, we suspect that the majority of people who believe this have never been poor and wouldn't last a day living the way the poor do. Even "pull himself up by his bootstraps" John Boehner grew up poor in a time when being poor was, according to Eugene Robinson, a less desperate and intractable position than it is today.[3] In short, Robinson is describing an important difference between the poverty of fifty years ago and the poverty of today. To borrow the concept of noted sociologist Erik

Olin Wright, today the poor are cordoned off in urban ghettos and isolated rural areas such that even middle-class Americans, let alone the wealthy and super rich, have almost no contact with the poor—not even as employees. In fact, most of the people that the wealthy hire to work in their homes and gardens and to care for their children are working-class and low-income individuals, who may indeed have difficulty making ends meet, but who do not qualify under government standards as "poor." One outcome of this lack of exposure is that very few upper-class, wealthy, or super-rich Americans have any way of understanding what it really means to be poor. Furthermore, from the perspective of those who are poor, because they are cordoned off in under-resourced schools and live in segregated housing, they lack the contact with people who work regularly, save money to buy a house, or send their children to college, and thus they have no real role models that would reinforce the mechanisms for pulling one up by one's bootstraps. Robinson asks the simple question:

> How is a teenager living in Abandoned dysfunction today supposed to escape? By follow-ing the sage advice of parents and other mentors? The teenager is likely being raised by a single mother, who herself was raised by a single mother. By attending first-class public schools, with constructive academic support at home? We know all about the failings of big-city public education. By landing a blue-collar industrial job with security, benefits and middle class wages? Those jobs can be found in China or Brazil, not in Cincinnati or Boston. The ladder that generations have used to climb out of poverty is missing its rungs.[4]

To the second point, and we will discuss individual decision making as a "cause" of poverty momentarily, is the fact that the "luxury" items cited in the Heritage report as evidence that the poor are not really poor, are available because of discount sup-pliers like Walmart. Quoting again from Robinson, who addresses the consumption patterns of the poor in a very straightforward manner, he notes:

> The wholesale transfer of manufacturing jobs to China robbed unskilled American workers of jobs, but that phenomenon, plus the rise of discount retailers like Wal-Mart, drove prices so low that former luxuries came within reach of practically everyone—tele-visions, household appliances, mobile phones, flashy "gold" jewelry made out of nickel or zinc. The poor certainly don't *look* as poor as they once did.[5]

Causes of Poverty

There are several things that cause poverty, and the majority of these causes fall into two distinct categories: structural causes and individual causes. We begin our discussion by focusing on structural causes.

Structural Causes of Poverty

There are several structural patterns in the economy and work that ultimately create poverty and lead to its unequal distribution in income such that African Americans are three times more likely to be poor than whites. One of the factors that creates poverty is low wages. Discussions of minimum wage are probably very familiar to most readers. But it is worth revisiting the actual numbers here so that we can see their connection to poverty. In 2011, a minimum wage job paid $7.35 and hour. A minimum wage, full-time job yields an annual income of $15,288. A single mother of two, working a minimum wage job, forty hours per week, fifty-two weeks per year, will still find herself and her children officially living in poverty. Of course trying to make ends meet on this minimum wage job, which yields just under $1,200 a month, will be even more difficult than the figures suggest. Imagine for yourself having to pay for rent, daycare, food, and transportation for a family of three on $1,200 a month. In many urban areas a studio apartment will rent for more than her entire monthly salary. Though we are well aware that the kinds of reforms necessary to raise minimum wage to a "living wage" are complicated, we do point out that as of 2011, the average CEO now earns 550 times his (or less often her) average employee. This disparity has increased tenfold over the previous fifty or sixty years; in the 1950s and 1960s, the average CEO made only fifty times more than his average employee. Yet, in those same fifty or sixty years, minimum wage has only risen by a factor of three or so. Clearly, then, the structure of the economy in which minimum wage has stagnated is a far bigger cause of poverty than the individual decision to buy a satellite dish or an Xbox.

Why do African Americans end up more often working in minimum wage and low-wage work than whites? There are two key facts that lead to this phenomenon (1) disparities in education, as we discussed in a previous chapter, and (2) continued segregation at work. As we highlighted in chapter 4, African Americans earn less education in a society in which they not only need to earn more, but their need to earn more education is greater than for their white counterparts who can achieve the same success with less education. Second, the fact remains that African Americans and whites continue to work in relatively segregated parts of the economy. This plays out in many different ways. First, African Americans and whites work in entirely different sectors of the economy. At the lowest level of the economy, white men with nothing more than a high school diploma are more likely to work in skilled trades and union jobs, whereas African American men with the same education are far more likely to work in unskilled labor jobs that are nonunionized and as a result pay far lower wages. Conversely, white women with only a high school diploma are more likely to work in low-level office work where as African American women are most likely to do the work of taking care of others: in daycare centers, as home health aids, and caring for the elderly. The professional environment of the office that white women inhabit pays better than the severely undervalued "care work" that African American women perform.

Second, for all the strides African Americans have made in every profession and industry, they still remain underrepresented in the higher earning professions and more lucrative institutions while whites, and white men in particular, remain over-represented. An examination of the CEOs of Fortune 500 companies is an example of both; despite making up more than 10 percent of the US population, African

Americans make up only 1–2 percent of the CEOs of the Fortune 500. African Americans are even less-well represented among the Fortune 100 the most prestigious of the this already prestigious group of companies. Another illustration comes from government or public service. Here, for example, African Americans have had more success gaining seats in the US Congress through the less prestigious house than the more prestigious senate—an issue to which we shall return at greater length in chapter 10.

As Robinson points out, when African Americans do reach positions in which they can open doors of opportunity for other African Americans, when they become transcendents—as CEOs, head football coaches, or as college and university presidents—the African Americans they are most able and likely to help are those in the middle class. There is virtually nothing they can do to help the abandoned. In fact their lives become increasingly isolated from each other.

Unfortunately, flat-out old-school discrimination is still alive and well in the United States. The data on job discrimination are quite clear: When everything else is equal—education, desire to work in a particular job, qualifications, the information contained in one's background check and so forth—African Americans are less likely to be hired, at all levels of the economy, than whites. This is demonstrated by experiments that artificially manipulate the application process. Specifically, research teams create two identical résumés varying only one thing: the name of the applicant: "Jamal" and "James." The researchers then identify jobs and apply for them online or by mail. In a typical study, Jamal will receive almost no "callbacks" indicating an interest in hiring him while James will receive a substantial number of "callbacks."[6] Anecdotally, the *New York Times* periodically publishes stories about professional African Americans who are having trouble finding work discover that when they "whiten" their résumés, the trouble suddenly disappears! For example, a story that ran at the end of 2009, well into the recession, features Tahani Tompkins. When she changes her name on her résumé to her initials, T. S. Tompkins, she suddenly found that prospective employers are calling back![7]

Finally, lawsuits continue to be filed that reveal discrimination in hiring and promotion. Though this case was filed by white employees, it ended up revealing racism in the internal system of promotion. One of the most widely publicized cases in recent years involved white firefighters who sued the New Haven, Connecticut, Fire Department in which they claimed reverse racism. The lawsuit revealed that the test used to select firefighters for promotion was racially biased. Identifying the bias, the fire department threw out the test, which meant that white firefighters were not promoted either—the basis of their lawsuit. Though the US Supreme Court ruled in favor of the firefighters in a controversial 5–4 decision, the fact that the test was revealed as racially biased serves as yet another reminder of the ways in which discrimination can occur; in ways that are both deliberate and obvious as well as subtle and sometimes presumably unintentional.

It is difficult to estimate with any degree of accuracy how much "old school" discrimination and the kinds of subtle, perhaps unintentional discrimination like biased tests, plays in depressing the income of African Americans, but unfortunately it continues to play some role. We will revisit this discussion when we examine the issue of wealth.

IMPACT OF THE RECESSION AND REGRESSIVE TAXES

It almost goes without saying that the recession has hit African Americans harder than most other racial and ethnic groups. The recession produced unemployment rates that are higher than the United States has seen in decades; and as troubling as a national unemployment rate of 9.1 percent is, economists all agree that the unemployment rate is at least twice that high for African Americans and may actually be three times higher for young African American men.

It's not just unemployment and underemployment hurting African Americans. We want to draw the reader's attention to the way in which government policies disproportionately impact African Americans. Specifically, because African Americans have significantly lower incomes than whites, they pay a greater percentage of their income on certain types of taxes, primarily sales taxes. A simple example will suffice.

Let's consider two families of four. Each spends $1,000 a month on groceries. They live in a state where food is subjected to the full state and local tax rate; let's say it's 7 percent. Thus, each family pays $70 each month in taxes for their food for a total of $840 per year. The family who earns $40,000 a year will pay 2 percent of their income on food taxes, while the family earning only $20,000 a year will pay 4.2 percent of their income on food taxes for the same food bill. Thus, a poor family will pay twice the percentage of their income in taxes on food as a middle-class family will pay. Because African Americans are more likely to be poor, they are more likely to lose when it comes to this type of regressive tax.

To make matters worse, because states set their own laws about taxes on food, the degree to which food is taxed varies from no tax on food to full state and local taxes on food—the example we just shared. As one would have it, African Americans are far more likely to live in states with food taxes; in fact, the vast majority of the states that tax food are in the South and these are the same states that have the highest percentages of African American residents, each state in which these taxes are in place has a population that is more than 30 percent African American. In fact, the two states that charge the full tax on food are Alabama and Mississippi—the "blackest" states in the United States and also the poorest. In the end, because money doesn't grow on trees, and food budgets are often the first to "go" we can speculate, based on our illustration, that when times are tough, African Americans who live in these states probably end up being able to spend 7 percent less on food to accommodate for the tax. In other words, if a family's monthly food budget is $1,000, to pay the $70 in taxes they will be forced to buy only $930 worth of food instead of the $1,000 they could afford if there were no tax. This has grave consequences for health; a topic we will devote chapter 9 to. It is interesting that in the fall of 2011, while we were writing this book, then-presidential candidate Herman Cain, the only African American running for the Republican nomination, argued for reforming "taxes" using an 9-9-9 model: setting income tax at 9 percent, taxing corporations at 9 percent, and instituting a national 9 percent sales tax. He argued that this was "fair" because everyone pays the same amount of taxes. Well, Mr. Cain, according to our example, not quite, at least not in terms of the percent of one's income, whereby the poor pay double or triple the percentage of their household income than the middle class.

UNFAIR BANKING PRACTICES

We will address predatory lending practices and the roles they play in homeownership rates, foreclosures, and so on, here we briefly address other types of banking practices that contribute to poverty. Specifically, because the poor obviously have few assets they often frequently have poor credit. Thus, when they have a need to borrow money—to purchase a car, make a down payment on a rental unit, or pay medical expenses—they are virtually locked out by traditional banks and they are forced to rely on payday lending institutions. Payday lending institutions are happy to lend the money, but to do so the borrower has to agree to exorbitant interest rates, sometimes paying nearly 100 percent interest. This practice contributes to poverty because it takes advantage of those who have no other options and puts them in a position of never being able to catch up or get ahead. We are especially perplexed by an article in the *New York Times* in the spring of 2012 that reported that mainstream banks, including Wells Fargo, are adopting these types of practices as well. Essentially they seek out low income borrowers and lure them inside the shiny bank only to offer them loans that are tied to instruments such as prepaid cards with extremely high interest rates. That there is no public outcry demanding banks to adhere to fairness in lending is extremely disturbing. This practice will likely contribute to the long-term poverty experienced by many African American families.

INDIVIDUAL CHOICES

Whites, but also many middle-class African Americans, are attracted to individual explanations for differences in earnings; they blame low income African Americans—the members of the abandoned—for making poor choices by dropping out of high school, ending up in prison, and having children without the benefits of marriage or at the very least a stable partnership. Henry Louis "Skip" Gates, President Barack Obama, and actor/comedian Bill Cosby have all, in one way or another, pleaded with young African American men to keep their pants zipped up, to stay in school, and to stay out of trouble.

Though we agree that at the individual level some of the hardships we see could be avoided by making better choices, this message is dangerous for many reasons. Most importantly because it ignores the structural barriers that African Americans continue to face. This message resonates for middle-class African Americans for reasons that are different but that are equally dangerous. This message leads to a false sense of individual accomplishment and a fierce blaming of those individuals who fail. Whites, especially whites who espouse liberal beliefs about race, would like to think that we have entered a postracial society, where they no longer have to feel guilty for their own successes or take responsibility for working to level the playing field for African Americans. Successful African Americans would also like to interpret their successes as due to their own efforts because individual efforts are perceived to be in some ways protected from the structural unfairness that has for so long plagued the lives of African Americans. If those who achieve believe they have gotten there all on their own then they can relax knowing that no one can take the accomplishments away; they are no longer subjected to the irrationalities of racial discrimination. They can pour all of their energies into helping their children make the same kinds of good decisions without having to worry that the gains they have made will be undone in the next generation by the vestiges of racism. One can only imagine the relief to believe that the dragon one has fought so hard to defeat has now been defeated and individual efforts—which can be controlled—are all that matter.

In the end, however, buying into this myth has terrible consequences for the African American community. For one thing, as Robinson points out, it drives the wedge between middle-class African Americans and the abandoned; and the abandoned continue to be blamed, by both whites and African Americans, for their circumstances. For those who continue to be blocked by inequalities in the system—hiring discrimination, wage discrimination, and the like—being blamed for their lack of success must be discouraging beyond belief.

Perhaps the worst outcome of espousing individual explanations for success is the fact that it creates a false sense of security for those who are doing well; and the lessons in this have never been more clear than in the recession of 2007. For the first time millions of middle-class African Americans found themselves unemployed or underemployed; ranging from those laid off from manufacturing and factory work that has moved to Singapore and China as well as to those who have graduated from college or professional school, those with so much promise, who find that the jobs they trained for, saved for, and went into debt for are no longer available as law firms, schools, and many other reputable, honorable professions reduce their labor forces to save the jobs they can.

Another problem with the proclamations of transcendents like Bill Cosby is that it fails to reach the intended audience, the abandoned. Rather than serving as a rallying cry to the very people who are making poor decisions that contribute to their dismal circumstances, the message serves to embitter middle-class African Americans who are embarrassed by and disappointed in their underachieving family and friends who fail to make choices that lead to prosperity. As for the other transcendents who absorb this message, those who have the power to affect social change, their belief in individual explanations not only sets their minds at ease, but it leads them to conclude that not only did they make it on their own, but anyone who wants to make it like they did simply needs to work harder.

This focus on individual efforts detracts from a focus on persistent structural disadvantages, which in turn tends to produce an intense abhorrence of programs, like affirmative action, designed to level the playing field and open doors of opportunity for those groups facing structural disadvantages and outright discrimination for decades, if not centuries.

A BRIEF DISCUSSION OF WELFARE

Before we leave the discussion of income and poverty and turn to our discussion of wealth, it is important to have a brief discussion of welfare and point out a few key issues.

Based on the data on income and poverty it will come as no surprise to the reader that though numerically white Americans make up the largest group receiving welfare benefits, African Americans are disproportionately likely to be receiving welfare. Approximately 12 percent of whites participate in forms of "welfare" but nearly 40 percent of African Americans do, with the two most commonly used programs being Medicaid and food stamps. In 1996 the system of welfare, Aid to Families with Dependent Children (AFDC), was completely revamped and renamed Temporary Assistance for Needy Families (TANF). Some of the key differences between AFDC and TANF include:

- time limits for the receipt of welfare: two years continuously and five years total
- work requirements: recipients must be enrolled in school or looking for work at least thirty hours per week
- a "cap" that *excludes* children born to mothers on welfare from *ever* receiving benefits

We highlight just a few problems with these revisions to welfare policies. The time limit restrictions have posed serious difficulties since the beginning of the recession. The reader may recall that several times in 2010 and early 2011 the Congress debated whether to extend one type of assistance, unemployment payments, to the long-term unemployed. In the end, the benefits were extended, but buried beneath the debate is the reality that tens of thousands of people's unemployment benefits expire every month. This means that not only the worker, but his family, including children, find themselves without any income and they will undoubtedly then turn to other programs, including cash assistance and food stamps simply to make ends meet, or sort of meet.

Another issue we'd like to highlight is the "cap" baby revision. In short, this stipulation was designed to discourage women currently receiving welfare from having more children. Though this might seem like a good idea, in the end the person who is hurt is the baby. Because the baby is not eligible for any TANF programs, her mother will *not* receive additional cash support or food stamps once her new baby arrives. This means that the family will have to feed one more mouth with no additional funds. We can only imagine this hardship. In the end, it is the child, as well as the other children in the household who suffer.

Despite the reality that it is the children who will most likely suffer when the "cap baby" restriction is imposed, and despite the fact that most reasonable Americans do not want to see children go hungry, the stereotype of the "welfare queen," a slur that President Ronald Reagan promoted, identifies the typical recipient of welfare as an African American single mother who is stereotyped as lazy and promiscuous. This stereotype of the welfare queen reaffirms the wrongly held belief we described earlier that African Americans are more likely to be poor than whites because of individual choices they make. Two clear examples of this are: (1) accusations that many Republican presidential hopefuls have made that Obama is the "welfare president," and (2) the case of "octo-Mom" Nadia Suleman.

In the case of Obama, it actually makes sense that welfare spending would increase and the number of Americans receiving welfare would also increase during the greatest recession of the last century; a time characterized by high unemployment rates, high rates of foreclosure, and an increased cost of living resulting in part from the gas crisis. In the case of Nadia Suleman, the mother of fourteen children, eight of whom were born as a result of single artificial insemination, Americans expressed their outrage that she would have more children than she could afford to raise. She responded by promising that she would never seek welfare to meet the needs of her family. Yet, in early 2012, she announced that she was in fact receiving welfare, to the tune of $2,000 a month in food stamps, and this sent the blog-o-sphere through the roof. Situations like Suleman's fuel conservative concerns that led to the implementation of the "cap baby" restriction. Her case, because of its outrageousness, enraged many liberals, who normally detest policies like the "cap baby" restriction, as well.

WEALTH

Most of the research on race and economic inequality focuses on the poor, noting the fact that African Americans are twice as likely to be poor as whites. In contrast, few scholars or policy makers are concerned with the fact that the gap is actually greater among the affluent: where whites are 2.5 times more likely to earn high salaries than are African Americans a situation that translates directly to differences in wealth and ultimately in access to the American dream.

Wealth and the Recession

Historically, and for many obvious reasons, including the right to own a home, there has been a racial gap in terms of wealth, with the average white family holding more wealth than the average African American family. Anyone who watches the news is aware that a great deal of wealth has been lost since the beginning of the recession. Though both white households and African American households have lost wealth during the recession, data released in early 2012 by the Pew Research Center are startling.[8] Since 2005, African American wealth has declined by 50 percent and the racialized gap in wealth has *doubled.* The median net worth for whites is $113,149 whereas the median wealth for African Americans is a paltry $5,667; in other words, the average white family now has twenty times more wealth than the average African American family, a figure that was only ten times just a few years ago. About a quarter of African American households have *no assets at all,* compared to only 6 percent of white households.

The causes of the decline in wealth are many, but the two most significant causes are (1) the failing stock market, which leads to huge losses in all kinds of investment accounts, including retirement accounts, and (2) the declining housing market. The Pew Research Center report noted that in 2005, nearly 60 percent of the wealth African Americans had was in housing. The bursting of housing bubbles and sky-rocketing foreclosures has been devastating to African American families.

The Causes of the Wealth Gap

Regardless of the devastating impact of the recession on African American wealth, which is in and of itself deeply disturbing, what is equally perplexing is the fact that a tenfold gap in wealth between whites and African Americans has existed for as long as anyone has kept track, and data prior to the recession indicated that the gap persisted at every income level, even among the wealthiest African Americans.

It is not difficult to see how the poor can fail to accumulate wealth, but how can we explain this gap among the affluent? The likely explanations hinge on at least two differences between African Americans and whites. First, because of the history of slavery and Jim Crow segregation, as we noted previously, whites have been able to work in the professions, build businesses, and accumulate wealth over several hundred years (many generations) whereas African Americans have only recently been able to do so. Because you "need money to make money," as one of the author's grandfather was fond of saying, African Americans had a much later start at the moneymaking game than whites. Second, among the affluent who *work* for a living—the professional classes, as opposed to those living on an investments—African Americans are more likely to have started out in lower- and middle-class backgrounds than their white counterparts and thus they have had to personally invest more in preparing for entry into the profession. For example, many professional African Americans were born into middle- and lower-income families and they often must invest more of their own money for the education that ushers them into the professional classes—as physicians, lawyers, college professors, and bankers—and thus they accumulate greater student loan burdens than their white counterparts. Because debt is a part of the wealth equation, this difference explains part of the disparity in wealth among the affluent. This is illustrated repeatedly in scenarios similar to that described by Kai Wright who writes about his father, a prominent African American physician who died at age fifty-seven, without a pension, and with no real assets:

> At least we held our ground: Troy and Grandma got my father to college, and my parents did the same for us. But none of us [African Americans] will take part in the historic wealth transfer now under way in America: According to another study Shapiro likes to cite, [white] parents will pass on a total of more than $10 trillion to their adult kids between 1990 and 2040.[9]

HOMEOWNERSHIP

As noted, homeownership is one of the most important elements of wealth, and this is especially the case for African Americans. Therefore it is important to explore not only the role that homeownership plays in the African American community, but also the barriers to it.

First, as noted, homeownership is the most common form of wealth. But not only that, homeownership also provides the type of security against disaster as well serves as a sort of built-in personal bank. Families can borrow against the equity in their homes to pay college tuition for their children or to provide the money necessary to weather a crisis such as a layoff or illness. Homes are also one of the most commonly inherited forms of wealth—thus homeownership contributes significantly to the accumulation of wealth across generations.

According to the US Census, in 2010, 66 percent of Americans owned a home. When we examine the data by race, we learn that whereas 75 percent of whites owned their own home, only 45 percent of African Americans did. African Americans are the least likely of all racial groups to own their home, even Native Americans, the racial group with the highest poverty rate, own homes at a rate that is 10 points higher. Though there are likely many different reasons for this, we are particularly struck by the difference in homeownership between blacks and Native Americans—the two poorest groups in the US population. We suspect that the primary difference for Native Americans is that the majority of their property is on reservations and therefore controlled by them; in contrast African Americans face two kinds of discrimination with regards to housing: predatory lending practices and redlining.

Housing Discrimination

African Americans face discrimination with regards to access to housing; there are 2 to 10 million individual incidents of racial housing discrimination each year according to sociologist Joe Feagin.[10] Discrimination includes redlining (refusing to show or sell homes in predominately white neighborhoods to African Americans), refusing to rent or sell to African Americans, and unfair mortgage practices.

A study by the Center for Responsible Lending published in 2006, just before the housing bubble burst, which according to many economists was the trigger to the recession, African Americans were the target for many types of discriminatory and predatory lending practices. Their study estimated that as a result of *predatory mortgage practices* African Americans lose upward of $25 billion annually.

> Borrowers of color are more likely to get higher-rate subprime home loans—*even with the same qualifications as white borrowers*. After accounting for credit scores, African Americans and Latinos are commonly 30 percent more likely to get the most expensive financing.[11]

In addition to these subprime mortgages, another form of predatory lending was the loosening of banking laws that allowed banks to relax the typical requirement that a buyer put down 10–20 percent on their mortgage and allowed bankers to lend nearly the entire cost of purchasing a home. Not only were the monthly payments extraordinarily high, but when the housing bubble burst and the prices of homes plummeted, many people found that their homes were worth less than their mortgages. Of course when the recession hit in full force, many people found themselves unemployed and unable to make the monthly mortgages. This led to millions of foreclosures, which in turn drove housing prices down even further—what a devastating cycle. Lastly, we remind the reader that we were all harmed by this practice of predatory lending, for the newly invented practice of selling subprime mortgages—called derivatives—is ultimately what caused the failing of banking giants like Bear Stearns and Morgan Stanley, something we are all paying for today. These illegal practices also restrict many low-income African Americans from buying a home at all and as a result they end up renting apartments and homes, which prohibits the accumulation of wealth.

There have been many studies of racial discrimination with regards to renting. Just like with the employment studies we described earlier, the typical design involves sending white and African American "testers" out into local markets to see if they experience discrimination in access to units or in terms of price. One such study involved e-mailing inquiries to rental companies in the Los Angeles area. When researchers varied the *name* of the potential renter, there were significant effects for both availability and price. Potential renters with white-sounding names were significantly less likely to be told the unit had already been rented and they were also less likely to be quoted an inflated rent. Potential renters with African American-sounding names were the most likely to be told that the unit had already been rented and they were also the most likely to be quoted inflated rents. Potential renters with Middle Eastern-sounding names fell in between whites and African Americans.[12] This was particularly surprising given the post-9/11 climate (the study was conducted in 2003) and thus serves to reinforce the overall finding, replicated many times, that African Americans continue to face severe housing discrimination.

Housing Segregation

Scholars have continued to document the fact that long after the *Brown v. the Board* decision that effectively outlawed legalized segregation, housing patterns in the United States remain highly segregated. An analysis that anyone can perform using the mapping tool in American Fact Finder at the US Census website (www.census.gov) reveals that most Americans live in neighborhoods that are comprised of 80–90 percent of people of one racial group. Whites live in white neighborhoods and African Americans live with African Americans. We encourage the reader to do this on one's own neighborhood. It can be very revealing.

One outcome of severe housing segregation is that whereas whites are more likely to live in neighborhoods that are also homogenous by social class, African Americans, even those who are solidly in the middle class, are more likely to live in low-income neighborhoods. Because whites do not buy homes in African American neighborhoods and because middle-class African Americans are restricted to buying homes in segregated, socioeconomically diverse neighborhoods, housing values in African American neighborhoods remain deflated; this is one of the primary causes of the wealth gap. Racial segregation in housing also exacerbates the impact of foreclosures. Specifically, when homes are foreclosed the overall value of homes in the neighborhood declines; because African Americans have significantly higher rates of foreclosure, those who do retain ownership of their homes see the value decline. Furthermore, owning a home that is of little value is not much better than not owning a home at all because in the time of a crisis or when it is time to pay college tuition a home with little equity cannot be liquidated or borrowed against to provide the cash that is needed. In some research we did on housing in Mississippi, we found that the average home value in several rural, mostly black counties was less than $40,000; homes were worth less than the price of most luxury cars or one year's tuition at a private college.

A CLEAR ILLUSTRATION: HURRICANE KATRINA

The disparities in wealth and especially homeownership that we have been describing were played out clearly and in plain view in the fall of 2005 as images of Hurricane Katrina were broadcast into our living rooms. It can be argued that based on firsthand accounts displayed on American television sets all around the country that it was African Americans who were hit the hardest when Hurricane Katrina devastated New Orleans. Hundreds of thousands of African Americans were left homeless or worse, dead. People lost their properties, loved ones, pets, access to normal day-to-day living arrangements, and as a consequence of the mishaps of the Federal Emergency Management Association (FEMA) found themselves scattered all over the country waiting for the signal that it was safe to return home.

The television scenes from New Orleans after Hurricane Katrina were horrific. The American public saw devastation and hopelessness in front of their very eyes. The poor, mostly African American men, women, and children were literally crying out for help and assistance on live TV. Months later we finally got the rest of the story and it was not just the poor, unable, homebound, and those without cars who were stranded in flooded New Orleans. With the return of Mardi Gras in February

2006, we learned that middle-class and professional African Americans, many of whom were dentists, lawyers, medical doctors, and corporate managers, were also flooded out of their neighborhoods. Most lost not only their homes but also their businesses and professional careers. This piece of the story was not told on CNN.

Why? Because we want to believe that there is a separate place for middle-class and affluent African Americans, away from those we did see on CNN. What we forget is that as a racial group African Americans of means are more likely to live with or near those who are poor. This is not the case for whites. The African Americans in the professional class living in what has been described as New Orleans East—a racially segregated community—lost their livelihoods and their businesses and clients not only because of Hurricane Katrina but also because of racial segregation. Willard Dumas, a dentist, recounts what happened to him and others he knows in New Orleans East:

> You spend 45 years building a life and then it's gone. Your home was flooded; your business was flooded. And this happened not only to you but to practically everyone you know, so your patients or clients are gone, your friends are scattered, and your relatives are somewhere else.[13]

The media had us believing that the reason we saw so many black faces on TV was because Hurricane Katrina disproportionately impacted the poor, most of whom were African American. In other words the conclusion was that this social problem was more about poverty than about race. What we learn is that in the final analysis *it is about race*. The middle class and affluent of New Orleans who were most affected by Hurricane Katrina were in fact African Americans living and working in the racially segregated city, alongside their poorer African American brethren. Racial disparities persist across class boundaries.

In concluding this section on "wealth" we have to underscore the fact that wealth differences are more unequal than income differences for African Americans and whites. Although pronouncements have been made about the decline in the meaning (and mostly negative meaning of race in American society), it is still important to note that our review of survey research on "race relations" tells us that for most of the big important decisions that African Americans and whites make, like where to live, where to send our children to school, what careers to pursue, which YMCA to join and even what sports to sign our children up for, are all, in the final analysis, shaped by race.

CONCLUSIONS

When analyzing, poverty and wealth we have to ask this question: does the election of the first African American president affect African Americans with regards to issues of social class, namely income, wealth and the likelihood of living in poverty, and in what ways? In short, does this election signify that we have now entered a postracial America with regards to wealth and poverty?

It is terribly concerning that a quarter of all African Americans hold no assets, but only 6 percent of white households have no wealth. Though the reasons for this are similar to the explanations laid out for the affluent, the consequences are more severe. Because the poor live on the proverbial economic edge, living paycheck to paycheck, any emergency, be it medical, a layoff, a short trip to jail, or even something as routine as having to miss a shift at work because the babysitter is sick, can plunge these families over the edge, into homelessness. Thus, many African American families live every day with severe threats to their very existence.

Returning to our ever familiar question, we ask how has the election of Barack Obama impacted African Americans in terms of income and wealth? Though Obama likes to remind us all that he inherited the recession, like it or not, African Americans are not only worse off than they were three or four years ago, but the wealth gap between African Americans and whites has doubled since it was last measured in 2005.

As the reader is no doubt aware, one of the key triggers to the recession was the collapse of the housing market. This has been devastating on many levels, most notably the decline in the value of the single greatest contributor to wealth, and the loss of one's place to live through foreclosures.

Disappointingly, in the fall of 2011, the *Washington Post* reported that despite Obama's attention to foreclosures and promises to assist families facing the loss of their house when he was still a senator and presidential hopeful, President Obama's intentions have fallen disappointingly short. Obama the candidate promised to help the more than 9 million Americans facing foreclosure, but three years later his administration has spent only $2.4 billion of the $50 billion he promised and helped only 1.7 million people.

All of this is devastating news for African American families. One of our biggest concerns is that this may not be reversible. As Eugene Robinson and others have noted, many of the jobs lost are simply not coming back. Most families may never recover the hits to the investment accounts or the decline in the value of their homes. Those most able to weather the storm will be those with more wealth: whites. What this means practically, is that the gap between the rich and the poor will widen, and with it, the gap between whites and African Americans.

8

Incarceration

Blacks Commit More Crime Than Whites

Darryl Hunt, nineteen, a Negro from Winston-Salem, North Carolina, was sentenced June 15, 1985, to life in prison for the rape and murder of Deborah Sykes, a white female, on August 11, 1984. In the summer of 1990 Darryl Hunt was granted a new trial. He was convicted again, this time by an all white jury in rural, western North Carolina. In 1994 he was granted permission to have his DNA tested and he was excluded as the rapist. Despite this evidence, the judge ruled that DNA was not scientifically sound. Darryl Hunt was offered the chance to plead guilty to second-degree murder and be released based on the time he had already served. He refused, saying that he would not admit to such a horrible crime that he did not commit. Nearly ten years later, after a lengthy investigation by the local newspaper, the same newspaper Deborah Sykes worked for when she was murdered, Darryl Hunt's lawyer was able to get permission from the court to have the DNA from the case run against the CODIS database. The CODIS database contains DNA samples for all convicted sex offenders and many convicted felons. Miraculously there was a partial match to a man who was the brother of one of the original suspects in the crime. Hunt's attorney was able to obtain a DNA sample from the original suspect who was, at the time, in prison serving time for other crimes. This time the match was identical. Despite having been excluded as the rapist and murderer in 1994, only when the real perpetrator was identified—and he later confessed to the crime—was there any light at the end of the tunnel for Darryl Hunt.

On Christmas Eve 2004, after serving nearly nineteen years in prison for a crime he did not commit, Hunt was released from prison. On February 6, 2005, Darryl Hunt was officially exonerated. On May 13, 2012, Hunt received an honorary doctorate from Duke University.

This story is a brief summary of the experiences of Darryl Hunt as laid out in an eight part series published in 2004 in the *Winston-Salem Journal*.

Myth: African Americans are more likely to be in prison because they commit more crimes.

Reality: The primary reason for the overrepresentation of African Americans in jails and prisons is not so much that they are more likely to commit crimes but because they face discrimination at every level of the criminal justice system including racial profiling, facing higher rates of prosecution for nonviolent offenses, higher rates of conviction and longer sentences. But, the primary cause of the over-incarceration of African Americans are the inequities in the drug laws especially as they pertain to the possession and sale of crack cocaine versus powder cocaine.

In this chapter we will discuss one of the most pressing issues facing African American families today: incarceration. Rapidly rising rates of incarceration in the United States since the mid-1970s have proved damaging to the nation's poor and minority communities and especially damaging for African American families. The effects of this prison boom have been concentrated among these families already on the periphery of American society, the abandoned. We will begin by providing some data on the number of incarcerated African Americans; we will then address the causes of incarceration, focusing specifically on the "crack cocaine" debate. We will conclude the chapter with a discussion of the impact of mass-incarceration on the African American family.

THE STATE OF INCARCERATION IN THE UNITED STATES

The rate of incarceration in the United States has been steadily increasing since 1980, primarily due to the inception of felony drug laws and "Three Strikes You're Out" laws. States like California, New York, and Texas each incarcerate more citizens than all of the other U.S. states combined. In the last few years, the rate has been especially steep, notably for African American men and, to a lesser extent, Hispanics. In 2008, more than 2.3 million Americans (0.7 percent of the US population) were incarcerated, in nearly 1,700 state, federal, and private prisons, and more than 5 million Americans were under other forms of custodial supervision, including probation and parole, for a total of 7.2 million Americans—3.2 percent of the US population—under some form of custodial or supervisory control of the criminal justice system.[1]

Contrary to what most people would assume, the United States incarcerates a greater percentage of its population (nearly 1 percent) than any other country in the world, more than Russia, China, and all other nation-states that are often associated with over-incarcerating their citizens.

As a point of reference, the United States incarcerates more of its citizens on *drug convictions alone* than the entire incarcerated population of the European

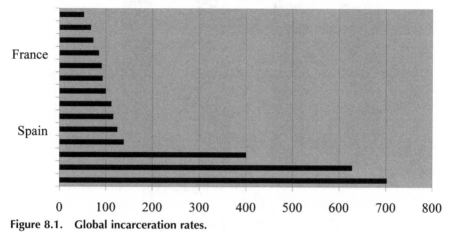

Figure 8.1. Global incarceration rates.

Union, which has a population significantly greater than the United States. If predictions hold, the recession will result in even higher rates of incarceration, because people in desperate times take desperate measures to meet their basic needs for food, clothing, and shelter; and with unemployment rates so high people may turn to property crimes or to selling drugs to meet these needs. We are, in short, addicted to incarceration.

In the United States, on any given day, 5 percent of all African American men are incarcerated, compared to less than 1 percent (0.5 percent) of their white counterparts. In other words, African American men are *ten times* more likely to be incarcerated than white men. Not surprising, women are far less likely to be incarcerated than are men, and this holds for all racial and ethnic groups in the United States. Yet, race differences persist across gender lines such that African American women are more likely to be incarcerated than are their white counterparts. It is interesting to note, however, that the racial gap for women is significantly narrower than it is for men.

When we examine the makeup of the prison population and compare it to the US population as a whole, we see that although African American men make up approximately six percent (6 percent) of the total US population they make up approximately half (50 percent) of the prison population. In other words, African American men make up more of the US prison population than white men, and all women, combined.

As shocking as these data are, the probability of incarceration over the lifetime of individual men and women is even more severe. Over their lifetimes, nearly *one-third of African American men will spend time in prison*, directly impacting the probability of establishing a healthy family unit or breaking up the family unit already established.

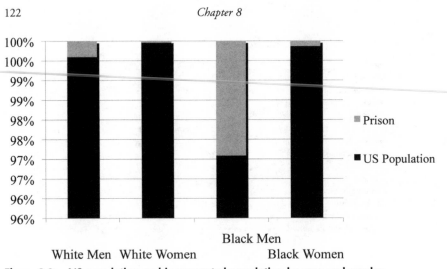

Figure 8.2. US population and incarcerated population by race and gender.

Causes of Over-Incarceration

Many Americans assume that African American men commit more crimes and therefore it is logical that they make up the bulk of the US prison population. And, in fact in opinion poll after opinion poll, including one conducted in 2011 by New Century Foundation (Color of Crime), white Americans say they believe blacks commit more crimes than whites. If everything were equal, this would be a logical conclusion for any thinking person. Yet, as it turns out, the picture is far more complicated than what it appears to be. Once we examine the data, we see that although African American men may be somewhat more likely to commit crimes, especially of certain types, the real cause of their overrepresentation in the prison population is the discrimination they face at every stage of the process, from being identified as suspects to being arrested, charged, and sentenced. We devote the next section of the chapter to a discussion of these issues.

African Americans Commit More Crimes

African Americans do commit certain crimes more often than whites. For example, homicide is now one of the leading causes of death for African American men. The data on homicide indicate that more often than not the perpetrator in these homicides is also an African American male. In fact, an examination of the data on all violent crimes (rape, homicide, assault) reveals that violent crimes are primarily intraracial; in other words both the victim and the offender are of the same race. However, when one examines the range of statistics on crime, one finds that just as African Americans are disproportionately likely to commit certain crimes (homicide), whites are disproportionately likely to commit others. Though some of these are nonviolent, financial crimes like those that executives such as Bernie Madoff (the ponzi scheme master) and Ken Lay (Enron Corporation) were convicted of, their nonviolent nature does not mean these crimes do not have victims. In fact, these crimes harm millions of American victims; many of whom have lost their life savings. For those unsuspecting folks who were employed in these firms, they lost their weekly paychecks, health insurance, and indeed their livelihoods when the firms collapsed as a result of the scams. Perhaps more perplexing is the fact that whites are also more likely to be serial murderers, child molesters, and school shooters. In fact the dominant profile of the perpetrators in all of these horrible crimes is not just white, but male. White men commit these crimes at disproportionately high rates. When we look closely at the treatment of child molesters—who are primarily white men—by the criminal justice system, we learn that the average child molester serves *shorter sentences* than crack offenders, who are primarily African American men. Child molesters are sentenced to an average of six years, and serve, on average, only 43 percent of their full sentences whereas the average person convicted of *possession* of crack is sentenced to eleven years and serves 80 percent of his sentence. In practical terms this means that the average child molester serves just under three years where as the average person convicted of possessing a small amount of crack serves nearly three times longer, just under nine years. Because the length of the sentence shapes the overall number of people in prison—those serving longer sentences contribute more to the overall incarcerated population than those who serve shorter sentences, the racial gap in incarceration rates cannot be explained entirely by the rate of committing crime. Part of the incarceration rate is driven by differences in sentencing that keep certain people in prison for longer periods of time than others.

Racial Profiling

Over the last decade or so, significant attention has been paid to the catch-all category of "racial profiling." Typically racial profiling refers to the targeting of African Americans, Hispanics, and since the tragedy of September 11, 2001, Middle Easterners, in "pulling over" a person for no apparent reason, searching private property such as a car or home, and arresting that person. Anecdotal evidence suggests that since September 11, nonwhites are more likely to be subjected to more extensive searches in airports and train stations. The most reliable data come from the Bureau of Justice Statistics. Beginning a decade or so ago (in the mid-1990s), the law required local law enforcement agencies to collect data on the race, ethnicity, and gender of all people involved in traffic stops. The latest report, released in April 2005, reported that there were no racial differences in the probability of being stopped, but that African Americans (and Hispanics) were more likely to be subjected to "forced search" of their cars and more likely to have "force used against them" during the traffic stop. The relationship between racial profiling and racial disparities in incarceration is significant and clear. Part of the higher rate of incarceration for African Americans is a *direct outcome* of the higher probability that they will be searched, arrested, and charged with a crime. Furthermore, we note that the discussion of racial profiling is politically charged. In August 2005 the director of the Bureau of Justice Statistics, Lawrence Greenfeld, was *fired* over a dispute regarding his agency's research on racial profiling. The Bush administration, and President George Bush in particular, did not want data on racial profiling released and sought to repress it. When Greenfeld refused to suppress this important information he was fired. We find it interesting that this issue, which is a clear demonstration of bias in the criminal justice system, in a climate when everyone is aware that African Americans are more likely to be incarcerated, is something an administration desires and demands be repressed.

Sentencing Disparities

Along with differences in traffic stops and arrest, there is also substantial evidence to support the argument that African Americans receive stiffer sentences than their white counterparts who commit the same crime. For example, among people convicted of drug felonies in state courts, whites were *less likely* than African Americans to be sent to prison. Specifically, in his testimony to the US Sentencing Commission on Racial Disparity in 2012, Marc Mauer reported on his research on sentencing demonstrating that in state courts 33 percent of convicted white defendants received a prison sentence whereas 51 percent of African American defendants received prison sentences for the same drug convictions.[2] In addition, in a review of forty recent and methodologically sophisticated studies investigating the link between race and sentence severity, many of the studies, especially at the federal level, found evidence of direct discrimination against minorities that resulted in significantly more severe sentences for African Americans than their white counterparts.[3] Therefore, we conclude that part of the explanation for differential rates in incarceration is *racial disparities in sentencing.* More African American men are in prison than their white counterparts because when convicted of the same crime they are more likely to receive harsher prison sentences.

The racial mix of the criminal justice system: Part of the problem in the criminal justice system is the overall lack of representation of African Americans in the very system that discriminates against them. At all levels of the criminal justice system, from law enforcement, to prosecutors, to judges, African Americans are grossly underrepresented. Anecdotally we know that even when they are present—especially as police officers and prison guards—there is a great deal of pressure on them to hold African American suspects and convicts to a more severe standard than whites. Routinely, despite a constitutional right to a jury of their peers, many African Americans are convicted and sentenced by all-white juries, even in the South where African Americans make up 20–30 percent of the population. Darryl Hunt, whose story opens this chapter, experienced this.[4]

Beliefs about Criminals

Those who defend racial profiling note that if African Americans are more likely to commit crimes, then it makes sense for law enforcement agents to target African Americans with police surveillance and systematic traffic stops. Unfortunately, as the previous examples illustrate, in many cases the targeting or treatment of a population is based more on myths or stereotypes about that ethnic population than on empirical evidence. In other words, beliefs around race and crime are so powerful that they create perceptions about African Americans and crime that significantly influence the behavior of whites reporting crime, identifying suspects, and in the case of police officers, engaging in racial profiling.

We illustrate our point here with two examples that should be familiar to most readers, both involve cases where whites blamed African American men for crimes they themselves had committed. In the fall of 1994 when Susan Smith drowned her sons in a lake in South Carolina, she appeared on TV publicly proclaiming that she had been carjacked by a black man. In 1989, when Charles Stuart murdered his pregnant wife in Boston, he, too, blamed it on a carjacker: a black man. Most recently, Amanda Knox, the American college student who was tried twice and ultimately declared innocent in the murder of her roommate in Italy, fingered an African man who owned the bar where she worked and where she spent the last night before her roommate was found murdered in their apartment. The man Knox falsely accused not only spent time in jail, but as a result he lost his business. This practice is so widespread that there are research reports on these racial hoaxes that find evidence to substantiate 100 cases, most falsely identify African American men of crimes like assault, robbery, and rape. We also point out that the only real explanation for these racial hoaxes is the power of the belief in the social stereotype of the African American criminal. Without this belief, there would be no safety in choosing to deflect one's own crime on an unidentified African American man.

Exonerations

One by-product of many of these causes, including differential treatment in the criminal justice system, beliefs about African American men as criminals, and the lack of African American representation in any aspect of the criminal justice system, is the issue of wrongful conviction. As the story of Darryl Hunt reveals, black men are incarcerated wrongly. Though for a variety of reasons—including a lack of DNA evidence in most crimes—there is no way to estimate the number of wrongful convictions; some scholars who study the issue estimate that 6 percent of those in prison were wrongly convicted. To be clear, this does not mean people who were sent to prison for the wrong charge—armed robbery instead of simple robbery—this refers to people who are factually innocent; they did not commit any crime. Even if only 6 percent of the half a million African American men in prison are actually innocent, the years of life lost in prison is supremely significant to those men and to their families.

THE ROLE OF DRUG USE AND DRUG LAWS

We could not adequately answer the question of the over-incarceration of African Americans and the concomitant destruction of the family unit without discussing the role drugs, and especially the disparities in sentencing associated with crack versus powder cocaine, play. Perhaps the major cause of the overuse of incarceration, and the over-incarceration of African Americans in particular, is the aptly named "War on Drugs."

Drug Use

Across the twentieth century, Americans' attitudes around drugs (and alcohol) have changed in terms of both drug and alcohol use as well as in terms of the use of the criminal justice system to regulate drugs and alcohol. One common misperception is that the dramatic rise in arrests, convictions, and incarceration for drug charges reflects an overall increase in the number and percent of Americans using controlled substances. In fact, research by the White House Office of National Drug Control Policy (ONDCP) Information Clearinghouse,[5] which has collected data on drug use, from 1975 to the present, shows overwhelming, in every category, that drug use rose from 1975 to 1979 and then dropped off significantly in the 1980s, 1990s, and early 2000s. These declines occurred in every age group and for every period for which data were collected. For example, the percent of Americans over the age of twelve who reported using an "illicit substance" in the last thirty days declined from 14 percent in 1975 to 7 percent in 2002. The evidence is overwhelmingly clear that the threefold increase in drug convictions between 1980 and 2008 are not in response to increased drug use, but rather to changes in the criminalization of substances (which occurred slowly across the entire twentieth century) and changes in the policies designed to address drug possession.

Drug Policies

The "War on Drugs" officially began in 1972 with a formal announcement by President Richard Nixon. The "War on Drugs" was significantly ramped up under the administration of President Ronald Reagan who added the position of "Drug Czar" to the President's Executive Office. The War on Drugs did not so much criminalize substances as that had been happening across the early part of the twentieth century. What these laws did do was put into place stiffer sentencing guidelines that required (1) longer sentences, (2) mandatory minimums, (3) moving certain drug offenses from the misdemeanor category to the felony category, and (4) the institution of the "Three Strikes You're Out" policy. Taken together, these drug laws result in:

- *Longer initial sentences:* Today crack cocaine defendants receive an average sentence of eleven years.

- *Longer overall sentences that result from "Mandatory Minimums":* The most frequently cited example is the sentencing guidelines for possession of crack-cocaine. As part of the War on Drugs, a conviction of *possessing* five grams of crack now mandates a five-year minimum sentence.
- *Felonizing drug offenses:* Small possession convictions, particularly of crack cocaine, were recategorized from misdemeanors to felonies in the 1986 Drug Abuse Act.
- *"Three Strikes You're Out":* This law allows for *life sentences* for convicts receiving a third-felony conviction. Coupled with the recategorizing of some drug *possession* offenses (i.e., crack cocaine) as felonies, the result has been that many inmates serving life sentences are there for three drug possession offenses; in effect, they are serving life sentences for untreated addictions.

The Crack Cocaine Dilemma

One of the most important and decisive changes to the drug policies that began implementation in the 1980s revolved around drawing distinctions between two forms of cocaine: crack (or rock) and powder. Crack is created by cooking powder cocaine with baking soda; the residual, or "rocks," are what we commonly refer to as "crack." It is commonly believed that crack was developed as a way to deliver a similar high in a cheaper form. Because crack is less pure than cocaine its street value is significantly lower. Many men and women we interviewed about their drug addictions talked about buying or selling a "rock" for around $20. As a result, the crack epidemic of the 1980s and early 1990s exploded with the heavy marketing of crack in low-income black communities, much as "meth" is today in rural white communities. By the early 1980s, around the same time that the Rockefeller Drug Laws were developed, crack had become associated with black urban ghettos and with that image of the "crackhead" being an African American man or woman. In contrast, the more expensive powder cocaine was largely associated with the upper-class professional community as well as with Hollywood. Readers may remember that by the late 1980s it was common to see the latest victim of a cocaine binge—often a child actor like Dana Plato who appeared in the television hit show *Different Strokes*—in handcuffs or in a mug shot displayed on the nightly news.[6] Those studying drug policy argue that as a result of racialized differential use of crack versus cocaine, drug policies regarding crack and cocaine developed in a racialized manner as well.

Additionally, New York City has a "zero tolerance" policy with police arresting individuals with as little as 25 grams of marijuana, causing an upsurge in arrests, from fewer than 1,500 in 1980 to 50,000 today. The human cost of zero tolerance has been devastating to New York City African American families.[7]

In sum, federal drug policy draws a distinction between crack and powder cocaine and sets a 100 to 1 sentencing disparity between the two forms. This means that possession of just five grams of crack cocaine (about a thimble full) yields a five-year mandatory minimum sentence, while it takes 500 grams of powder cocaine to trigger the same five-year sentence. *Crack cocaine is the only drug for which there is a federal mandatory minimum sentence for mere possession.* In contrast, the laws around the illegal possession of narcotic prescription drugs, such as oxycontin, for example, do not vary based on the number of milligrams of the drug per tablet. Yet, this is just what the crack cocaine laws do.

The impact of these drug policies on the lives of African Americans and their families are not only severe, but they are way out of line with other postindustrial nations. Currently, in the United States, 450,000 of the more than 2 million inmates (45 percent) in state and federal prison are incarcerated for nonviolent drug offenses. In contrast, this is more people than the European Union, an entity with a 100 million more people than the United States, has in prison for *all crimes combined.* States and the federal government continue to spend about $10 billion a year imprisoning drug offenders, and billions more on the War on Drugs. These costs do not include the impact incarceration has on the economic and social life of the country, individual states, and communities. Because inmates incarcerated for nonviolent drug offenses are disproportionately likely to be African American, the impact on the African American family, and community, is devastating.

THE IMPACT OF INCARCERATION
ON THE AFRICAN AMERICAN COMMUNITY

One way to understand the impact of the over-incarceration of African American men is to examine the losses that occur and the disadvantages that accrue in the African American family when these men are removed in such large numbers. As with any accumulation of disadvantage, such as the steep rise in incarceration for African American men, comes an accumulated advantage for someone else. For example, whites, implicitly or explicitly, benefit from the sending of hundreds of thousands of African American men to prison. One big advantage that can be measured empirically is that these high levels of incarceration effectively remove these men from the competitive labor force, and upon release they are disenfranchised in the political system.

Second, advantage can accrue to communities. For example, the prison boom—both in terms of the number of prisons built and the escalating numbers of citizens sent to prison, and the locating of prisons in deindustrialized communities and rural communities—is an economic advantage that accrues primarily to whites in the form of jobs (e.g., prison staff) and in terms of building contracts and other services that are necessary when a town builds a prison. These advantages by and large do not accrue to the families where African American males have been removed nor do they accrue to their communities.

Loss in the African American Community: Economic Costs

The economic and family consequences of incarceration affect more than just the individual and his family. As a result of the hyper-residential segregation we described earlier in the book, African American communities will by default have higher rates of male incarceration than white communities. As noted by Jonathan Kozol in his book *Ordinary Resurrections*, in Mott Haven, New York, *half* of all the children in this neighborhood routinely make visits to prisons like Rikers Island to visit their fathers, and we note, with more and more also visiting their mothers.

Furthermore, incarceration has a social class component as well. The 25–33 percent of African American men who are incarcerated in their lifetimes are not spread evenly across all social class groups. Drawing again on Eugene Robinson's way of categorizing the African American community, the rates of incarceration are much lower among middle- and upper-middle-class and professional African American men and they are much higher among low-income and poor African American men. Thus, in a poor African American community—inhabited by the abandoned—perhaps as many as 50 percent of the men will have been to prison. If 50 percent of men in a single community have been incarcerated and have felony records, then half the families in this community will face the consequences of the chronic unemployment and underemployment these men face as a result of their incarceration. Thus incarceration contributes significantly to the devastating poverty that plagues these families and communities. With reduced capacity for earning a living wage, entire communities will struggle just to have enough income to survive and there will be little to no chance of owning homes or establishing businesses in the community, leaving the entire community vulnerable to other oppressive forces such as slum landlords and exploitive labor practices that force workers to go outside the community to find jobs. We would add to Robinson's argument that incarceration is a major force in both creating the "abandoned" and in separating them from the rest of the African American community in jails and prisons.

Loss in the African American Community: Human Capital

A major part of the prison problem is that an enormous amount of human capital is lost with the incarceration of African American men who go to prison in their most productive years. Human capital refers to the education, skills, and experience one has that can be leveraged for wages in the labor market. In prison, these men learn few transferable skills and when they are finally released, as most of them will eventually be, they are useless to themselves and to others, at least in terms of their ability to earn a living wage.

One of the most obvious and devastating outcomes of incarceration on human capital is seen in the labor market. Protected by law, employers are allowed to ask prospective employees if they have been convicted of a felony. Additionally, in some states and in some industries, we note that employers can also ask about misdemeanor records and arrest records (with no conviction). To examine the impact of felony records on employment, sociologist Devah Pager designed an experiment to test the relationship between race and incarceration history on the likelihood of getting a "call back" after submitting a job application. What she found is terribly disturbing.

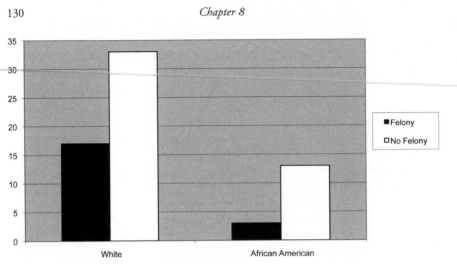

Figure 8.3. The mark of a criminal record.

Pager designed an experiment in which she sent out "testers" to apply for jobs. In one case the job applicant indicated that he had a felony record and in the other he indicated that he did not have a felony record. Both African American and white men played both roles. Her study revealed that whites were more likely to be called back for an interview regardless of incarceration history. White men without a felony were, not surprisingly, the most likely to be called back of all groups. The shocking finding from her research is that whites *with a felony record* were more likely to be called back than African Americans *without a felony record*. Fewer than 5 percent of African American men with a felony record were called back (compared to 15 percent of whites with a felony record). Incarceration is problematic for anyone, but the effects are devastating on the employability of African American men and ultimately on the families they are hoping to support.

Loss in the African American Community: Social Capital

Related in many ways to the human capital loss is also the loss of "social capital." The loss of social capital to the African American community and to African American families is immense. According to Harvard sociologist Robert Putnam and French sociologist and philosopher Pierre Bourdieu, social capital refers to the social networks or connections among individuals. These social networks provide access to information, support, advice, and so forth. Bourdieu, Putnam, and others argue that these social ties and networks impact most aspects of our daily lives from finding housing to finding employment to finding an intimate partner. One of the most important sources of social capital is one's family.

These very important "reciprocal social relations" are lost when African American men are sent to prison. More often than not, inmates are removed from their home communities to be incarcerated, often hundreds of miles away. This makes regular contact, especially face-to-face visits, difficult if not impossible. Though some may argue that this is what an inmate deserves, isolation from family and friends, we must remember two key points. First, the inmate is not the only person suffering this isolation. His intimate partner, parents, children, siblings, and everyone else in his life also suffers. Second, social networks are critical to successful reentry once an inmate is released. Those who reenter the "free world" without social ties are far more likely to recidivate and end up right back in prison. We explore the impact of the loss of social capital through incarceration on African American individuals, families and communities with two examples. We begin with the perspective of an inmate.

Social Capital: An Inmate's Perspective

For the last decade we have taught a course in which we take college students on a two-week "off campus" experience through the Deep South. A significant part of the course is a visit to the Mississippi State Penitentiary at Parchman. "Parchman Farm" is located right in the heart of the Mississippi Delta. Parchman is a 20,000-acre men's prison with the capacity to house 6,000 inmates. Parchman holds all death row inmates in Mississippi and has executed prisoners using a roving electric chair, a notorious gas chamber, and now, by lethal injection. Parchman was founded more than 100 years ago on the Parchman family plantation and is entirely self-sustaining. The inmates sew all of their own clothes and bedding, they make all of the tack and saddles for the horse patrol, and they grow all of their own food including corn, okra, hogs, and more recently catfish. Because Parchman is 85 percent African American and its population has historically fluctuated with the labor needs of the agricultural season, it is often described as a plantation.

While at Parchman, we and our students meet with inmates and learn lessons firsthand from prisoners doing a stretch of time that is unimaginable. Walter Lott spoke to our class on several of these visits to the prison, and in these discussions he made it clear that his life was ruined from the first day he was sent to Parchman. The lives of his family members were also ruined. Walter has been imprisoned in Parchman since he was nineteen years of age. Walter was finally paroled in 2009 after serving nearly thirty years at Parchman.

When we first met Walter in 2003 he was working in the Parchman chapel and thrived on his position as a spokesman—giving "scared straight" talks to groups like our own. When we saw Walter two years later, in 2005, he had lost his living space with a reorganization in the cell blocks. This reorganization resulted in a structural reduction in his privileges. His connections with prison officials, a form of social capital on the inside, were his *only hope* for being reassigned to a different unit and having his privileges reinstated. Thus, for inmates, social capital is as important on the inside as it is on the outside.

As noted, social capital is one of the primary factors necessary for successful reentry. For many inmates like Walter, with no social support on the outside, reentry to the "free world" can be as daunting as the thought of entering prison when they were first sentenced. When we visited Parchman in 2009, just after Walter had been paroled, we asked those staff who knew him about his reaction to being paroled. Ms. McIntyre, the Parchman reception center administrator and tour guide, told us that Walter, after thirty years of incarceration, was afraid of leaving Parchman as he did not know how to live on the outside. This is akin to the fictitious character, Brooks, in the film *Shawshank Redemption* who is paroled after a long time in prison and shortly thereafter hangs himself in a halfway house because he felt unable to figure out how to make it outside of the institutional life to which he had become accustomed.

All of Walter's family members (mother, father, sisters, and brothers) are either dead or had disowned him and have severed contact with him. He has virtually no social ties or social networks in the "free world." He had actually been granted parole earlier, in 2007, but could not be released because he failed to meet a condition of that parole: he had to move in with a family member. Thankfully, in 2009, he was able to find a family member who would accept him.

It should be clear that an extensive social capital network is necessary for survival inside prison; it is also the case that the physical relocation of these men from their own communities to other communities, often far from home, breaks their social networks and renders them alienated and unable to connect with others in their social network groups and families on the outside.

Social Capital and Inmate Relocation: An Illustration from New York

New York is one of the states with the highest rates of incarceration of all of the United States. Additionally, because one author was raised in New York and is familiar with the geography, we choose it as our illustration. Maintaining relationships with family and friends on the outside is one of the major predictors of both surviving incarceration and successful reentry. Therefore, to better understand some of the barriers and struggles faced by inmates and the families they leave behind we designed a "thought" exercise in which we simulated a likely scenario based on the data on incarceration in New York. In short, the vast majority of people inhabiting New York state prisons are not only African American but they are from the five boroughs of New York City. The vast majority of prisoners are housed in the white, rural communities of upstate New York. Thus, overall, as a direct result of incarceration, tens of thousands of African Americans are "relocated" from their own communities to communities that are almost entirely populated by whites. In other words in New York, as in other states, inmates are required to serve their time outside of their communities of origin and far away from their families.

This is the thought exercise.

We decided to determine what it would be like for the family of an inmate who fit this description: the family lived in New York City or the Bronx or Suffolk County. The inmate is incarcerated in St. Lawrence County, close to the Canadian border. Depending on the exact specifications, this is a nearly 500-mile "relocation."

As part of our thought exercise we assumed that the family does not have access to a car. According to many inmates we have spoken with this is fairly typical as so many of the incarcerated are from low-income families and because it is unusual for all types of families residing in New York City to have regular access to a car, never mind owning one. According to the *New York Times*, we found that there are privately chartered buses that travel to Ogdensburg Correctional Facility, in St. Lawrence County, at least once a month. The round-trip travel time, by bus, from New York City was approximately twenty-three hours and the fare, per person, was between $50–75 for the adults and half of that for kids. Thus, it would be difficult for a family to travel from New York City to the prisons in upstate New York on any kind of regular basis.[8]

Clearly the geography of prison locations—which may be in part designed to isolate inmates from families—disrupts family life, isolates innocent victims, including the intimate partners, parents, and children of inmates, and leads to an overall decline in social capital in many African American communities. Furthermore, this practice has a significant impact on reentry and recidivism for the 750,000 individuals who are released back into their communities annually. We turn now to a discussion of political capital.

POLITICAL CAPITAL: CENSUS RECALCULATION AND FELON DISENFRANCHISEMENT

Incarceration depletes political capital, both of the individual and of the community from which the individual comes. This depletion of political capital is critical both symbolically and practically. The disenfranchisement of felons has symbolic power because it takes away a right, the right to vote, that is the quintessential symbol of being an American citizen. Furthermore, because of the high rates of incarceration of African Americans, disenfranchisement also takes away the power of *African American communities* to choose their political representation at the local, state, and national level. According to sociologists Chris Uggen and Jeff Manza, the outcome of the 2000 presidential election was shaped in part by felony disenfranchisement.[9] Finally, the relocation of inmates from their home communities to prisons in other counties, in other parts of the states, changes the way that resources are allocated by the state and federal government. Though many people know that inmates are relocated for the purposes of incarceration, the way that this shapes resource allocation is less well known, but extremely important and thus worthy of discussion.

The Impact of Incarceration on the US Census

Currently, the Census, which is used every ten years to, among other things, redraw congressional districts to ensure that districts are proportional, allows rural communities with prisons to "count" inmates as citizens. In New York, like most states, prisons are in rural regions but the majority of inmates originate from urban communities, thus the relocation of inmates to rural prisons has significant outcomes for the Census and ultimately for both the counties that house the prisons and the counties from which the inmates originate. This practice allows rural counties to "grow" and thereby get more congressional representation while urban communities "dwindle" and get fewer representatives and fewer tax-based economic resources. This is despite the fact that the inmates counted as *citizens* of rural communities are disenfranchised and thus cannot vote. Therefore, they are in no way "citizens" of these rural communities. Again, New York State provides a useful illustration.

New York City loses 43,740 residents *annually* to the districts of upstate legislators where they are incarcerated in rural areas. Inmates have been moving up there for decades, but since 1982, all new state prisons in New York are built upstate. As a result of Census rules, rural upstate communities counting the prisoners as "citizens" are actually *overestimating* their populations beyond the 5 percent rule established by the US Supreme Court. In fact, the population of some upstate towns comprised mostly of inmates. The majority of the population of Dannemora, New York, is incarcerated in its "supermax" prison and almost half (3,000) of the town of Coxsackie's population (7,000) is in prison.

As many as twenty-one counties in the United States have more than 21 percent of their population incarcerated as recorded by the Census. In four counties, the percentage is nearly one-third. We note that these counties are both rural and for the most part, southern; thus the poorest regions of the country are able to actualize and access government resources by decimating urban ghettos.

This process is racialized as well. For example, the majority of inmates coming from the boroughs of New York City are African Americans who live in predominately African American districts. They are relocated and counted in predominately white counties. Thus, congressional representation and federal and state resources are rerouted from predominately African American districts to predominately white districts.

Felony Disenfranchisement

Most Americans know that there is some relationship between felony status and the political system. For example, ex-felons cannot be elected to the Office of the President. Fewer people understood the relationship between felony status and voting until the 2000 presidential election when the issue rose to the national scene as part of the voting debacle in Florida that resulted in the outcome of the presidential election being determined in the US Supreme Court.

It is not surprising that most Americans do not know much about the relationship between felony records and voting since the disenfranchisement laws vary tremendously from state to state. All but two states (Maine and Vermont) have some sort of restrictions on voting for people with felony conviction affecting 47 million people or one-fourth of the adult population.[10] The restrictions vary:

1. a restriction on voting while incarcerated (twelve states)
2. restrictions on voting while incarcerated and/or on parole (twenty-four states)
3. a lifetime ban on voting for all convicted felons (twelve states)

This becomes even more complex because some states, including seven of the states that impose a lifetime ban on voting, have a process of restoration that can be invoked at a later point in time. In some states this process is easy and straightforward, and in others it is a process that is nearly impossible to navigate. For example, in North Carolina where felons are banned from voting until they complete their entire sentence (including parole or probation), the Department of Corrections supplies felons being discharged with the information about reinstating their right to vote. All that is required is for the ex-offender to reregister to vote. In other states the process is lengthy and involves filing paperwork at the state department of corrections or the state capitol.

How important was the disenfranchisement debacle in Florida in 2000? Uggen analyzed what he first identified as the demographic characteristics of the pool of *wrongly disenfranchised* and then examined the previous voting patterns for these groups. By extrapolating the voting records on top of the election outcome, his research demonstrates that had African Americans who were wrongly disenfranchised in Florida in the 2000 presidential election had their right to vote restored and recognized, the outcome of the election would have been clearly in favor of Vice President Gore. Thus, the consequences of felony disenfranchisement are significant and affect the lives of all Americans. Regardless of one's opinion regarding felony disenfranchisement, it is clear what a powerful policy it is.

Furthermore, as noted throughout this chapter, because of the concentration of incarceration among low-income African Americans coupled with hyper-residential segregation, felony disenfranchisement can effectively disenfranchise whole communities, and as Robinson would no doubt acknowledge, these are communities of the abandoned. We can only guess as to the role that incarceration has played in furthering the plight of the abandoned and separating them from the larger African American community. We can conclude, however, that this has been significant.

Interestingly, tracing the history of felony disenfranchisement reveals the fact that these laws were enacted at precisely the moment that African Americans were freed from the oppressive structure of chattel slavery and first seeking the right to vote. Thus, felony disenfranchisement has a powerful and deliberate impact on the political capital of African American communities.

CONCLUSIONS

When analyzing incarceration today we have to ask the question: does the election of the first African American president affect convictions, arrests, sentencing, or any other aspects of the criminal justice system for African Americans, and in what way? In short, does this election signify that we have now entered a postracial America in terms of incarceration?

The answer, in short, is that the election of the first African American president has done absolutely nothing to address the wrongs in the criminal justice system. While this may be seen as a harsh statement, it is a true statement. The United States is addicted to incarceration and African American men remain the most likely of all subgroups of the population to go to prison. African Americans are still subjected to discrimination at every turn in the criminal justice system. They are more likely to be stopped, arrested, prosecuted, convicted, and they are given longer sentences than their white counterparts for the same crimes. Despite increased attention on two main issues facing African American men—the crack powder cocaine debate and exonerations—little has been done by anyone, including the federal government or the White House to address either issue.

We close this chapter by considering the impact of incarceration on the African American family. Quite simply it is nothing short of devastating. Because incarceration is concentrated in the communities of the abandoned, it also has devastating impact on larger communities, many of which already face so many challenges including minimum resources, low incomes, declining infrastructure, and so on. We can say without a doubt that the mass incarceration of African American men contributes significantly to and exacerbates the plight of the African American families and the communities they live in. How do we know this?

It is not hard to demonstrate that incarcerating young African American males, ages sixteen to thirty-five, directly affects family life. It can be underscored in a "what if" scenario: One in nine African American men between the ages of sixteen and thirty-five is behind bars. According to 2009 data from the Census Bureau we learn that 70.5 percent of African American women between the ages twenty and thirty have never married. Is this a direct correlation? Probably. If men and women marry mostly members from their own race group, something is going on here.

Stanford University professor Ralph Richard Banks, in his book *Is Marriage for White People? How the African American Marriage Decline Affects Everyone*, sheds light on the reasons why African American women are the most unmarried group of people in the United States. The answer is not because African American men are with white women—as spouses or boyfriends—as some wrongly believe. It is, to be sure, what Harvard sociologist William J. Wilson means when he argues that the male marriageable pool is depleted. Women of all races, including African American women, don't marry men who are jobless and they sure can't marry them if they are in jail or prison or dead.[11] Thus, the over-incarceration of African American men contributes to many of the issues plaguing the African American family that we have explored elsewhere in the book, including low marriage rates for African American women, high rates of single-parenting, and poverty.

Perhaps the greatest irony of all is the fact that a black man is named President of the United States and yet mass incarceration and the disenfranchisement that results mean far too many African Americans can't vote. African Americans are more disenfranchised today than any other racial or ethnic group in America. The legacy of voting rights, fought for and won on the backs and with the lives of so many African Americans across the twentieth century, has effectively been lost through mass incarceration.

9

Health, Nutrition,
and Chronic Diseases

Access to Healthy Food and
Well-being among African Americans

My father came a long way to arrive at his deathbed at the age of 57. Fifteen years ago, he ranked among Indianapolis' premier physicians, treating a largely working-class black clientele in this same hospital. But the way he griped about it, you would think he spent the day sweeping floors instead of doing surgery.

As disabling diseases go, diabetes is among the most insidious. If it runs its course, as it did with my father, it will shut down most bodily functions: mobility, sight, kidney, and finally the heart. More than 2.5 million African Americans have it, which is 80 percent higher than the disease's prevalence among whites. More than 9 out of 10 black diabetics have type 2, the version that develops in adulthood.

From heart disease to AIDS, African Americans are dying from preventable illnesses in disturbing numbers. The diabetes mortality rate is 20 percent higher for black men than white men, and 40 percent higher for black women.

Toward the end, when his illness gave him all the time in the world to sit and think, my father was keenly aware of the irony of his situation: He had spent his career counseling black folks about how to stay healthy. I'd ask him why he never followed his own advice, and he'd twist his face into that same disbelieving stare, shocked I couldn't do the math on my own. "When would I have the time to go to Fall Creek and take a walk, Kai?"

True, but the answer was never quite sufficient. In his medical practice, he witnessed every day the hidden tragedy of the late-20th-century tale of racial progress. Since the civil rights movement, African Americans have improved their lot in life by almost every measure: Black and white incomes are more equal, the racial gap in school dropout rates has been cut by a third, the glass ceilings of many professions have at least cracked. But in that same period, black America has made no progress on what may be the most important measure of all: living to see old age.

As you move up the economic ladder, black health drastically improves, but the disparities between blacks and whites do not.

The answer, a growing number of researchers say, is that the vaunted black middle class simply ain't all it's cracked up to be. Black strivers have a much harder time turning their paychecks into the status, opportunity, and security that white yuppies take for granted.

Despite all of the material success he achieved in life, my father died deeply in debt, largely from unpaid taxes on the symbols of middle-class life he had once accumulated—a nice house, a nice car, his own business. By the time he got hold of his dream, he could no longer stay healthy enough to keep it.

Kai Wright. 2006, May 24. *Upward Mortality*. Mother Jones. http://motherjones.com/politics/2006/05/upward-mortality

Myth: African Americans are more likely to develop chronic diseases like diabetes and die sooner because they are lazy and eat too much McDonald's.

Reality: As Mr. Wright's description of his father's life—and death—makes clear, African Americans do suffer more often from chronic diseases in part because they are less likely to exercise and eat a healthy diet. As the case with so many issues we've addressed in this book, when we focus on individual explanations, we miss the role that structural factors play. In this case, much of the explanation has to do with poverty—including the lack of health insurance, the inability to afford to join a gym, and the inability to afford healthy food. Our focus in this chapter will be on the role that access (or not) plays in shaping the health and mortality of African Americans. We shall see that just as with housing, which we explored in chapter 7, segregation also significantly shapes access to healthy food. Lastly, we note the intangible argument Wright makes and that others confirm, that there are hidden health costs to being African American. Today, the average American can expect to live five years longer than a Palestinian—unless that American is a black male, in which case he can expect to die three years sooner.[1]

In this chapter we will examine and analyze the state of health in the African American community, specifically the role that lifestyle—nutrition specifically—plays in shaping the health of African Americans. The health of a community has many important consequences for family life. For example, when poor health leads to early mortality families are robbed of years with grandparents or even parents. Poor health is expensive; it often prohibits employment, leads to reliance on social welfare programs including Social Security Insurance (SSI), and can become the greatest expense a family faces. Those who are uninsured or face medical costs that are not covered by insurance often incur huge credit card debts or take out second mortgages on their homes. As with everything else, healthcare costs can be especially devastating in the current recession.

Despite living in the most advanced economy in the world with the most advanced healthcare system in the world, many Americans live with chronic diseases and health crises that are similar to citizens of developing nations. Yet, even within the United States health and illness are not distributed randomly: in fact African Americans are more likely to suffer from chronic diseases, to lack access to healthcare, and to die earlier than their white counterparts. In this chapter we will explore some of the ways in which nutrition and access to healthy food shapes the disease landscape faced by African Americans. Additionally, we will include a case study: an examination of "food deserts" as they exist in rural and urban African American communities and the role they play in shaping the health outcomes of African Americans. We begin with an overall summary of the state of the health of African Americans in the twenty-first-century United States.

THE STATE OF HEALTH AND WELL-BEING IN AFRICAN AMERICAN CIVIL SOCIETY

As we look out a decade into the third millennium, the state of the health of African American *citizens* living in the United States is grim indeed. For a variety of reasons African Americans suffer from higher rates of the most lethal chronic diseases: cardiovascular disease (leading to heart attacks and strokes), diabetes, and certain forms of cancer.

Health disparities between African Americans and Americans of other racial or ethnic backgrounds have existed since these various groups began to populate—as colonists, settlers, and slaves—what is now the United States of America. The power of lingering disparities can best be understood in the context of the US economy and the US system of healthcare. One of the reasons that the life expectancy for all Americans nearly doubled during the twentieth century was because of the changing nature of the economy. During the long period of agriculture that dominated the economies of the eighteenth, nineteenth, and early twentieth centuries, many laborers died in work-related accidents. According to the Occupational Safety and Health Administration (OSHA), farming was and remains one of the most dangerous occupations. Data from the National Safety Council still shows the dangers of farming, which are surpassed as an occupational hazard in today's economy only by those associated with mining.

Manufacturing occupations, such as mining and steel mills, which replaced agricultural work, were safer, but still dangerous. The reader is certainly familiar with the accidents in mines. In the summer of 2010, on August 5, more than thirty miners were trapped in a mine in Chile. They spent an unimaginable sixty-nine days underground until they were dramatically rescued on October 13, 2010. It took nearly an entire day to bring them all up through a narrow tube using a contraption that looked like a very narrow basket or a ride at an amusement park. It was so small that miners were fed a liquid diet in the days leading up to the rescue so that they would fit into the cage.

At the close of the twentieth century, as the economy shifted to its current postindustrial service phase, occupational fatalities continue to decline. Yet, as work becomes safer, and life expectancies grow longer, African Americans, and *African American men in particular lag behind*. Thus the probability is high that men, fathers, grandfathers, uncles, and brothers will die prematurely and be less likely to be part of their families, disrupting African American family life.

RACIAL DISPARITIES IN CHRONIC DISEASES

We begin by briefly reviewing the data on the most serious and prevalent chronic diseases as they exist by race and gender groupings in the United States (all statistics on health come from the Centers for Disease Control). These data are important because they tell us something about the overall health and well-being of African Americans. Furthermore, as the data will show, a major *cause* of the chronic diseases that many African Americans live with and ultimately die from is poor nutrition.

After cardiovascular disease, diabetes ranks as the next most significant chronic disease among Americans. Diabetes is of particular importance for both its prevalence but also for the impact it has on people's lives. Type 2, or what was previously called "adult onset diabetes," has reached epidemic proportions in the United States, affecting nearly 20 million Americans. Diabetes, if not controlled through diet and oral medications, afflicts many significant systems in the human body, most notably the circulatory and excretory systems. The outcomes for patients include lower body amputations (toes, feet, and legs) and kidney failure. Kai Wright's story illustrates this precisely.

On average, African Americans are 1.6 times more likely to have diabetes as are whites of similar age. The rate of diabetes is important because it is related to so many other diseases. Patients with diabetes are two to four times more likely to develop heart disease—which is the single leading cause of death for all Americans—four to six times more likely to suffer a stroke, and it accounts for 60 percent of all nontrauma-related amputations.

LEADING CAUSES OF DEATH

Another way to examine health and well-being is to examine causes of death. One reason it is important to examine causes of death is because they tell us something about how various individuals and groups cope with illnesses. For example, though whites and African Americans develop certain forms of cancer at similar rates, African Americans are more likely to die from the disease than whites. The presumption among researchers is that higher mortality rates may be a result of poorer health to begin with, but may also be related to lack of access to early diagnosis and treatment. The case of diabetes is illustrative as well. If 8 percent of whites have diabetes, but few die of the illness (or related complications), then we can assume that they have the support (financial resources, access to medical care, access to a nutritious diet) needed to control the disease. In contrast, if African Americans are significantly more likely to die of diabetes and diabetes-related illnesses than their likelihood of developing it to begin with, then we can assume they lack access to the support they need to manage the disease.

INFANT MORTALITY

One measure of health and well-being is the infant mortality rate, which refers to the probability that a child will die before his or her first birthday. The rate itself is calculated as the number of children/infants who die before their first birthday *per* 1,000 live births. Thus, an infant mortality rate of 7.1 (the US average) means that of every 1,000 babies born alive, seven will die in their first year of life.

The infant mortality rate is considered by researchers to be a good measure of poverty and access to healthcare because of what it represents as well as the fact that it is (1) a clear measure, and (2) it is comparable across geographic region. What do we mean by "clear measure?" We mean that unlike many other measures of poverty such as literacy or malnourishment, it is clear whether an infant has died by her first birthday or survived to celebrate it. Second, unlike measures of income that are difficult to standardize because of variance in cost of living and other factors, infant mortality, the death or life of an infant, has the same meaning across all geographic regions and all cultures and societies on the planet.

Finally, though some infants die accidentally or because of genetic birth defects, or sadly, some are murdered by a parent, the majority of infants die *because of preventable causes* such as infections that go untreated, birth defects that are preventable through prenatal care and a healthy diet for both mother—pregnant or nursing—and the young child.

Internationally, infant mortality rates vary from a low of 2.28 deaths per 1,000 live births in Singapore to a high of 192.5 deaths per 1,000 live births in Angola. To put the infant mortality rate in perspective, the United States ranks thirty-six of the 208 countries for which there are infant mortality data. The United States is outranked by all of the western European countries and many countries in Asia such as Singapore, Japan, and Hong Kong. The infant mortality rate in the United States, the wealthiest country in the world, is slightly higher than that in the countries of the former Soviet bloc and only slightly lower than many Caribbean nations. We learn that there are significant disparities in the infant mortality rate for different racial and ethnic groups within the United States. The infant mortality rate for African American babies is twice as high—14 percent—as it is for white babies.

More data reveal that infant mortality rates also vary by region of the country. The infant mortality rate for African American babies born in highly segregated, poor, Southern counties of the United States are more than double those experienced by

blacks living in other regions of the country that are less segregated and more affluent. *An African American infant born in parts of the Deep South is more likely to die
before his first birthday than a baby born in many developing nations.* At the extreme,
only four *countries* in the Western Hemisphere have infant mortality rates *higher* than
Tippah County, Mississippi (40 percent): the Dominican Republic (41); Guyana
(45.2); Bolivia (66); and Haiti (88.9).

As noted, the infant mortality rate is affected primarily by poverty and access to
healthcare. The role that poverty plays in infant mortality is related to at least two key
factors: maternal diet and infant diet. Women without adequate nutrition during pregnancy are more likely to deliver low birth weight babies or babies with particular birth
defects (mostly related to the consumption of folic acid). These low birth weight babies
are more likely to die in their first year of life. Second, new mothers who do not have
adequate nutrition during the period of lactation will be unable to produce enough
nutrition-rich breast milk to nurture their infants. Third, mothers who are unable to
produce enough nutrient-rich milk may need to rely on formula. If they cannot afford
formula or do not have access to a clean water supply, their infants will be at serious
risk for death during the first year. Access to healthcare, both prenatal and postnatal,
is also significantly linked to infant mortality. Mothers who receive prenatal care are
more likely to deliver healthy babies of normal birth weight. Similarly, when mothers
and their babies receive healthcare, checkups, and vaccinations in the first year of life,
the babies are far less likely to die. Finally, the mother's age is also a significant predictor
of low birth weight and ultimately of infant mortality. Because teen childbearing is a
siginificant factor for infant mortality and because African Americans have higher rates
of teen pregnancy than whites, this is most likely another factor that produces racial
disparities in infant mortality.

OUTCOMES OF POOR HEALTH: PREMATURE DEATH

We have already discussed the primary outcome of poor health in the African
American community and that is death. Because we will all die some day, what
becomes important are the causes of death that (1) are preventable and (2) result
in premature death.

Another of the standardized measures of health and well-being is life expectancy.
Life expectancy is a statistic that represents the *average* number of years a person born
in a particular year can expect to live. Life expectancies are calculated for each new
year. The life expectancy for a child born in 2012 is significantly longer than the life
expectancy of a person born in 1940.

As Kai Wright noted in the piece we excerpted at the beginning of the chapter,
many scholars talk about the cumulative stress associated with racism. One outcome
of that accumulated stress as well as of poverty (lack of access to healthcare, poor
nutrition, etc.) is a lower life expectancy. For Americans born in 2002, whites can
expect to live longer, as can women. White women have the longest life expectancy

and African American men have the shortest; African American men can expect to live nearly twelve years fewer than white women. What is also interesting about this data is the interaction effect of race and gender. We see, for example, that the gap between African American and white women is narrower (white women can expect to live five years longer than their African American counterparts) than it is for African American and white men. Thus, African American women, for example, share some of the protections that all women have relative to men, but they suffer some of the negative health outcomes that we associate with racism and poverty.

CAUSES OF POOR HEALTH AND DEATH

There are a variety of causes of poor health and death for all Americans. Many experts argue that obesity is the number one health problem of all Americans. Today 65 percent of Americans are overweight or obese, a 16 percent increase over the rate just a decade ago. African American women have the highest rate of obesity of all race or gender groups: 77.1 percent are overweight, and they are 20 percent more likely to be overweight than white women, 57.2 percent of whom are obese. Men, both African American and white, fall between these two extremes, with white men being somewhat more likely to be overweight (69.4 percent) than African American men (62.6 percent).

Overweight and obese individuals are at increased risks for many diseases and health conditions, including hypertension, type 2 diabetes, coronary heart disease, stroke, and some cancers, including endometrial, breast, and colon.

Comparing the health conditions associated with being overweight or obese and the leading causes of death for Americans, it is clear that one of the major causes of poor health (and even death) in the United States is lifestyle: eating too much, eating an unhealthy diet, and not getting enough exercise. Though this is less of a problem for African American men, it is a serious problem for African American women. And, though some have been critical of Michelle Obama's decision to make the "First Lady's Issue" obesity because it is characterized as a "fluffy" issue, it is clear from the data we reviewed for this chapter that obesity is a huge issue in the African American community and it has enormous consequences for African American women in particular and the children and grandchildren they leave behind.

Poverty and Lifestyle

The relationship between lifestyle causes of poor health and race is confounded by social class. To disentangle this set of relationships we will begin with a brief discussion of the relationship between social class and lifestyle. The relationship is complex and occurs at both the individual level and the societal level.

At the societal level, America is the land of wealth and abundance. Americans eat more meat, for example, than people in most other nations: both developed and developing. Fewer and fewer Americans have jobs that require much if any physical activity, and as the literal land of the automobile, except for those Americans living in major cities (New York, Chicago, Washington, D.C.), few Americans walk anywhere. Thus, compared to citizens in other countries, both developed and developing, Americans eat more, especially calorie-rich foods, and get less physical activity.

Like most everything else, however, even this is shaped by social class. The affluent, for example, are the least likely to have jobs that are physically demanding, but they are the most likely to own memberships to exclusive gyms and country clubs where they can exercise, play golf and so forth. Similarly, though the affluent have the resources to purchase more meat and "rich" foods, it is the poor who find it difficult to afford or even find healthy food such as fresh fruits and vegetables, leaner cuts of meat and fish, and lower fat dairy products. Thus, in this land of plenty, social class shapes lifestyle, in particular access to healthy food and exercise. Because African Americans are more likely to be poor and less likely to be affluent, these patterns are also highly racialized.

Nutrition

Because African Americans are disproportionately likely to be poor, they are less likely to eat healthfully and exercise and more likely to suffer diseases such as stroke, diabetes, and heart disease and more importantly, to die from these diseases. Though the data on nutrition as a "cause" of obesity and obesity-related diseases and deaths is mixed overall, there is a high degree of certainty with regards to the overall relationship among nutrition, obesity, morbidity, and mortality; and there is a reasonable degree of certainty regarding the relationship between certain foods and specific diseases. For example, according to the American Cancer Society, though the data are "mixed" on the relationship between the consumption of fruits and vegetables and colon cancer, the data are clear that those who eat processed meats—bacon, sausage, ham—are at greater risk for developing colorectal cancers than those who limit the consumption of these specific foods. As noted, the relationship between the consumption of fruits and vegetables and colorectal cancer is mixed. Some epidemiological studies find a relationship whereas others find only an association. Based on our anecdotal experience living and traveling extensively through the Deep South, an area that is also commonly referred to as the "stroke belt"—we wonder if the "mixed" findings are a result of the fact that many Southerners, including African Americans, eat fruits and vegetables as a regular part of their diets. However, the majority of Southerners prepare these foods in ways that decrease their nutritional value and may in fact contribute to higher rates of chronic diseases and cancer. For example, vegetables including greens, okra, and beans are typically boiled—which leaches the vitamins—with salt and fatback (pork fat), creating a wonderful taste, but adding fat, and in particular the fat associated with processed meat, to the vegetables. Literally everything on a Southern menu can be and often is fried. Thus, the preparation of the vegetables reduces their nutritional value and may in fact contribute to the development of diabetes, stroke, and colorectal cancer and may help to explain the "mixed" findings in vegetable consumption.

A similar relationship can be found when we consider the role that carbohydrates play in the diets of the poor. Not only are carbohydrates a relatively inexpensive source of calories, most poor people around the world depend on variations of carbohydrate heavy dishes—samp and beans in South Africa, rice and beans in Latin America, and lentils and rice in India, for example—to meet their caloric needs. However in the United States, the poor are significantly more likely to eat highly processed carbohydrates because they are cheaper and easier to obtain. Highly processed carbohydrates, including bread and pasta, are usually prepared with white flour and high levels of sugar or similar sweeteners. Thus, highly processed carbohydrates are typically high in calories, low in fiber, and consuming them regularly and as a significant portion of one's overall diet probably contributes significantly to higher rates of obesity and diabetes. It is clear that access to healthy food, the ability to afford healthy food, and historical preferences for less healthy preparations of food all contribute to significantly higher rates of obesity and obesity-related diseases that afflict African Americans disproportionately.

CASE STUDY: FOOD DESERTS

The term "food deserts" describes the variability in accessibility of healthy, high quality food in urban and rural areas. A food desert is an area in either a rural or urban community in which several conditions exist either independently or simultaneously: (1) a lack of grocery stores that stock healthy, nutritional food; (2) a high number of "fast-food" restaurants; (3) a high number of convenience or other types of "grocery" stores that stock food that is cheap but not high in nutritional value; and (4) the ratio of availability of healthy food to unhealthy food is low.

Scholarly attention on food deserts began when urban researchers observed that one consequence—most likely unintended—of white flight and "ghettoization" was the consequent flight of chain supermarkets that offered a variety of food choices to local residents. Of course, the variety was not always of the best quality, as news exposés such as the 1996 *ABC Primetime* with Diane Sawyer investigation showcasing Food Lion revealed. In the exposé, hidden cameras were placed in Food Lion stores in North Carolina, and revealed the stores stocking and selling spoiled meat and fish that had been treated with bleach and other chemicals to remove the smell, cheese that had been nibbled on by rats, and produce that had been retrieved from the Dumpster. Nevertheless, chain supermarkets had at a minimum provided some access to produce and fresh meat and dairy products, even if the quality and nutritional value was somewhat diminished, relative to these same supermarkets in the upscale wealthier neighborhoods and suburbs. In low-income and poor neighborhoods, for the most part, traditional grocery stores have been replaced by convenience stores and "bodegas" that carry some produce and dairy products but for the most part carry only

packaged and prepared food items that are both more expensive and less nutritionally complete. Along with the demise of the supermarket in urban "ghettos" is the
rise of fast-food restaurants, ranging at the "high" end with McDonald's, which in
its attempt to stay competitive has added "healthy" options to its menu, to the "low"
end, which includes Church's Chicken and other similar restaurants that specialize
in selling deep fried gizzards at extremely low prices.

Figure 9.1, based on a study of the city of Chicago, paints a graphic picture of
this for us. As the data in the figure clearly illustrate, compared to all other racial or
ethnic groups, African Americans had about equal access to fast-food as other racial
groups, but their access to stores that sold healthy food was significantly reduced by
the barrier of distance. Whereas most whites lived within one-third of a mile of a
supermarket, African Americans lived nearly twice as far.

What is the impact of living in a food desert? Based on the research done in
Chicago and reflected in the following figure, living in a food desert contributed
significantly to higher rates of "diet-related death." Yet, as with everything we have
discussed in this chapter, the impact varies by race or ethnicity.

There is no significant difference between the rates of diet-related deaths among
whites regardless of whether they live in a food desert or not—as represented by
the "food balance" columns, which captures the ratio of the accessibility to healthy
versus nonhealthy food. In contrast, African Americans who live in food deserts are
significantly more likely to suffer from diet-related deaths than those who live in
neighborhoods with regular access to healthy food.

This finding is important because it underscores and reinforces some research
we did in the Deep South on the impact of housing segregation on well-being. We
found that whites who lived in majority "black" counties did not differ significantly
in terms of overall well-being (educational attainment, employment, wealth, infant
mortality) than those who lived in majority "white" counties. In contrast, for African Americans the impact of living in a majority "black" county was devastating

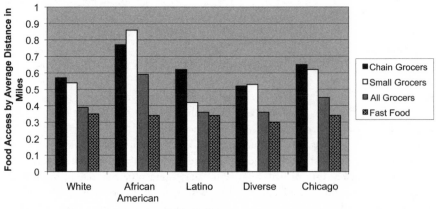

Figure 9.1.   Food access by average distance.

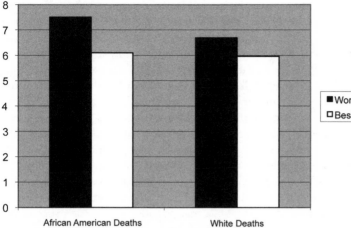

Figure 9.2. Deaths per tract by race and food balance.

on all measures of well-being, including education, employment (or not), income, the likelihood of living in poverty, and as we mentioned in the previous discussion, infant mortality.[2]

What's interesting is that most of the focus on food deserts has been on urban areas like Chicago. Perhaps the lack of attention to rural food deserts is attributable to both the relative invisibility of rural America, especially the rural South, or perhaps it is due to the misconception that food deserts could not possibly exist in the regions of the country where the bulk of our food is grown. In fact, food deserts do exist in rural, farming communities especially across the Deep South where the majority of African Americans continue to live and where rates of obesity and diet-related diseases are the highest in the nation. In fact, the Delta counties of rural Mississippi and the Black Belt counties of Alabama are referred to by public health scientists as constituting the "stroke belt" for this very reason.

Anecdotally we can confirm, after spending many weeks each summer driving through and living in the Mississippi Delta, that rural food deserts are indeed expansive. Even moderately sized cities such as Clarksdale, Mississippi, offer only one supermarket for the entire city. With no public transportation, it is out of reach for most of the African American population, who instead rely on a series of Seven Eleven–style convenience stores and local takeout restaurants that boast "meat boxes" and every conceivable fried food to meet all of their nutritional needs. In the rural communities that dot the Delta between the moderate cities it is difficult even to find a "healthier" fast-food option such as Subway or McDonald's. The vastness of rural food deserts is incomprehensible to those who have not witnessed them. The impact on health is clear; these counties, many of which have not a single stop light in the whole county, "boast" the highest rate of obesity, diet-related diseases, and infant mortality. Because a substantial portion of the African American population lives in these communities, the impact on African American health is devastating.

To many, one of the things that is so surprising about rural food deserts is that they exist in one of the most agriculturally rich areas on the planet. Based on research that we supervised in the Delta in the summer of 2010 we learned that one of the major barriers to growing food for local consumption is the history of the slave plantation and sharecropper systems that were in place until relatively recently in this hidden part of the United States. Folks who were interviewed in the Delta indicated that they were not interested in growing their own food because they interpreted this as a step backward toward the oppressive lives their parents and grandparents had lived as former slaves or sharecroppers. Additionally, because the land has always been cultivated with commercial crops—cotton and now soybeans—there is very little collective history or experience with growing *food that one can consume* or sell at a local farmer's market. Lastly, though many of the larger communities, like Clarksdale, offer weekly farmer's markets, rich with healthy and nutritional food, access is limited for many because of a lack of public transportation and barriers such as the inability of farmers' markets to accept "food stamps" both of which limit the access of poor African Americans to the bounty grown in their own "backyards."[3]

Additionally, our research project confirmed that the main barriers to adequate food are: (1) lack of transportation, (2) the lack of high quality food stocked in local markets, and (3) the inability of local markets to accept food stamps. For example, according to the folks living in Friar's Point, Mississippi, the major barrier to accessing healthy food was transportation. Friar's Point, a historically African American town, does not have a single grocery store; the closest mainstream grocery store, Kroger, is a forty-mile drive away in Clarksdale. For a community in which, according to the US Census, the median household income is under $20,000 annually, or 40 percent of the national median, access to transportation is a major barrier to accessing healthy food. Secondly, for the community of Friar's Point and others like it, where half of the residents live below the poverty line, the food stamp program should be a primary solution to the nutritional problems associated with food deserts. Yet, because the community lacks a grocery store and the residents lack reliable, consistent transportation to nearby towns with mainstream groceries, where their food stamps are accepted, it is a failed solution at best. Residents of Friar's Point reported that despite receiving food stamps monthly, they were rarely able to use them to purchase food. Tragically, a highly necessary program fails in its goals because of the lack of transportation and the presence of grocery stores that accept food stamps.

Finally, as is likely familiar to anyone entering convenience stores in their hometowns or while traveling, convenience stores cannot rely on regular customers nor delivery, and thus they stock foods that are primarily nonperishable. As a result, the food that is available in a local convenience store in places like Friar's Point, is likely to be primarily canned foods that are higher in fat and sodium. Folks visiting the convenience store are unlikely to find fresh fruits and vegetables, and as residents of Friar's Point reported, when they did buy fresh fruits and vegetables in the local convenience stores where they shopped, the food quickly rotted once they got it home. Facing severely constrained food budgets, no family wants to purchase fresh fruits and vegetables that spoil in days and cannot be consumed. To do so doesn't make logical sense. Thus, even when "fresh" foods are available in these convenience stores and low-end groceries, they are rarely purchased, and thus storeowners rarely stock them; all of this creates a feedback loop that contributes to the lack of fresh food in communities like Friar's Point. In sum, the tragedy of many rural food deserts is that well-intentioned government programs like the food stamp program, which are expensive but palatable even to many conservatives because they make sense theoretically, fail miserably in practice. To solve the problem of food deserts in rural America, researchers and policy makers will have to spend time in rural food deserts to understand more fully the barriers that residents face to accessing healthy and nutritious food.

CONCLUSIONS

When analyzing the question of health generally and nutrition specifically, we have to ask this question: does the election of the first African American president affect African Americans' access to better health—health insurance, medical care, healthy food—and if so, in what way? In short, does this election signify that we have now entered a postracial America with regards to health?

In this chapter we have provided an overview of issues related to health and well-being in the African American community. Unfortunately, on nearly every front, the story is dismal. African Americans are more likely to suffer from many lifestyle-related chronic diseases such as cardiovascular disease and diabetes, and they are more likely to be among the uninsured, which severely limits their access to healthcare that would both prevent these diseases in the first place and treat them when they develop.

African Americans die earlier than white Americans. And for different reasons. Whereas 90 percent of the leading causes of death for whites are diseases of lifestyle and age, 20 percent of the leading causes of death for African Americans are preventable and premature: AIDS and homicide. Furthermore, African Americans are significantly more likely to die prematurely of diet-related diseases such as diabetes and heart disease because they lack the resources for proper care, they experience discrimination in treatment and delays in diagnosis, and they lack the resources to control the diseases through diet and exercise.

The African American community is being devastated by illness and premature death. The effects on African American families are extraordinary. Because African Americans are more likely to face health crises and live with chronic diseases, the burdens on family members are tremendous. These burdens include both financial and emotional strains as well as the burnout associated with long-term care giving, as without expensive health insurance and the even more expensive long-term care insurance, most folks dealing with chronic diseases will be cared for at home. Clearly, the greatest impact is the disruption that premature death causes in families. Children grow up without parents and grandparents, partners are widowed and live out their lives alone. It is impossible to measure the full impact of this on African American families.

Though we begin and end the chapter with discussions of the role that poverty plays in chronic diseases and death, as Kai Wright makes clear: race trumps class. This is partly explained by the fact that housing remains significantly segregated. As noted in our discussion of poverty and wealth, even middle-income African Americans are often forced because of discrimination in both lending and renting to live in low-income neighborhoods that are often characterized as "food deserts." Additionally, with significant racial disparities in wealth accumulation even middle class African Americans may face additional financial barriers to housing and food security. We must also acknowledge, as is in the case in any group, the role that history and traditions around "food" that shape African American's risk for diet-related diseases as Kai Wright so poignantly describes.

What role has or will the election of Barack Obama play on the health and well-being of African Americans? We submit that the impact will remain to be seen. There are some reasons to be hopeful; for example, depending on the ways in which Obamacare is implemented, it may address some of the barriers that African Americans face in accessing healthcare. Additionally, we are pleased with Michelle Obama's choice of childhood obesity as a focus and are cautiously optimistic that at a minimum it will shed light on a critical problem facing the next generation of African Americans. The NFL has launched a new program called "60 Play" encouraging children to get sixty minutes of play and exercise each day. It is intuitive that an organization dominated by African American players, many of whom are significantly overweight, would choose this focus.

That said, for all the reasons we can find to be optimistic, none of the programs that we have described would deliver the kind of universal approach that this problem needs. Certainly healthcare is an important piece of the puzzle, but if food deserts remain and people can't find or afford healthy food then much of it will be for naught. In short, we believe that the food distribution system in the United States needs a radical overhaul. This will be expensive, and it will take dedication, but it is doable.

We argue that access to nutritionally healthy food is a human right that must be expanded in the United States. In the "land of plenty" where much food is discarded every year before it gets to market, where fields are left fallow as part of price support programs, and where the legacy of slavery has created ideologies around food that negatively impact African Americans, especially those living in the rural South, the issue is clearly not predicated on the amount of food grown—as it often is in drought-ridden East Africa—but the access and distribution of that food to segments of our population. Reconstituting access to healthy food as a human right would be one step in shaping food policies in ways that would reduce the impact of diet-related illness among all Americans and African Americans in particular.

Practically speaking, we recommend the following:

- Rendering illegal the practice of supermarket chains that as part of their delivery cycle remove rotting and nearly expired food from upscale neighborhood stores and restocking these items in their stores in low-income neighborhoods.
- Creating zoning laws that restrict the number of fast-food restaurants based on geography and population density.
- Creating zoning laws that require supermarkets or local food markets be built or retained based on geography and population density.
- Creating incentives for local food producers and farmers' markets to sell in low-income neighborhoods; for example, the government could make available, for free to participating farmers' markets the simple machine that processes food stamps.
- Create delivery services for farmers' markets. Many affluent Americans order their food online and have it delivered to them each week. We propose that the government subsidize local farmers' markets or grocery stores to prepare boxes of healthy food to be delivered to food stamp recipients each week. This would actually reduce the overall cost of the food stamp program and at the same time reduce the access issues people who live in food deserts face.
- Require health courses—and provide the staff to teach them—in all public schools.
- Adjust the requirements of school lunch programs to restrict access to unhealthy food and increase the healthy food offerings; this is especially critical given the percentage of African American students who qualify for and receive free or reduced lunch.

A bright spot: We conclude our chapter by highlighting the initiative in Clarksdale, Mississippi. With the help of several programs, including Delta Initiatives and the placement of a HealthCorps staff, a garden program has been developed at the local high school. During the school year, students participate in an after-school program and during the summer they are paid to raise food in the high school garden. During the spring, summer and fall, the students sell the food at the local farmers' market. This produces income for the program, provides employment for a few students, teaches skills ranging from farming practices to business practices, and improves the eating habits of the young men. The early indications are that this program is successful, and perhaps can stand as a model for both rural and urban communities in efforts to improve health, changing ideologies, and increasing access to healthy food.

10

Politics

Will African Americans Now Dominate Government Like They Do the NBA?

Barack Hussein Obama was elected the 44th president of the United States on Tuesday, sweeping away the last racial barrier in American politics with ease as the country chose him as its first black chief executive . . . it was just as much a strikingly symbolic moment in the evolution of the nation's fraught racial history, a breakthrough that would have seemed unthinkable just two years ago.

"It's been a long time coming," the president-elect added, "but tonight, because of what we did on this date in this election at this defining moment, change has come to America."

"This is a historic election, and I recognize the significance it has for African Americans and for the special pride that must be theirs tonight," Mr. McCain said, adding, "We both realize that we have come a long way from the injustices that once stained our nation's reputation."

As the returns became known, and Mr. Obama passed milestone after milestone—Ohio, Florida, Virginia, Pennsylvania, New Hampshire, Iowa and New Mexico—people rolled spontaneously into the streets to celebrate what many described, with perhaps overstated if understandable exhilaration, a new era in a country where just 143 years ago, Mr. Obama, as a black man, could have been owned as a slave.

"I always thought there was a potential prejudice factor in the state," Senator Bob Casey, a Democrat of Pennsylvania who was an early Obama supporter, told reporters in Chicago. "I hope this means we washed that away."

Adam Nagourney, "Obama Elected President as Racial Barrier Falls." November 4, 2008. Elisabeth Bumiller contributed reporting from Phoenix, Marjorie Connelly from New York and Jeff Zeleny from Chicago. www.nytimes.com/2008/11/05/us/politics/05elect.html?pagewanted=all

Myth: The election of Barack Obama as the forty-fourth president of the United States will open opportunities for African Americans in politics at the national level.

Reality: The election of the first African American leader of the US government has done little to change the complexion of our leadership at any level; national or state, elected or appointed.

This story is simple enough. The remarkability of this story is that it is unique on several levels, the most obvious being race. Until now, every single president of the United States has been not only male but also white. The story of Barack Obama is even more unique in that it is not the story of an overt privilege on any level. Perhaps only the story of former President Bill Clinton rivals that of Obama in terms of growing up in a single-parent household, being educated in a public university, and rising to the highest position of power in the free world. We do acknowledge that though both men earned their undergraduate degrees at public universities, both men *are* graduates of Ivy League law schools (Yale, Clinton and Harvard, Obama) which have provided access for a small and exclusive group of American men who control not only the government but also banking, industry, and higher education.

For others, the story of Barack Obama might as well be "a dark and stormy night." The acrimony, to put it mildly, in the president's day-to-day life from racist cartoons to social movements calling for his birth certificate all cast a long, gray shadow on the highest office in the United States now occupied by an African American.

The late legal scholar Derrick Bell, known for his use of allegory in his legal writings, just prior to his untimely death in 2011 spoke to the students at Yale University School of Law. In the speech entitled "On Celebrating an Election as Racial Progress," he said:

> In our media-obsessed society, every aspect of Barack Obama's election and inauguration was covered like a heavy rain on a parched landscape. It was a historic landmark, with Obama receiving more electoral college votes than any president in history and more popular votes than any president except Ronald Reagan. His taking office as the first black president was hailed as a racial breakthrough. And it was a unique moment, one even most civil rights progressives did not believe would occur in their lifetimes. My great appreciation for having lived to see a day I thought would never come is, however, diluted by experience.
>
> The question that history, even fairly recent history, requires that we ask is this: Is Obama's elevation to the White House more than just another unique moment when the fervent hopes of blacks coincide with the needs of whites and other nonwhites? Is even an individual with his enormous talents, coupled with those of so obviously gifted a woman as Michelle Obama, equal to the task of salvaging a society that by so many measures is on its way down?[1]

Professor Bell raises the very questions we grapple with throughout this book. First, does the election represent a coincidence, a time in which the self-interests of whites and blacks converged, or does it represent something more? This is a question we will focus on in the final chapter. Second, Bell wonders, what has been and what will be the impact of the Obama election? Will it usher in a postracial America, and for the purposes of this chapter, change the complexion of governing bodies? For us, in this chapter, the question is clear, will the election of Obama change, in any measurable ways, the experiences of and opportunities for African American families?

A WATERSHED MOMENT?
THE COMPLEXION OF OUR GOVERNMENT

The question is unfortunately rather simple to answer; but before we look at the changing (or not) face of government since the election of Obama, we provide a brief history of African Americans in government to date. Though it may seem irrelevant, since our focus has been on looking forward, in fact, this brief history provides an interesting lesson.

Blacks in Politics

From the beginning, African Americans were denied the right to vote. Even the passage of the fourteenth amendment, which legally gave African American *men* the right to vote, was effectively dismantled by poll taxes and other legal blockages that prevented African American men from actually voting.

One measure of status in our society is a group's representation in the political arena. Since African Americans have this unique history unknown to other racial or ethnic groups in America, that of chattel slavery, peonage, systematic segregation, and holding legalized second-class citizenship, their local and national representation in the political arena has been almost nonexistent. Even today.

We do acknowledge that as part of the conditions that ended the Civil War one of the requirements of reconstruction, though very short-lived, was the election of African American men to state and national congressional seats—a sort of quota system. Once the immediacy of reconstruction ended, the story of African Americans holding any elected (or appointed) positions in government is really a story that begins in the second half of the twentieth century. Most important, it is a story that has three main themes: (1) a lack of power, (2) African Americans can only represent black people, and (3) stagnation.

A Lack of Power

This theme is best represented by examining the trajectory of African Americans attaining what one would think would be a position of power: the mayorship of a large, US city. Interestingly, this is one of the first elected positions that African Americans were able to attain. Some of the first African American mayors included: Carl B. Stokes (Cleveland, Ohio), Richard G. Hatcher (Gary, Indiana), and Walter Washington (Washington, D.C.). To date, African Americans have held the helms of seventy-six cities, including Washington, D.C.—who can forget Marion Barry—and Chicago (Harold Washington), and Atlanta. Some cities have had more than one African American mayor, among them Washington, D.C., and Atlanta.

Yet, unfortunately, it is a story of the decline in power. Quite simply, just as African Americans were able to get elected as mayors in cities across the United States these cities experienced two major shifts: a loss of jobs (and thus economic power) and white flight. Thus, what African Americans thought they were getting—the leadership of a major city—was nothing short of a very hollow prize. They were elected to govern cities that were losing or had already lost their white populations. Which bring us to the second point.

African Americans Can Only Govern Black People

Okay, this is not *quite* true. But it is the theme of blacks in politics. The best illustration of this is looking at the national level, specifically at the US Congress. While there have been a good number of African American women and men in the US House of Representatives, there have only been four African Americans senators:

- Edward William Brooke III, Republican, Massachusetts
- Carol Moseley Braun, Democrat, Illinois
- Barack Obama, Democrat, Illinois
- Roland Burris, Democrat, Illinois

Though there are certainly many different explanations for this, the obvious one is that US representatives are elected from very small subsets of the entire state, and they are elected with the express purpose of representing the people in their district. In contrast, US senators are elected by the whole state and with the express purpose of representing all of the citizens of the state. As the reader is by now familiar, the United States remains a highly segregated society, especially with regards to housing. What we know about both housing patterns and redistricting for election purposes, leads us to conclude that African Americans are elected to the US Congress as representatives because they run, for the most part, in districts that are predominately African American. For example, Charles Rangel, who we will discuss momentarily, represents, as his predecessor did before him, Harlem, New York, and John Lewis, a long-standing member of Congress, represents a section of Atlanta that is 56 percent black. In contrast, when it comes to running for US Senate, not only have there been only four African American US senators in the modern era, but apparently, there is some sort of unwritten rule—as their terms do not overlap—that only one can be elected at a time. This reinforces the comments by Derrick Bell that African Americans will not be elected to statewide offices until whites in those states see his election *as being in their best interest.*

Stagnant

One of the major themes of US politics is that unlike the story for women, for African Americans once an initial barrier has been overcome, there is no flood of

African Americans rushing into new territory. The data on the US Senate are also revealing on this point. Not only have African Americans struggled to be elected to represent an entire state, but there has been zero growth in the number of African Americans in the US Senate since they first arrived. Ironically, for the first time in more than twenty years, there is not a single African American serving in the US Senate. Clearly, in this regard at least, the election of Barack Obama has not been a watershed moment. And, of course only time will tell, as there has only been one mid-term election since he entered the White House, but when we look out on the political landscape at the time of his campaign for a second term, there is no evidence that there is much change on the immediate horizon.

This last question, which raises the issue of whether whites see African American politicians as representing their best interests, can also be explored by applying a lens to examine the roles that African Americans who serve in the US Congress play in this legislative body. In short, though some, including Charles Rangel, have held relatively powerful positions—for example as chairs or members of influential committees—most often they gain their greatest notoriety as spokespeople for "the race."

For example, as part of the Obama government, African American Congress men and women are often asked to comment, from the "black" perspective, on Obama's decisions. In the fall of 2011, after the "jobs speech" that President Obama delivered to a joint session of Congress on Capitol Hill in which he announced a $447 billion jobs bill, Representative Maxine Waters (D-California), a frequent and vocal, and African American critic of the president, voiced her displeasure over the lack of specific content in the speech.

> Rep. Maxine Waters, D-Calif., said President Obama should have specified the African American community in his address on jobs to Congress Thursday night, similar to how he signaled out veterans and small business owners. "I wanted him to say something about the intolerable rate of unemployment in the African American community. He didn't quite get there."[2]

Probably one of the most visible African Americans in the US Congress is Georgia Democrat John Lewis. Yet, most of the notoriety that comes to Lewis is tied to the fact that he marched with Martin Luther King Jr. He is most often visible in the press when he comments on his impressions of Obama's impact on the black community. In contrast, despite the fact that he has taken a visible position on mortgage debt relief and overhauling the tax code, he is rarely asked to comment in the press on these issues—of relevance to all Americans, and disproportionately to African Americans.

PRESIDENTIAL APPOINTMENTS

One of the areas in which the president has a great deal of power is in making nominations and appointments to powerful positions, most notably the US Supreme Court and the cabinet. In an unusual turn of fate, President Obama had

the opportunity not once, but twice, in his first two years of the presidency to appoint justices for life to the US Supreme Court. Though we applaud his decision
to appoint not one but two women, and he will go down in history as appointing
the first Hispanic justice—Sonia Sotomayor—he chose *not* to appoint an African
American man or woman. Not to put too fine a point on it, but despite the potential "excuse" that there is already an African American on the court, Justice Thomas
has a record of being extraordinarily conservative on issues of race and he has voted
and written opinions that have undone many of the advances for African Americans
since the passage of the civil rights legislation in the 1960s, including the virtually
overturning of *Brown v. the Board* in several school districts around the country. In
short, Obama's appointments to the Supreme Court mimic the overall pattern in affirmative action; the vast majority of the doors of opportunity are opened for white
females not African Americans.

When we turn to the appointments Obama has made to his cabinet, the primary
pattern that has emerged is that he has appointed fewer African Americans, especially
to the most powerful inner cabinet positions, than the two white men who occupied
the White House prior to him—George W. Bush and Bill Clinton. In fact, it is
important to remember that Bush actually appointed two African Americans, whose
terms were overlapping, to the *two most powerful* cabinet positions: Secretary of State
(Colin Powell) and National Security Advisor (Condoleezza Rice).[3]

The only appointment Obama has made of an African American to a position of
any note at all is that of Eric Holder who has the position of Attorney General. This
vacuum of appointments, especially to high level cabinet positions of extraordinary
power and influence has certainly been disappointing to the African American community. But it also may serve to undermine the fear expressed on the part of some
whites; in reality the election of an African American president did not open up
the floodgates for African Americans in government. Just as whites often express
concern that appointing an African American athletic director will lead to his hiring
all black coaches—especially for football and men's basketball—this rarely happens in either sports, or now we know in politics. As a cursory comparison of the
administrations of Barack Obama and George W. Bush reveals, African Americans
had more power—Colin Powell, Condoleezza Rice, and even elected Senator Barack
Obama—under a white president.

POLITICS IN HOUSING

Though we devoted a section of the wealth and poverty chapter to housing, we
return to this issue here to examine the politics of housing. One measure that we
continuously turn to when assessing the status of one's social and economic well-
being is housing. Housing, still the measuring rod for middle-class Americans, has
become central to the debate over whether the current leadership really cares about
the American people.

For example, when the president or his spokespeople are out talking with the American people at rallies or at town hall meetings, they like to point to the number of construction jobs in housing that have been created or sustained across a certain time. The clear implication here is that if new houses are being built this must be evidence that we have climbed out of the housing crisis and that our climb out of the recession cannot be far behind.

What is usually missing from this message is the number of Americans, and especially relevant to our discussions in this book African Americans, who have had their homes foreclosed. That is to say, as we noted in a previous discussion, that every month African American families lose not only their singular investment, but many also, become "homeless."

This recession has seen some $6 trillion in housing wealth lost among all Americans.[4] For African Americans, the recession created an economic crisis felt literally *in the home*. One example that resonates here are the subprime mortgage loans, which we mentioned in chapter 7, made by two of the biggest banks in America: Wells Fargo and Countrywide Financial Corporation. A formal investigation of their lending practices uncovered that between 2003 and 2007 both banks had sold mortgage loans to African Americans at approximately three percentage (3 percent) points above the US Treasury standard. That the interest rates associated with these loans are higher means, in short, that so are the mortgage payments. In this investigation carried out by the *Chicago Reporter*, investigators also found that mortgage loans to whites were in the normal range 4.92–5 percent interest.[5] An additional problematic practice involved loaning homebuyers the down payment on top of the usual mortgage. In many cases mortgages, which are normally based on a 10–20 percent down payment, and thus the mortgage is 80–90 percent of the home value, were made at 100–120 percent of the home value. It's not rocket science to figure out that these mortgages are at a very high risk for foreclosure—the buyers were given loans that were far too expensive for them to pay back—and for going underwater. All it takes is a slight drop in home values for a home with a 100 percent mortgage to go underwater.

In research conducted by the Center for Responsible Lending,[6] we learn that in one of the country's largest African American municipalities, Prince George's County near Washington, D.C., African Americans are hit the hardest by foreclosure. Prince George County which is 64 percent African American is called the "Subprime Capital of Maryland."

A story in their report looks at what happened to an elderly couple. The couple believed that they had a fixed-rate mortgage—the interest rate is flat across the life of the loan, typically thirty years—when in fact their mortgage was an adjustable rate mortgage (ARM). In short, an ARM is designed to have a low interest rate for the first five years of the loan—typically a rate far below "market" value—but the interest rate "resets" after the initial period, often to a rate significantly higher than "market" value. For example, a loan may jump from a 5 percent interest rate to a 15 percent interest rate at the five-year mark. What this means is that an affordable monthly mortgage payment can quickly become far too much for the borrowers to handle. In the case featured by the Center for Responsible Lending, the couple's monthly mortgage jumped from $1,000 a month to $1,700. Tragically, this jump occurred at the same time that the husband died. The monthly payment was more than the widow received in monthly income, and consequently she lost her home. ARMs are one of the most notorious of the predatory lending practices; and they contributed significantly to the crash on the housing market.

In late October 2011, it was reported on the national morning news that during 2011 alone US homeowners experienced nearly 2 million foreclosures; and 10 million more homes were reported to have mortgages that were underwater or upside-down: the homeowner owes more on the home than it is worth.

Professor Anita Hill, who we know for her courage in standing up in the Senate confirmation hearings in the nomination of Clarence Thomas to the Supreme Court, has an illustrious academic career. Her career has taken a variety of different trajectories, among many other things, her most recent work focuses on the politics of housing.

In her book *Reimagining Equality: Stories of Gender, Race, and Finding Home*, Hill centers her analysis on the 2007/2008 recession and the housing bust that devastated the United States. She is concise and to the point in telling the reader stories about the deep personal loss that comes when a home is no longer yours to claim. Hill tells the story of Anjanette Booker, owner of the Vixxen Hair Salon in the Belair-Edison neighborhood of Baltimore, Maryland. Hill recounts the conversations in the Vixxen Hair Salon, mostly among single black mothers with children, talking about what Booker calls: "money and foreclosures." In her own words, Anita Hill gives her impressions of these conversations:

> For me, the revelation spells more than a crisis in the housing market; it signifies a crisis in home, one that threatens our country's belief in its promises of fairness and prosperity for generations to come. At the heart of the crisis is the ideological disconnect between home as a basic element of the American Dream and pathway to equality, and home as a market product.[7]

Why, then, do we discuss and analyze "housing" in this chapter on politics? A good question and one that should be asked more forcefully. We feel that the leadership of this country has played politics with peoples' lives via the two major agencies that provide housing for middle-class Americans: the banks and their mortgage lending units and the two federal funded agencies that are supposed to provide oversight for these banks, Freddie Mac and Fannie Mae. Freddie Mac and Fannie Mae control almost half of all home mortgages and have received over $130 billion in taxpayer dollars to offset home loan losses—as part of the now infamous "bank bailout." Yet, the sitting administration has been shown to be guilty of negligence when it comes to fixing the housing crisis in America and especially among poor and minority homeowners. In a *Washington Post* story that ran in the fall of 2011, it was revealed that not only did Obama fail to address the tragedy of millions of Americans losing their homes, but it was his appointee to the position of Secretary of the Treasury, his friend and former Goldman Sachs CEO Timothy Geitner, who expressed reluctance at government intervention with the banks. In short he was concerned that if the government intervened it could be misconstrued as the government *helping* the banks.[8] Yet, by not intervening, clearly the government didn't help the millions of Americans who have lost their homes. We wonder what the conversation with Geitner would be like if we asked him to reconcile these two competing interests: (1) the potential that Americans might perceive specific measures as helping out the banks, and (2) the lack of real help for real Americans.

Finally, though it is not the point of this book to critique individual appointments, we simply point out that the Geitner appointment raises all kinds of issues around the politics of the first African American president and the degree to which his election has helped the average African American; and implicit in the fears expressed by many whites, that in turn his election would hurt the average white American.

CONCLUSIONS

In all previous chapters and in this one we ask the following question. When analyzing politics we have to ask this question: does the election of the first African American president affect how African Americans access politics, and in what way? In short, does this election signify that we have now entered a postracial America regarding access to political power?

In politics, probably more than any other substantive area we examine in this book, African Americans have been on the outside looking in. To have little to no access to the formal political arena—at least not in any significant way—holds African Americans hostage for assistance in terms of what they get, not what they need.

Politicians serving African Americans in heavily black districts like Harlem and neighborhoods in Atlanta, Washington, D.C., Detroit, and elsewhere, have shortchanged their constituents who have had to put up with their representatives being in the political game for themselves more than for their constituents.

How is this you might ask? Adam Clayton Powell Jr. represented Harlem, New York, in the US Congress from 1945 to 1971. Powell, during his approximately thirty-year reign in Congress, rose to powerful committee assignments such as Chairman of the Education and Labor Committee, one of the most powerful positions held by an African American in Congress.

Powell is credited with integrating lunchrooms, helping hospital workers get employment at Harlem Hospital and being influential with getting the John F. Kennedy and Lyndon Baines Johnson administrations to pay attention to poor African Americans.

Yet, by the mid-1960s, Congressman Powell was being criticized for the mismanagement of his Congressional committee's budgets, for taking far too many trips abroad on the tab of taxpayers, including an allegation that he was spending too much time at his hideaway in the Caribbean, Bimini, the Bahamas. He was further criticized for missing meetings in Congress and failing to work as hard as he had in service of the needs of his constituents. Powell's actions become so egregious that he even came under heavy attack from his supporters.

In early January 1967 the House of Representatives—following the action of the Democratic Caucus that stripped Powell of his committee chairmanship—refused to seat him, but Powell fought back and remained a member of Congress. He was ineffective. In June 1970, he was defeated by Charles B. Rangel, an African American who has represented Harlem since his election in 1970.

That blacks are running against each other, competing for that *one* position, illustrates poignantly the limited access that African Americans have to political representation. More so, as we emphasize here, not only did Powell lose his power and become ineffective, he let a lot of African Americans—his constituents who had dreamed of the day they would have "one of their own" in Congress—down by his aberrant behavior.

Likewise, Charles Rangel, who as we noted took over from Powell, has been in Congress since 1971. Charles Rangel is one of the longest serving members of the House of Representatives. In 2007 he became the chairman of the powerful House Ways and Means Committee, the first African American to do so. By the end of 2010 he was officially censured and by all the formal rules of the House of Representatives Rangel effectively lost his powerful chairmanship.

The charges against Rangel range from tax evasion—misreporting and underreporting of his income—abusing the New York City rent stabilization program by holding far more apartments than one is entitled to hold, using government stationery for fund-raising purposes, and using federal buildings to store his Mercedes-Benz automobile without paying the fees. Embarrassingly, he was hording rent-controlled apartments for himself and his many mistresses. But the most serious charge against the congressman was his questionable fund-raising for the Charles B. Rangel Center for Public Service at City College of New York.

Unike Powell before him, Rangel still serves in Congress but he has lost his leadership positions. In so losing, so do the African Americans in the 15th Congressional District of New York who have lost a powerful advocate all because of his own greed and his putting his own needs ahead of theirs.

Finally, we also point to the case of Congressman William J. Jefferson, Democrat of Louisiana. Now a prisoner, former congressman, William J. Jefferson was convicted of corruption charges in a case made famous by the $90,000 in bribe money stuffed into his freezer and a legal battle over the raid of his Washington office—a first in US history, the office raid of a sitting member of Congress, that reached the highest levels of the US government. Federal jurors found the Louisiana Democrat guilty of using his position as a high-ranking member of the House Ways and Means trade subcommittee and his congressional office as a criminal enterprise to enrich himself, soliciting and accepting hundreds of thousands of dollars in bribes to support his business ventures in Africa. Several members of Jefferson's family were also convicted in the bribery schemes.

Certainly, we would never argue that African American politicians are any more corrupt or any more likely to abuse their positions of privilege and power than white politicians, or politicians of any race or ethnicity for that matter. Especially in this time of economic crisis and facing a set of challenges most Americans have never faced before, we need more than anything and deserve political leaders who are truly committed to service: putting the needs of their constituents ahead of their own personal self-interests. The crisis in the American political system has perhaps never been greater and the evidence for that is everywhere as we enter the final phases of the 2012 election. Faith in government has perhaps never been lower.

That said, we point to the Powell, Rangel, and Jefferson cases to highlight and demonstrate the recklessness of these political leaders who we believe have a responsibility to effectively represent their constituents as this applies to their overwhelming social, political, and economic needs. All were representing mostly poor African Americans in African American communities, both in New York and Louisiana, in dire need of government assistance to sustain themselves. We ask: If not their representative, then whose? It may not be fair to hold African American leaders to a higher standard, but the truth is that white Americans have many ways of accessing what they need and many advocates focused on their needs. Though a white senator from North Carolina may be focused primarily on his constituents, because many of them share the same needs as their fellow citizens in Virginia and South Carolina, in essence, he may be an advocate for whites in these states as well. In contrast, African Americans, and especially those living on the economic margins, who have few if any advocates, manage to elect leaders who take advantage of the power inherent in these positions and use it to further their own needs and not the needs of those they serve, the wound is that much more painful.

Perhaps if the election of Barack Obama had served as a watershed moment and allowed access to a pipeline of African American leaders willing to serve, then African Americans and their families, like whites and their families, would be less reliant on the goodwill (or not) of the few leaders that advocated for them in the public arena. Because this has not been the case, and for many other reasons as well, the African American family is no better off today than they were before Obama entered the White House. We have no reason to believe that any significant, positive shift in their well-being is on the horizon.

11

Recommendations and Conclusion

President John Fitzgerald Kennedy reigned over the height of the multidecade civil rights movement. On June 11, 1963, approximately five months before his assassination on November 22, 1963, he delivered his famous Civil Rights Address. In it he stressed that blacks, like all other US citizens, ought to have the same citizenship rights as every American, regardless of race, ethnicity, and skin color.

> It oughta be possible for American consumers of any color to receive equal service in places of public accommodation, such as hotels and restaurants and theaters and retail stores, without being forced to resort to demonstrations in the street, and it oughta be possible for American citizens of any color to register and to vote in a free election without interference or fear of reprisal. It oughta be possible, in short, for every American to enjoy the privileges of being American without regard to his race or his color. In short, every American ought to have the right to be treated as he would wish to be treated, as one would wish his children to be treated. But this is not the case.
>
> The Negro baby born in America today, regardless of the section of the State in which he is born, has about one-half as much chance of completing high school as a white baby born in the same place on the same day, one-third as much chance of completing college, one-third as much chance of becoming a professional man, twice as much chance of becoming unemployed, about one-seventh as much chance of earning $10,000 a year, a life expectancy which is 7 years shorter, and the prospects of earning only half as much.
>
> This is not a sectional issue. Difficulties over *segregation and discrimination* exist in every city, in every State of the Union, producing in many cities a rising tide of discontent that threatens the public safety.[1]

His speech, along with national TV coverage of violent and disturbing attempts at school integration, including Little Rock High School and the University of Mississippi, generated much broader and far-reaching support for civil rights for African Americans, especially among white Americans.

Taking up the mantle upon his tragic assassination, President Lyndon Baines Johnson shepherded some of the most progressive and important civil rights and social welfare legislation of the twentieth century.

- "War on Poverty" programs such as Medicaid and Medicare.
- 24th Amendment to the Constitution, which effectively banned poll tax in federal elections.
- Voting Rights Act of 1965, which put an end to literacy tests, especially in the South.
- Several pieces of legislation addressed the concerns over inhabitable housing, including the Omnibus Housing Act under the establishment of the Department of Housing and Urban Development.
- Executive Order 11246, the precursor to affirmative action as we know it today.
- Primary legislation of the civil rights movement, the Civil Rights Act of 1964; a landmark piece of legislation that outlawed all major forms of discrimination against African Americans, including social segregation. It ended unequal application of voter registration requirements and racial segregation in schools, at the workplace and by facilities that served the general public (e.g., movie theaters, restaurants, transportation centers).

Myth: Nothing can be done to improve the lives of African Americans and their families in the second decade of the twenty-first century.

Reality: We have argued throughout this book that there is much that can be done, but to change the state of the African American family in the United States there will have to be structural changes—not individual changes. Though we should all strive to improve our lots in life, true change will only happen through government policies and programs that address universal issues. As with so many other human rights issues in the United States contemporarily and historically, there is often a tension between public support (or opposition) and the role of government in creating and enforcing programs designed to address inequalities. For example, the history of school integration is one in which public opposition lasted long after policies were decided and enacted. As the reader is well aware, this tension led to the use of military interventions that forced integration in places like Little Rock, Arkansas, and the University of Mississippi. In contrast, public support for interracial marriage, at least outside of the South, outpaced the historic Supreme Court decision in *Loving v. Virginia* that struck down antimiscegenation laws.

Why is our opening "story" in this concluding chapter a brief summary of the civil rights legislation of nearly fifty years ago? Because, as we have seen in this book, much of this legislation, which we thought forever changed the landscape for African Americans, is now being effectively eroded; all during the first occupancy of the

White House by an African American president. Let us be clear, we are not arguing that Obama himself has proposed or enacted policies that have eroded the rights of African Americans; but his presence as the leader of the United States, and the "free world," is not sufficient to stop or curtail the legislation and Supreme Court decisions that have turned back the clock on many affirmative action policies that were designed to level the playing field for African Americans and many others. In fact, as we have argued throughout the book, for a variety of reasons, including the sluggish economy, the pushback from conservative politicians who label Obama's policies as socialism, and perhaps an "overcorrecting" factor on the part of Obama himself, many African Americans and their families are no better off—and many are worse off—under the Obama presidency than they were in the previous decade.

We also acknowledge that the critiques contained in this book are made with the clear understanding that many of the problems that face African American families, and all families, are a direct result of the incredible recession that has gripped the twenty-first century, and intensified to levels that were unimaginable just prior to Obama's inauguration. We must be clear that we do not believe that fixing the economy and returning it to the robustness of the 1990s is a one person job nor is it likely to happen in one presidential term, no matter how gifted the individual holding that position. Finally, we point out that our analysis is set in the historic moment of the election of the first African American president. It is likely that the full impact of his election and presidency may not be felt or seen for years to come.

This concluding chapter summarizes the overall state of the African American family in the contemporary United States during the period of the Obama presidency. The primary focus will be to reconsider the assertions we set out to address at the beginning of the book: (1) has the United States entered a period that can be characterized as "postracial," and (2) has the election of an African American president improved the conditions of African Americans overall, and the African American family in particular? We argue that neither is the case. The election of Barack Obama does not signal a movement into a "postracial" period. If anything it helped to generate a renewed racism and consequent racist acts that we had not seen since the struggles of the civil rights movement. For example, nooses have been found hanging in both workplaces and in universities; there are reports of white workers designating workplace restrooms as "white" and "colored," and there has been a great deal of violence that appears to have some racial component, of which the controversial killing of Trayvon Martin by community watch captain George Zimmerman is just one example. Many would argue, as do we, that the midterm elections of 2010, which were highly influenced by the ultra conservative Tea Party movement, suggest that Obama's election has ushered in a new fear among whites and a reignition and radicalization of white racism.

In terms of the second question, the overall impact of the Obama election and presidency on the African American family, we will demonstrate that African American families are worse off than they were prior to the election of Obama. Though much of this can be explained by the recession, which Obama inherited, though in reaction he has not engaged in policy making that has targeted the African American underclass, and he has made decisions that seem to favor the very institutions—including Wall Street and big banks—that target African Americans through programs such as predatory lending practices. African Americans have every reason to be discouraged and whites who were worried about the election and the fallout for them seem to have nothing to fear. This sentiment is powerful and interesting, and we should also point out that though the types of racism that African Americans face is somewhat unique, many low-income whites are also, for the most part, hurt by the same policies that harm poor African Americans—including bank bailouts, the extension of the Bush tax cuts to the wealthy, the discontinuation of long-term unemployment benefits, and so forth. In this sense, white families have also not seen their situation improve under the presidency of Obama. But interestingly, the focus, at least among radical racist groups and highly conservative politicians, is not on *that* fact, but rather on the myth that Obama would somehow deliver "the goods" to his own people at the exclusion of others, namely white Americans. We begin with a discussion of the question of "postracial" America.

POSTRACIAL AMERICA?

Americans seem fond of using the term "postracial," probably because our racial history is so painful and the term seems to imply that we have moved past this incredibly painful period. We wonder what do people mean when they use this term? What is a postracial society and what would it look like?

A postracial society would be one which is devoid of racial preferences or discrimination. It does not mean that race would cease to exist or cease to have meaning. It would be characterized such that every decision we make as individuals and as a society would be made without consideration of race.

What would this look like?

It's actually very hard to imagine. We are probably more comfortable, as a society, thinking about race not mattering—what is often referred to as being "color-blind." But "postracial" is different from "color-blind." Whereas a "color-blind" society would be one in which race disappeared—"I don't see race"—a "postracial" society would be one in which we "see" race, we acknowledge its importance individually, collectively, and in our history, but race is *not* factored when we make decisions. Given the fact that we believe most traits are distributed more or less equally across all racial groups—withholding the possibility that there might be some mild exceptions to this rule—here's what this might look like:

- Congress would be 64 percent white, 12 percent African American, 13 percent Hispanic, 4 percent Asian, and the remaining seats would be held by Native Americans and Alaskan Natives

- The NBA would have a similar complexion
- The boardrooms of Fortune 500 companies, same complexion
- The complexion of people who serve our food, clean our hotel rooms, and mow our grass would be similar to that reflected in boardrooms
- As would churches, country clubs, and every other conceivable social institution
- Rates of interracial marriage would climb, especially interracial marriages involving African Americans

This is pretty hard to imagine because all of the categories we use to sort human beings—racial categories, gender, nationality, religion, sexuality, region of the country—carry with them a set of both positive and negative stereotypes. These stereotypes become what sociologists term "reified"; and in that process they become real and they exist independently of the people whom they were originally developed to describe. To illustrate we provide some stereotypes so deeply embedded in our cultural ideology that they have become reified. Asians, especially Asian men, are good at math, African American men are good at sports, white men are intellectual and good at running things and making decisions, and African American women are lazy. When stereotypes become reified and take on a life of their own, the qualities of individuals cease to become relevant. Though perhaps our illustrations are a bit of an overdramatization, we still live in a culture in which many, many decisions are based on stereotypes rather than individual qualities. As we have demonstrated, stereotypes shape the way people are treated when they apply for jobs and mortgages or admission to college, when they are arrested, or when they run for public office. Thus, for us to enter a postracial society, we will have to dismantle stereotypes and remove the power they have to exist independently of real people.

In addition to dismantling stereotypes, several other social and structural changes would have to take place as well; we focus on two such changes: (1) social class, and (2) leveling the playing field. These changes would both contribute to a movement toward a postracial society and impact in very obvious ways the lived realities of African American families. Specifically, in a postracial society the opportunity for African Americans to make enough income to buy a home, feed their families healthy food, ensure the health and safety of their young children, and eventually send their children to college would be "real" and attainable.

Once again, we refer to the framework of Eugene Robinson. As Robinson aptly describes, there is no longer one black community. He suggests, the major issue that divides and subdivides the black community is social class. Compared to the Jim Crow era, when, as required by segregation, African Americans of all social classes lived in relative proximity and they encountered each other in everyday life—in segregated schools, hospitals, and businesses—today, the physical distance between poor African Americans and middle-class African Americans is great, but it is dwarfed by the distance that exists for the upper-class professionals and the transcendents. And, though of course all African Americans, regardless of their social class, face discrimination as a result of long-held and deeply entrenched racial stereotypes, low-income and poor African Americans face many other barriers as well. As we have discussed throughout this book, not only are poor African Americans dislocated from the larger black community, they live even farther out on the margins of mainstream American life. As long as they continue to live on the margins, not only is a postracial society impossible to achieve, but even if it were, they and their families would simply live on the margins of that society as well.

Perhaps the best illustrations come to us from examining two things we have already discussed, the aftermath of Hurricane Katrina and prisons. People who live in these "places," and they are disproportionately poor African Americans, are relatively invisible to the rest of America. We suggested that Hurricane Katrina laid bare, on national TV, streaming into all of our living rooms, what had existed invisibly for years: an isolated community of mostly poor, but also moderate-income African Americans who were more or less cut off from the rest of New Orleans and from mainstream America more generally. This was both physical—the barriers and dykes designed to keep the lower ninth ward from flooding—and symbolic.

Similarly, those who live inside the walls, fences and chains of prisons are *almost always invisible to us*. Just like those in the lower ninth ward, their contact with mainstream America is almost nonexistent. Thus, we would contend that until low-income people of all racial and ethnic groups are more integrated into mainstream American society, even if we enter a postracial society, they and their families will continue living on the margins.

As important, we would argue, is their integration to *create* a postracial society. For it is clear that despite all of their best efforts, racial and ethnic minorities who do succeed and enter the ranks of the wealthy and powerful continue to be plagued by racial stereotypes. The treatment of President Barack Obama is case in point. Having achieved enormous professional success, he continues to have his face characterized like a monkey and his mother and father's relationship described similar to dog breeding. Despite the fact that the transcendents violate virtually every negative stereotype we hold about African Americans, whites continue to associate them with the kinds of behaviors and stereotypes that are built more around poverty than race. Thus, to move into a postracial society, the poor will have to be liberated from poverty and the negative stereotypes released from coloring our impressions and judgments about all African Americans.

Of course it may seem like a chicken and egg question, but we contend that the playing field must first be leveled for the United States to enter a postracial society. After 250 years of slavery, another 100 years of Jim Crow segregation, and the continuation of racial discrimination into the twenty-first century, we highly doubt that a postracial society will be ushered in, which will in turn level the playing field; an environment in which race will no longer be a factor in our decision making. Why? Because the ushering in of a level playing field will *require* whites to recognize the ways in which the system of racism preferences them and they will have to collectively agree to eliminate those privileges and offer all Americans the same opportunities; for an education, for a good job, to buy a decent house in any neighborhood, and to be treated fairly when they get into trouble. What is more likely is that policies that level the playing field will come first, and as African Americans seize the opportunities and are successful they will throw off the stereotypes they are bound by, and this process will usher in the postracial society so many desperately seek. Like many other social changes in the tumultuous racial history of the United States all of these changes will require government policies designed to level the playing field. These policies will have to be enforced. For many reasons we are less than optimistic that this approach will work anytime soon.

For example, as we noted in chapter 8, in far too many cases and in every part of the criminal justice system, racism is still at work. It takes the shape of everything from racial profiling to disparities in sentencing for virtually every crime, but especially drug charges, to prosecutorial misconduct, which is often at the root of wrongful convictions.

One illustration will suffice. Prosecutorial misconduct has led to hundreds of men, more often than not African American, being wrongfully convicted and serving decade upon decade in prison for crimes they did not commit. In most cases of prosecutorial misconduct, the prosecutor intentionally withholds evidence that would have led to an acquittal. The Supreme Court ruled in a series of cases in 2011 and 2012 that prosecutors are immune from liability and therefore consequences, even when it can be demonstrated that their actions, which led to wrongful convictions and exonerations, were deliberate and purposeful.

We contend that this violates everything we teach our children about democracy and fairness as the cornerstone principles of the United States of America. In short, as with every other issue we have addressed in this book, the criminal justice system in the United States needs an entire overhaul so that justice is served fairly for all.

When it comes to the types of policies that will need to be enacted and enforced, we note, first and foremost, that the climate for affirmative action—a policy explicitly designed to level the playing field—has never been chillier. Second, policies that were enacted fifty and sixty years ago—including school desegregation—have been all but reversed in the last twenty years. The policies designed to level the playing field will have to be deliberate, purposeful, and enforced. These kinds of policies will ultimately require the buy-in of whites with the power to enact these policies and monitor their implementation. Given the way in which the bankers responded to the recession—by increasing their bonuses, for example, even while receiving public bailout money—we are less than optimistic that this buy-in will happen anytime soon. Clearly it is one thing to elect an African American president. It is quite another to open up the elite institutions of higher education, banking, the government and the professions to a broader range of African Americans, not just those who achieve transcendent status.

As many Americans do, we remember sitting in front of the television November 4, 2008, watching the election results come in. Like many people, we were both nervous but also cautiously optimistic. We wondered out loud if white Americans would have the courage it would take to vote for an African American president as there has been a long history of mispredicting elections based on polling data taken a few days in advance when the election involves a black candidate.

This phenomenon is referred to as the "Bradley Effect"; it was named after Los Angeles Mayor Tom Bradley, an African American, who lost the 1982 California governor's race despite being ahead in voter polls just days before the elections. This type of phenomenon is also an illustration of what many race scholars term "symbolic racism" or the frontdoor/backdoor talk. In other words, the majority of whites have learned how to talk the talk, but that doesn't necessarily mean they will walk the walk. We should note here that similar to gender examples—for example, presidential candidate Mitt Romney talks publicly about equality for men and women in the workplace despite refusing to support equal pay legislation—this can be very confusing for African Americans. Imagine how it feels to hear a white colleague talk about diversity in a meeting or vote for including diversity in the mission statement of an organization and then watch that same colleague raise concerns about a minority applicant's "qualifications." Thus the front or back talk can do significant damage to race relations.

Back to the television, like many people watching that night, it was very surreal watching Obama win state after state, wondering when reality would kick and McCain would begin winning states. The evening grew even more surreal as the analysts revealed that not only was Obama being elected by white voters—who make up the majority of the electorate and therefore are necessary to win any election—but also because "red" states, many in the South and rustbelt Midwest—were turning "blue," including states like North Carolina and Virginia. It seemed to be a miracle. Many people like us held out hope: maybe our country had finally passed over a major hurdle, maybe the election of the first African American president was indeed ushering in a new, if imperfect, era in our history.

TROUBLE BEGINS

For all the jubilation and optimism, it was clear that the election of the first African American president was, like so many other troubling events in our racial history, ushering in yet another period of intense, vitriolic white racism. After the election, again after Obama's inauguration, during the midterm 2010 election cycle, and at various intermittent periods in between, symbols of racism emerged. African Americans came into work to find nooses—a clear symbol of lynching—hung in their workplaces, even on their office doors as was the case of a Columbia University professor. Workers in a chicken processing plant in North Carolina found bathrooms labeled "white" and "colored." Then came the images of Obama looking like a monkey.

Who can forget the attempts in 2010 and 2011 by relatively high-ranking Republicans and pundits, spurred on by the Tea Party, demanding to see Obama's birth certificate. Many continue to contend that he's not really "American."

Hank Williams Jr., whose music opened Monday Night Football for twenty years, was "released" from his duties after he compared Obama to Hitler. If you ask us, the comparison didn't even really make any sense. But whether the comments make sense or not, they were clearly offensive. When confronted, Williams defended himself by reclaiming his "redneck" identity.

The Southern Poverty Law Center reports that in each year *since* the election of Barack Obama the number of hate groups rises by several percent, topping 1,000 in early 2011, which marks a 66 percent rise since 2000. This is deeply disturbing.

Just as every gain in civil rights for African Americans brings out the ugliest displays of racism by whites—from the *Brown v. the Board* decision to desegregate public schools, to the civil rights movement of the 1960s that brought, among other things, African Americans the right to vote—so did the election of Barack Obama.

There is no other conclusion to be drawn except that his election has not ushered in the ever-coveted "postracial" society.

Though we can be optimistic about the number of whites who supported Obama then and continue to support his reelection efforts now, we would remind the reader that every turning point in the struggle for civil rights in this nation has involved white allies.

In other words, though we acknowledge that the number of whites who support Obama, work on his campaign, and were willing to pull the lever and vote for him is a reason to be optimistic, we caution the reader that the presence of white allies in no way indicates that we are through or past the very painful racial history of the United States. What is discouraging is the obvious rise in expressions of white racism.

As optimistic as many of us felt in late 2008, it is quite clear that the election of the first African American president has neither ushered in nor does it symbolize a postracial America. Obama himself acknowledges this as well.

> "I never bought into the notion that by electing me, somehow we were entering into a post-racial period," Mr. Obama said in an interview with *Rolling Stone*. "I've seen in my own lifetime how racial attitudes have changed and improved, and anybody who suggests that they haven't isn't paying attention or is trying to make a rhetorical point," he said. "Because we all see it every day, and me being in this Oval Office is a testimony to changes that have been taking place."[2]

THE IMPACT OF THE ELECTION
ON AFRICAN AMERICAN FAMILIES

Has the election of Barack Obama improved the lives of African Americans and their families? Quite simply and on all accounts, the answer is a definite no. As we have demonstrated over and over, in chapter after chapter, on nearly ever measure of well-being and success, the lives of African Americans and their families have not only not improved since the election of the first African American president, the majority of families are worse off than they were in late 2008. Not only are individual families worse off, but disturbing trends, such as high school dropout rate, figures on median income—which has declined $3,000 in the last three years—and the racial gap in wealth have only gotten worse. The state of African American families is troubling to say the least, and for many African American families there seems to be little hope for the next generation. The abandoned fall further away from the mainstream, middle-class African American families are moving closer, in many cases, to the margins, and the chasm between the transcendents and everyone else is growing. Thus, leaving those African Americans who are in a position to open doors of opportunity, create access, and design and implement policies that would positively impact the lives of African Americans and their families so far removed that they no longer truly understand the problems that face many African American families today.

Of course, we must also be fair in our assessment and acknowledge that President Obama *inherited* a recession that was well under way and in all likelihood was significantly worse than most people—both regular Americans and frankly many economic experts—realized. Experts, rallying to defend Obama's economic record as he prepares to run for reelection, are quick to point out, recovery from a recession as deep and severe as that which we are currently experiencing will certainly not take place overnight; it will most likely be five to ten years before we can expect a full recovery. Fair enough.

The problems facing African Americans are associated with the recession and class issues as well as race. Thus, it is not reasonable to hold Obama entirely accountable for the state of African American families deep into the worst recession in a century.

Seeking to be measured and objective in our analysis, we must examine the issues that plague African American families. What we see is troubling and is both the lack of implementing and enforcing policies meant to address the vestiges of a racial history based on the clear and intended exploitation of African Americans by whites as well as an unwillingness to implement class policies that would help all poor, low-income, and middle-class Americans, regardless of race.

We feel it is unnecessary to revisit every issue and indicator that we have explored in this book. The myths that we have explored throughout this book are damaging to African American families. Believing, for example, that African American boys, in particular, are less likely to graduate from high school because they lack the intellectual capacity or because they are lazy or because they want to avoid the accusation that they are "acting white" unnecessarily prejudices the teachers who teach in predominantly African American schools as well as the school boards that fund them. On the other hand, underlying each myth is a troubling trend, that if we choose to ignore in an attempt to appear "postracial" only serves to harm those who need our attention and our proposals for changing the system now more than ever if they have any hope of surviving. We provide a brief summary or reminder to the reader of some of the trends that have the most potential to further damage African American families.

- Marginalized African Americans, those Robinson refers to as the "abandoned," live in austere isolation from the mainstream African American community.

- ○ Rates of teen pregnancy and single-parent households that are *triple* what we see in all other populations in the United States
- ○ High school dropout rates of nearly 50 percent
- ○ Incarceration rates between 30 and 50 percent
- ○ Poverty rates that are double and triple of all other population groups in the United States
- ○ Unemployment rates of nearly 50 percent
- • Middle-class African Americans continue to experience significant and demonstrateable discrimination in education, housing, employment, access to healthcare, and banking.
- • The recession has impacted *all* African American families more severely than other population groups.
- ○ Higher than average rates of child abuse and neglect
- ○ Higher than average rates of family violence, especially IPV
- ○ Higher rates of foreclosure and underwater mortgages
- ○ The depletion of wealth

So, what kinds of policies could the Obama administration have implemented that would have addressed the inequities facing African Americans and their families? First, as we noted in the previous chapter, Obama, though he had the opportunity to make two appointments to the US Supreme Court, did not appoint an African American. Why would this matter? As we have shown, the US Supreme Court has the ability to hear and rule on cases that arise out of institutionalized discrimination, specifically cases in education, employment, housing, mortgage lending, and incarceration. Though we would not expect changes overnight, we cannot ignore the role that key decisions, such as *Brown v. the Board* and cases related to the Civil Rights Act and Voting Rights Act, have played in moving toward a more level playing field. Though Clarence Thomas has a demonstrated record of turning back the clock on affirmative action and school integration in ways that put African American families at a disadvantage, all despite his personal experience with racism and poverty, it is critical to have judges who have either personal experience or the awareness of the issues that so severely threaten African American families. A more diverse court has the potential at least to return to a body that sees the potential to decide cases in such a way as to transform the very institutions where African Americans face the types of discrimination that produces inequalities in everyday life. Education and banking are two very real examples of this potential. For example, as we noted in our discussion of wealth, the choice by mainstream banks to begin engaging in payday loan practices further exacerbates the financial devastation plaguing poor and middle-class African American families. A court that would be willing to hear challenges to these practices and find them unconstitutional would almost immediately reduce some of the most serious problems facing low-income, middle-class, and even professional African Americans and their families.

No doubt the biggest criticism that Obama has received focuses on his inability to produce or create any measurable improvements in the economy. We would argue that this critique is an unreasonable one. Reviving the economy is more than a one-person job. Despite the belief that many of the Republicans campaigning for office seem to believe, we're not entirely convinced that it is a "job" any president is capable of doing through his office. What is troubling is that the persistence of the recession is devastating African American families in ways that may be permanently damaging. Of specific concern are the following:

- A deeply entrenched and persistent high unemployment rate
- A lack of any real improvement in jobs
- A lack of any real improvement in the housing market
- A lack of real regulation of the financial institutions, specifically banks and investments houses
- A lack of a policy or incentive to cap CEO compensation relative to average worker compensation
- A lack of a policy or incentive to increase minimum wage to a "living wage"
- An inability to modify the tax structure to shift more of the tax burden toward the super-wealthy

Taken together we share the concern that Anita Hill raises in her latest book *Reimagining Equality: Stories of Gender, Race and Finding a Home*. Because homeownership, like education, is one of the advantages or disadvantages passed across generations, the loss of one's home during the recession may lead to lower homeownership rates in future generations. It may take decades to reverse the trend and return to a time when most African American families own their own homes.

These areas of concern all point to one of the most perplexing issues facing America in general and African American families in particular: the growing wealth gap. The "occupy" movement that started in 2011 focuses our attention on this gap by talking about the 99 percent, a reference to the fact that the vast majority of the wealth in the United States is owned by the top 1 percent. *New York Times* Op-Ed writer Nicholas Kristoff argues that without a dramatic shift in course, the US landscape will move significantly to resemble the worst "banana republics" in the world; characterized by a small, but very powerful wealthy class, a huge population of poor, and a tiny middle class.

The wealth gap between white families and African American families has doubled since the beginning of the recession. In addition to the racialization of wealth, we are also troubled by the gap that contributes to the growing distance between the transcendents and all other African Americans as well as between the abandoned and all other African Americans. It is as if the most well off and the most marginalized stand as bookends to a community that no longer shares any common interest and therefore has no motivation for public outcry.

We reinforce what Robinson has pointed out, despite the racial ugliness of the persistence of Jim Crow during the post–World War II era, a time we would never want to return to, the relative income equality of this era meant that the average middle-class African American had a relatively higher standard of living than that same middle-class person has today. A robust economy, though it certainly cannot eliminate racial inequalities—the 1950s are an excellent illustration of that point, a time when African Americans continued to be subjected to severe racism, when they were denied access to college and universities, and they were forced to live in segregated neighborhoods—would, nevertheless, have a tremendous impact on many of the problems facing African American families today.

We conclude this book by returning to the point we opened the final chapter with: has the election of the first African American president—a barrier many thought they would never see overcome—had any impact on the lives of African American families? Secondly is a postracial society possible in the United States, and when might it arrive?

On the first point, we must acknowledge the psychological impact that the election of Obama has on African Americans, especially young people, and liberal whites as well. African American children can now see someone who looks like them sitting in the Oval Office and living in the White House. Many folks, African Americans and whites, feel emotionally buoyed by the fact that this barrier has now been overcome and perhaps there is reason to hope. Yet, on every measure we can identify, African American families are not better off since this historic election, and there is some evidence to suggest that they are worse off and that recovery of any significance is nowhere in sight.

To the second point, it would be far too depressing to believe that a postracial society could never be ushered in. Certainly, we cannot dismiss the importance of the first African American president in a society with such a toxic racial history. We believe that the evidence is clear: the election of the first African American president neither represents nor has it ushered in a postracial America.

Closing the book with a discussion of social class is not unintentional. As sociologists who study social stratification, one thing we can say with confidence is that any form of inequality—be it based on race, social class, gender, sexual orientation, or religion—tends to exacerbate *all forms* of social inequality. The reverse is true as well. It is not surprising that the greatest movement in racial civil rights occurred immediately after the ushering in of the strongest economic period in US history; equality begets equality.

Thus, we conclude by suggesting that the greatest chance we as a society have for improving the lives of African American families will be first and foremost to return this country to the strong economy that characterized the post–World War II period. A stronger economy and greater income and wealth equality, will immediately improve the lives of African American families, and if history holds, coupled with the strides in our racial culture that allowed for the election of the first African American president, would likely lead to improvements in the racial project as well.

No one is free when others are oppressed.

Epilogue

One of the challenges of writing any book like this one is making the tough decisions about what to leave in and what to exclude. We deliberately avoided the vitriolic debates that drowned out the serious, but critical, scholarship of the late 1970s in the work of sociologist William J. Wilson.

Any time authors write a book they receive input along the way, from reviewers, editors, and friends who commit the time to read a work in progress. This book underwent a similar process. During that process early readers raised a few questions about the topics we chose to include and those we did not discuss in depth. In case other readers have similar questions, we have decided to address them here.

First and foremost, as noted, the difficult task of deciding what to include and exclude is exacerbated by constraints on the length of the manuscript! The topic of African American families is broad and deep—much larger than can be addressed completely in this brief book. This makes the task of deciding what to include and what to exclude that much more difficult. Ultimately, the decision lies with the authors, and we stand by the decisions we made.

We share some of these questions that follow, in case other readers wonder about why we chose to discuss some topics in depth and leave others to be explored in different venues.

What do education, poverty, and most importantly incarceration have to do with black families?

Wow! For us this was an odd question. So, just in case it is lurking in the minds of other readers, here goes.

One of the universal challenges of family life, from the beginning of time all the way up until now and in every single culture, is how to feed, clothe, and shelter family members. In fact, family theorists consider these concerns so fundamental that they argue that the family structures that emerge in different times and places are a direct reaction to these specific needs. We offer a few examples that illustrate this point. During the height of the agricultural era, roughly 10,000 years ago until about 1800, polygamy was a very common family form. Why? Because the more wives a man had the more children he could father and the more children he could father the more labor he had to work his vast land. Additionally, because the agricultural era was also plagued by high rates of infant mortality and epidemics like the Black Plague that wiped out millions of people, this was also a way to ensure that enough children would survive to work the fields, tend the animals, and ultimately accumulate wealth that could be transferred down through the generations. In contrast, demographers know that one of the consequences of industrialization is the rapid decline in fertility. Families in industrial and postindustrial economies no longer need child labor, and their focus turns toward providing an ever-improving standard of living and ultimately, as characterized by the postindustrial American family, an education. Given these changing needs, families reduced the number of children they both desired and had to more efficiently meet the demands for food, housing, shelter, and increasingly an education.

African American families, like all families, battle every single day to meet these basic needs in their families and thus any book that *doesn't* include discussions on these issues, especially because of the racial disparities in education, poverty, and the ability to provide and pass on wealth to the next generation are so severe.

With regards to incarceration, one only needs to watch one or two episodes of the MSNBC show *Locked Up*, to understand the impact that incarceration has on families. Men who are locked up leave mothers, wives, girlfriends, sons, and daughters on the outside. The burdens that their incarcerations create for family life are tremendous. A potential wage earner removed from the labor force is unable to contribute to the family, even if his contributions were from the illegitimate economy, such as dealing drugs. The pressure that mothers and wives and girlfriends, but also children, feel to be in communication with the man during his period of incarceration is tremendous. Writing letters weekly, accepting collect phone calls weekly, and making the trek to the prison as often as possible can come to consume the family members and their resources. In addition, those family members feel enormous pressure to put money into the canteen accounts of their incarcerated loved ones so that he (or less often she) can purchase food and other "luxury" items that make the period of incarceration more tolerable.

Shockingly, nearly one-third of all African American men *between the ages of sixteen and thirty-five* will spend some time behind bars during their lives, with most being incarcerated during their most productive years and when they are engaged with their families. *Incarceration is a fact of life for many African American families.* To not address the impact of this experience on black families would be remiss. That said, incarceration is more or less invisible to those who aren't engaged with it or who don't study it. As a result, ours is one of the only books on the market that deals honestly with the impact that mass incarceration has on African American families. This makes us even more committed to including a full chapter on this burning issue. Lastly, we note that like so many other experiences, the racial disparities in incarceration are severe, thus making it that much more worthy of our attention and discussion.

Why aren't single fathers addressed in more depth?

One reader wondered why we did not pay more attention to the growing number of African American men who are raising their children alone. One of our colleagues, Roberta Cole, has written an outstanding book on African American single fathers called *The Best Kept Secret: Single Black Fathers*, and has edited another volume on the subject. Her work and the work of those scholars she includes in her book is valuable and allows us to move the discussion of black fathers forward. That said, the truth of the matter is that not only is the number of black men raising their children alone small (less than 10 percent), it is the other side of the equation that is far more disturbing: Black men who are not only not participating actively in raising their children but are less than responsible in procreation and meeting their child support obligations is a larger issue than male single-parenting. Not to overstate the point, but a growing number of black men have children with many different women (or baby mamas). And, lest the reader think this is simply an artifact of the celebrities who are featured every week in the news, from rapper Jay-Z to football players like Terrell Owens and Antonio Cromartie—who just added his tenth child, with eight different mothers, and has a *monthly* child support bill that is higher than the US median household income—this issue is a regular feature of "black" talk radio shows like the Tom Joyner Show, especially on Mother's Day. We chose not to include what would be a lengthy and mostly negative discussion in this book. We feel strongly that it is adequate to discuss, as we did, the impact of single-parent families on black children.

What about the Black Church?

Perhaps the most interesting, and we would argue problematic issues raised in a question, is our decision *not* to feature the Black Church in our book. Much like our decision not to highlight black single fathers, in particular, our decision is based on several important factors. First, as we will argue extensively in this book, the African American community in the twenty-first century is a very different black community than that of the 1940s, 1950s, and 1960s when the "Black Church" was in its heyday and at the center of the largely segregated African American community. We acknowledge that the Black Church once served a central function in the black community; it was not only a site of spirituality but also a physical place where African

Americans could legally gather—something they were denied under Jim Crow segregation—and it served as a training ground for black leadership. Most prominent African Americans, aside from athletes and celebrities, have long charted a path through the Black Church on their way to political and social prominence, including Martin Luther King Jr., Reverend Fred Shuttlesworth, Reverend Samuel Dewitt Proctor, Reverend Jesse Jackson, Reverend Wyatt Tee Walker, Reverend Al Sharpton, and so many, many others. Today, the African American community is no longer one community and therefore the Black Church no longer serves as a common meeting space for "the black community." Nor does it serve any longer as a route for black leaders to emerge. Consider some of the most visible black social commentators of the twenty-first century—Cornell West, Henry Louis "Skip" Gates, Melissa Harris-Perry, and Touré, even President Barack Obama. Not a one rose to serve as a spokesperson for "the" black community through the Black Church, even though many of these prominent blacks claim their faith is central to their calling. Rather, black leaders today are more likely to emerge from the intelligentsia—all have or continue to hold positions as faculty at some of the most prestigious universities.

Second, from our vantage point, the Black Church is plagued by all of the same problems that all churches are—sex abuse scandals, financial malfeasance, and domestic violence—and there seems no point in discussing these shortcomings here, primarily because we see them in all Christian, including Catholic, churches and thus it would be difficult to argue that these problems are unique to the Black Church.

Third, the Black Church, to the degree that it does exist as a monolithic institution, is on the "wrong" side of many pressing social issues facing Americans as we enter the final phases of the 2012 election cycle. Specifically, many, many leading black pastors (e.g., Rev. Emmett C. Burns Jr., Rising Sun Baptist Church in Baltimore; Rev. Wallace Charles Smith, Shiloh Baptist Church in Washington, D.C.; Bishop Harry Jackson Jr., senior pastor of Hope Christian Church in Baltimore, Maryland; and Nation of Islam leader Louis Farrakhan) have come out against marriage equality. However, survey data reveal quite clearly that when religion is controlled, nearly 60 percent of African Americans actually support some sort of marriage equality. Though it is easy to blame blacks for passing referendum after referendum that restricts marriage to one man and one woman it is obviously more complex than that. That said, the Black Church has come out strongly against both gay marriage and homosexuality in general. This is particularly disturbing given the fact that African American men and women have HIV rates that are higher than all other groups, and as we noted in our discussion on health, AIDs is one of the top ten leading causes of death among African Americans. By refusing to talk about AIDS because it might be tied to homosexuality is to do a terrible disservice to the African American community. Though an argument can be made that this is an important part of a discussion of family, for all of these reasons, and given space constraints, we stand by our decision not to include this discussion.

We believe that the emotional ties many African Americans feel toward the Black Church are primarily feelings of nostalgia for the Black Church as it existed during the civil rights movement and that any serious examination of the Black Church in the twenty-first century would reveal a very different institution and one that is very far removed from the churches packed with people planning bus boycotts and lunch counter sit-ins.

Again, in a brief book like this, it is impossible to completely address the complex picture of African American families. We thank the unsung heroes who gave us feedback in the review process, and we hope that this book will help readers begin to explore some of the important myths and realities facing black families today, as well as to work for positive change in the future.

Notes

INTRODUCTION

1. Tera W. Hunter. 2011. "Putting an Antebellum Myth to Rest." *New York Times*, August 1, 2011, www.nytimes.com/2011/08/02/opinion/putting-an-antebellum-myth-about-slave-families-to-rest.html?_r=1&nl=todaysheadlines&emc=thab1.

2. www.time.com/time/specials/packages/0,28757,2083745,00.html.

3. Ralph Ellison. 1995. *Invisible Man.* New York: Random House, 3.

4. Economist. 2004. "Meritocracy in America: Ever Higher Society, Ever Harder to Ascend." December 29, www.economist.com/node/3518560?story_id=3518560, Accessed July 3, 2011.

5. Jason DeParle. 2012. Harder for Americans to Rise from Lower Rungs. *New York Times*. January 4, www.nytimes.com/2012/01/05/us/harder-for-americans-to-rise-from-lower-rungs.html?pagewanted=all.

6. *Parents Involved in Community Schools v. Seattle School District No. 1*, 551 US 701 (2007) and *Grutter v. Bollinger*, 539 US 306 (2003).

7. We note that many scholars make this point as well. We chose to frame our discussion using Robinson's work because it is so accessible to the public audience.

8. Eugene Robinson. 2011. *Disintegration: The Splintering of Black America*. New York: Doubleday, 5.

CHAPTER 1

1. Information of both was taken from the official White House biographies, which can be accessed at: www.whitehouse.gov/administration.

2. Jefferson, Thomas. 1787. Notes on Virginia. In Merrill D. Peterson, *Writings of Thomas Jefferson*. New York: The Library of America, 1984, 264–66, 270.

3. We note that this need to accumulate land and other resources is the rationalization that has been used to explain patriarchal systems of inheritance: by limiting the pool of potential

people who can inherit to sons only, over time a family will split up the resources only half as often as if both sons and daughters were allowed to inherit. One hundred acres handed down to two sons, fifty acres each, rather than to all four children (twenty-five acres each) minimizes the dilution of resources.

4. Tara W. Hunter. 2011, August 1. "Putting an Antebellum Myth to Rest." *New York Times*, www.nytimes.com/2011/08/02/opinion/putting-an-antebellum-myth-about-slave-families-to-rest.html?_r=1&ref=familiesandfamilylife.

5. Jumping the Broom, www.african-weddings.com/jumping_the_broom.

6. Hunter. 2011. "Putting an Antebellum Myth to Rest."

7. Herbert Gutman. 1976. *The Black Family in Slavery and Freedom, 1750–1925*. New York: Vintage Books; Herbert Gutman. 1975. "Persistent Myths about the Afro-American Family." *The Journal of Interdisciplinary History* 6 (2), 181–210; Herbert Gutman. 1975. "The World Two Cliometricians Made: A Review Essay of F+E = T/C," *Journal of Negro History*, 60, 53–227.

8. Tara Hunter. 1997. *To Joy My Freedom: Southern Black Women's Lives and Labors after the Civil War*. Harvard University Press. 1997.

9. The single exception here is that single-father households are not more likely to be poor than their two-parent counterparts.

10. For a review of the struggles of welfare mothers to live by the rules of welfare, see Edin and Lein's *Making Ends Meet* (Russell Sage, NY, 1997) as they demonstrate that it is virtually impossible to live off welfare while adhering strictly to the requirements of no man in the household, no employment, and so on.

11. S. McLanahan. 1985. "Family Structure and the Reproduction of Poverty." *American Journal of Sociology* 90, 873–901; R. A. Moffitt. 1997. *The Effect of Welfare on Marriage and Fertility: What Do We Know and What Do We Need to Know?* (No. 1153-97). Madison, WI: Institute for Research on Poverty.

12. Nonresidential coparenting refers to the arrangement in which parents of a child do not live together yet they share parenting much like parents in two-parent households do.

13. Charles Murray. 2012. *Coming Apart: The State of White America, 1960–2010*. New York: Crown.

14. Arland Thorton, William G. Axinn, and Yu Xie. 2007. *Marriage and Cohabitation*. Chicago: University of Chicago Press.

15. Thorton, Axinn, Xie. 2007. *Marriage and Cohabitation*.

16. R. Kelly Raley. 2001. "Increasing Fertility in Cohabiting Unions: Evidence for the Second Demographic Transition in the United States?" *Demography* 38(1):59–66.

17. D. T. Lichter, Z. Qian, and L. M. Mellott. 2006, May. "Marriage or Dissolution? Union Transitions among Poor Cohabiting Women. *Demography* 43(2):223–40.

18. Carlson, Garfinkel, McLanahan, Mincy, and Primus, 2004."The Effects of Welfare and Child Support Policies on Union Formation." *Population Research and Policy Review* 25, 513–42.

19. Jeffrey S. Passel, Wendy Wang, and Paul Taylor. 2010, June 4. Pew Research Center Race Survey, Conducted October 28–November 30, 2009 (N=2884). "Marrying Out: One-in-Seven New U.S. Marriages Is Interracial or Interethnic." http://pewresearch.org/pubs/1616/american-marriage-interracial-interethnic.

20. http://publicpolicypolling.blogspot.com/2011/04/barbour-bryant-lead-in-mississippi.html.

CHAPTER 2

1. "Is Spanking a Black and White Issue?" *New York Times*, August 11, 2011. www.nytimes.com/roomfordebate/2011/08/14/is-spanking-a-black-and-white-issue/its-not-just-black-parents.

2. J. Goldman, M. K. Salus, D. Wolcott, and K. Y. Kennedy. 2003. *A Coordinated Response to Child Abuse and Neglect: The Foundation for Practice*. Washington, D.C.: Office of Child Abuse and Neglect, Department of Health and Human Services.

3. Children of Alcoholics Foundation. 1996. *Collaboration, Coordination and Cooperation: Helping Children Affected by Parental Addiction and Family Violence*. New York: Children of Alcoholics Foundation.

4. J. Goldman, M. K. Salus, D. Wolcott, and K. Y. Kennedy. 2003. *A Coordinated Response to Child Abuse and Neglect: The Foundation for Practice*. Washington, D.C.: Office of Child Abuse and Neglect, Department of Health and Human Services.

5. K. Edin and L. Lein. 1997. *Making Ends Meet: How Single Mothers Survive Welfare and Low-Wage Work*. New York: Russell Sage Foundation.

6. The entire report may be accessed at www.acf.hhs.gov/programs/opre/abuse_neglect/natl_incid/nis4_report_exec_summ_pdf_jan2010.pdf.

7. US Department of Health and Human Services Child Welfare Information Gateway: www.childwelfare.gov/pubs/usermanuals/foundation/foundatione.cfm no page number, accessed online, May 16, 2011 .

8. J. Goldman, M. K. Salus, D. Wolcott, and K. Y. Kennedy. 2003. *A Coordinated Response to Child Abuse and Neglect: The Foundation for Practice*. Washington, D.C.: Office of Child Abuse and Neglect, Department of Health and Human Services.

9. US Department of Health and Human Services Child Welfare Information Gateway: www.childwelfare.gov/pubs/usermanuals/foundation/foundatione.cfm; no page number, accessed online, May 16, 2011.

10. US Department of Health and Human Services Child Welfare Information Gateway: www.childwelfare.gov/pubs/usermanuals/foundation/foundatione.cfm; no page number, accessed online, May 16, 2011.

11. This is a distinctly different claim than that made by Newt Gingrich during the fall 2011 Republican primary season. Gingrich claimed that when children don't see adults working for pay they will have less interest in or commitment to going to work. Gingrich's comments had a more defeatist tone rather than recognizing, as Wilson's work does, that environmental factors can and do shape individuals' life chances and lived reality.

12. D. Cicchetti, M. Lynch, and J. T. Manly. 1997. US Department of Health and Human Services Child Welfare Information Gateway: www.childwelfare.gov/pubs/usermanuals/foundation/foundatione.cfm; no page number, accessed online, May 16, 2011.

13. M. Ehrensaft and P. Cohen. 2003. "Intergenerational Transmission of Partner Violence: A 20-Year Prospective Study." *Journal of Consulting and Clinical Psychology 7*, 741–753.

14. I. J. Chasnoff, H. J. Landress, and M. E. Barrett. 1990. "The Prevalence of Illicit-Drug or Alcohol Use during Pregnancy and Discrepancies in Mandatory Reporting in Pinellas County, Florida." *New England Journal of Medicine 322*, 1202–1206; D. R. Neuspiel. 1996. "Racism and Perinatal Addiction, Ethnicity and Disease." *New England Journal of Medicine 6*, 47–55.

15. L. M. Burton. 1990. Teenage Childbearing as an Alternative Life-Course Strategy in Multigeneration Black Families. *Human Nature 1*(2), 123–143.

CHAPTER 3

1. Kaiser Family Foundation Fact Sheet. 2005. www.kff.org/youthhivstds/upload/U-S -Teen-Sexual-Activity-Fact-Sheet.pdf.

2. Data come from Child Trends Bank, www.childtrendsdatabank.org/?q=node/120.

3. Guttmacher Institute, www.guttmacher.org.

4. Data come from Child Trends Bank, www.childtrendsdatabank.org/?q=node/120.

5. National Kids Count, http://datacenter.kidscount.org/data/acrossstates/Rankings .aspx?ind=3.

6. Guttmacher Institute, www.guttmacher.org/pubs/FB-ATSRH.html.

7. We note that despite the focus on African American girls having babies, Hispanic girls actually have the highest rate of teen childbearing, 78 out of 1000.

8. Data are from the Guttmacher Institute, www.guttmacher.org, and Child Trends Bank, www.childtrendsdatabank.org/?q=node/120.

9. P. Roper and G. Weeks. 1993. *Over Half of the Women on Public Assistance in Washington Reported Physical and Sexual Abuse as Adults.* Seattle: Washington State Institute for Public Policy.

10. Guttmacher Institute, www.guttmacher.org/pubs/FB-ATSRH.html.

CHAPTER 4

1. Shannan Catalano, Erica Smith, Howard Snyder, and Michael Rand. 2009. "Female Victims of Violence." US Department of Justice, Washington, D.C. Statistics collected and disseminated by the Bureau of Justice Statistics can be accessed online at http://bjs.ojp.usdoj.gov/.

2. Patricia Tjaden and Nancy Thoennes. 2000. *Full Report of the Prevalence, Incidence, and Consequences of Violence Against Women: Findings From the National Violence Against Women Survey.* Washington, D.C.: US Department of Justice.

3. Bureau of Justice Statistic, http://bjs.ojp.usdoj.gov/content/homicide/family.cfm.

4. Angela Browne. 1989. *When Battered Women Kill.* New York: Free Press.

5. Though African American women are more likely to be battered than white women, the highest rate of IPV is among Native American women.

6. We recommend two books to the interested reader: M. B. Pipher. 1994. *Reviving Ophelia: Saving the Selves of Adolescent Girls.* New York: Putnam Press; J. Raphael. 2004. *Listening to Olivia: Violence, Poverty & Prostitution.* Boston: Northeastern University Press.

CHAPTER 5

1. *Brown v. Board of Educ. of Topeka*, Supreme Court of the United States, 348 US 886; 1954 U.S. LEXIS 1467, Nov. 22, 1954; *Brown v. Board of Educ.*, No. 1, Supreme Court of the United States, 349 U.S. 294; 75 S. Ct. 753; 99 L. Ed. 1083; 1955.

2. For an excellent history of the desegregation process of schools, we recommend D. M. Douglas. 1995. *Reading, Writing, and Race: The Desegregation of the Charlotte Schools.* Chapel Hill: University of North Carolina Press.

3. J. C. Boger and G. Orfield. 2005. *School Resegregation: Must the South Turn Back?* Chapel Hill: University of North Carolina Press.

4. J. P. Greene, M. A. Winters, and Manhattan Institute for Policy Research. Center for Civic Innovation. 2005. *Public High School Graduation and College-Readiness Rates, 1991–2002.* New York: Center for Civic Innovation at the Manhattan Institute.

5. *Journal of Blacks in Higher Education*, Weekly Bulletin, August 18, 2011, www.jbhe .com/latest/index081811.html?utm_source=The+Journal+of+Blacks+in+Higher+Education &utm_campaign=e797316f55-JBHE_Weekly_Bulletin_for_4_7_114_7_2011&utm_ medium=email#racialgap.

6. "The Huge Racial Gap in College Graduation Rates." 2012. *The Journal of Blacks in Higher Education*, April 27, 2012. www.jbhe.com/2012/04/the-huge-racial-gap-in-college -graduation-rates/

7. Georgetown University Center on Education and the Workforce, http://cew.georgetown .edu/whatsitworth/.

CHAPTER 6

1. Roger Bannister's unfortunate remarks were picked up on the Associated Press and reprinted widely. See *Tacoma New Tribune*, September 14, 1995.

2. "Test Drive" by James Healy. September 16, 2011. Accessed online August 12, 2012. www.usatoday.com/money/autos/reviews/healey/story/2011-09-15/beetle-test-drive -healey/50419802/1.

3. Henry Louis Gates. 1991. "Delusions of Grandeur: Young Blacks Must Be Taught That Sports Are Not the Only Avenue of Opportunity." *Sports Illustrated*, August 19, 78.

4. The best source for this data are the annual graduation rate studies by Richard Lapchick at the DeVos School of Management at the University of Central Florida.

5. Lapchick, R. E. 2006. "Race in college sport." In R. E. Lapchick (Ed.) *New Game Plan for College Sport*. New York: Praeger, American Council on Education, 90–110.

6. Henry Louis Gates, 2004, August 1. "Breaking the Silence." *New York Times*.

7. Barkley is quoted in the *Sports Illustrated* story by Jack McCallum, March 11, 2002, entitled "Citizen Barkley" (see page 32).

8. *SportsWorld* is a term coined by Earl Smith in his award-winning book *Race, Sport and the American Dream* (Durham, NC: Carolina Academic Press, 2007/2009). It was developed to describe "sports" as a social, political, and economic institution that has power and implications far beyond the individuals who participate as coaches and athletes and draws attention to the institutions such as the NCAA and professional governing bodies that move sports from leisure to a multibillion-dollar business.

CHAPTER 7

1. Robert Pear. 2011, October 25. "Top Earners Doubled Share of Nation's Income, Study Finds," *New York Times*, www.nytimes.com/2011/10/26/us/politics/top-earners-doubled- share-of-nations-income-cbo-says.html?hpw.

2. Robert Rector and Rachel Sheffield. 2011, July 19. *Air Conditioning, Cable TV, and an Xbox: What Is Poverty in the United States Today?* The Heritage Foundation, www.heritage.org/ research/reports/2011/07/what-is-poverty.

3. Eugene Robinson. 2010. *Dis-Integration: The Splintering of Black America*. New York: Doubleday.

4. Eugene Robinson. 2010. *Dis-Integration: The Splintering of Black America*. New York: Doubleday, 195.

5. Eugene Robinson. 2010. *Dis-Integration: The Splintering of Black America*. New York: Doubleday, 195.

6. See, for example, Marc Bendick Jr., Charles W. Jackson, and Victor A. Reinoso. 1994. "Measuring Employment Discrimination through Controlled Experiments." *The Review of Black Political Economy* 23(1):25–48.

7. www.nytimes.com/2009/12/06/weekinreview/06Luo.html.

8. Paul Taylor, Richard Fry, and Rakesh Kochhar. 2011, July 26. "Wealth Gaps Rise to Record Highs between Whites, Blacks, Hispanics Twenty-to-One," Pew Research Center, www.pewsocialtrends.org/2011/07/26/wealth-gaps-rise-to-record-highs-between-whites-blacks-hispanics/.

9. K. Wright. 2006, May 24. "Upward Mortality." *Mother Jones*.

10. J. R. Feagin. 1999. Excluding Blacks and Others from Housing: The Foundation of White Racism. *Cityscape: A Journal of Policy Development and Research* 4(3):70–91.

11. *Unfair Lending: The Effect of Race and Ethnicity on the Price of Subprime Lending*, 2006.

12. A. Carpusor and W. E. Loges. 2006. Rental Discrimination and Ethnicity in Names. *Journal of Applied Social Psychology* 36(4):934–952.

13. J. Cass. 2006. "Notable Mardi Gras Absences Reflect Loss of Black Middle Class." *Washington Post*. p. A01.

CHAPTER 8

1. The Bureau of Justice Statistics provides the most current data on incarceration, www.ojp.usdoj.gov/bjs/correct.htm#findings.

2. Marc Mauer. 2012. "Testimony of Marc Mauer Executive Director of the Sentencing Project. Federal Sentencing Options after Booker." United States Sentencing Commission on February 16; M. R. Durose and Patrick A. Langan. 2001. *State Court Sentencing of Convicted Felons, 1998 Statistical Tables*. Washington, D.C.: US Department of Justice.

3. M. Marit Rehavi and Sonja B. Starr. 2012, January 15. "Racial Disparity in Federal Criminal Charging and its Sentencing Consequences," University of Michigan Law and Economics Working Paper; See also C. C. Spohn. 2000. *Thirty Years of Sentencing Reform: The Quest for a Racially Neutral Sentencing Process*. Washington, D.C.: National Institute of Justice.

4. Patrick Bayer, Shamena Anwar, and Rand Hjalmarson. 2012. "The Impact of Jury Race in Criminal Trials." *The Quarterly Journal of Economics*, 1–39, http://qje.oxfordjournals.org/content/early/2012/04/15/qje.qjs014.full.

5. www.whitehousedrugpolicy.gov/publications/factsht/druguse/

6. Paul Bracchi. 2010. The curse of Diff'rent Strokes. Mail Online. January 27, 2010. www.dailymail.co.uk/tvshowbiz/article-1246308/The-curse-Diffrent-Stokes-Frail-Gary-Coleman-leaves-jail-wheelchair-child-star-arrested-again.html#ixzz23Ard60E3

7. *New York Times* Op-Ed columnist Brent Staples covers this important topic on April 29, 2012, on page SR10 of the New York edition with the headline: "The Human Cost of 'Zero Tolerance.'"

8. Vincent Mallozzi. 2005, May 20. "On the Outside, Busing In." *New York Times*, www.nytimes.com/2005/05/20/nyregion/20bus.html?pagewanted=all.

9. C. Uggen and J. Manza. 2002. "Democratic Contraction? Political Consequences of Felon Disenfranchisement in the United States." *American Sociological Review* 67(6), 777–803.

10. Heather Thompson. 2010, December. "Why Mass Incarceration Matters: Rethinking Crisis, Decline, and Transformation in Postwar American History." *The Journal of American History*, 703–734.

11. Ralph Richard Banks. 2011. *Is Marriage for White People? How the African American Marriage Decline Affects Everyone*. New York: Dutton; William J. Wilson. 1987. *The Truly Disadvantaged: The City, the Underclass, and Public Policy*. Chicago: University of Chicago Press.

CHAPTER 9

1. National Center for Health Statistics. *Health, United States, 2005 with Chartbook on Trends in the Health of Americans*. Hyattsville, Md.: U.S. Dept. of Health and Human Services, Centers for Disease Control and Prevention, 2005.

2. The interested reader can read the entire paper: Angela Hattery and Earl Smith. 2007. "Social Stratification in the New/Old South: The Influences of Racial Segregation on Social Class in the Deep South." *Journal of Poverty Research 11*, 55–81.

3. For a podcast dealing directly with food deserts in rural Mississippi see: www.youtube.com/user/msussrc#p/a/u/0/i5ZnNMU72Sk.

CHAPTER 10

1. Derrick Bell. 2009. "On Celebrating an Election as Racial Progress." *American Bar Association Journal of Human Rights*, 36.

2. www.cbsnews.com/8301-503544_162-20103688-503544.html.

3. For an in-depth analysis of race and politics, including elected and appointed positions, we recommend Richard L. Zweigenhaft and G. William Domhoff. 2006. *Diversity in the Power Elite: How It Happened, Why It Matters*. Lanham, Md.: Rowman & Littlefield.

4. Anita Hill. 2011. *Reimagining Equality: Stories of Gender, Race and Finding Home*. Boston: Beacon Press.

5. www.chicagoreporter.com/news/2007/11/lenders-maintain-racial-mortgage-gap.

6. www.responsiblelending.org/mortgage-lending/research-analysis/foreclosures-by-race-and-ethnicity.html.

7. Anita Hill. 2011. *Reimagining Equality: Stories of Gender, Race and Finding Home*. Boston: Beacon Press, 116–117.

8. Zachary Goldfarb. 2011. "Obama's Efforts to Aid Homeowners, Boost Housing Market Fall Far Short of Goals." WashingtonPost.com, www.washingtonpost.com/business/economy/obamas-efforts-to-aid-homeowners-boost-housing-market-fall-far-short-of-goals/2011/09/22/gIQAoJdeAM_print.html; Accessed October 24, 2011.

CHAPTER 11

1. www.civilrightsdefence.org.nz/event/jfkaddress.html; accessed October 25, 2011.

2. Sabrina Tavernise. 2012, May 3. "4 Years Later, Race Is Still Issue for Some Voters." *New York Times*, www.nytimes.com/2012/05/04/us/politics/4-years-later-race-is-still-issue-for-some-voters.html?_r=1&nl=todaysheadlines&emc=edit_th_20120504&pagewanted=all.

Recommended Readings and Films

INTRODUCTION

Robinson, Eugene. 2011. *Disintegration: The Splintering of Black America.* New York: Doubleday.

Willie, Charles Vert, and Richard J. Reddick. 2003. *A New Look at Black Families* Walnut Creek, Calif.: Altamira Press.

Zuberi, Tukufu, and Eduardo Bonilla-Silva. 2008. *White Methods: Racism and Methodology.* Lanham, Md.: Rowman & Littlefield.

CHAPTER 1: MARRIAGE AND DIVORCE

Smith, Earl, and Angela J. Hattery. 2008. *Interracial Intimacies: An Examination of Powerful Men and Their Relationships across the Color Line.* Durham, NC: Carolina Academic Press.

Smith, Earl, and Angela J. Hattery, eds. 2012. *Interracial Relationships in the 21st Century*, 2nd ed. Durham, NC: Carolina Academic Press.

Williams, Brian, Stacey C. Sawyer, and Carl M. Wahlstrom. 2008. *Marriages, Families, and Intimate Relationships.* Boston: Allyn & Bacon.

Guess Who. Studio: Sony Pictures Home Entertainment. DVD release date: August 2, 2005. Run time: 105 minutes.

CHAPTER 2: CHILDREARING PRACTICES

Burton, Linda, Ronald P. Angel, Lindsay Chase-Lansdale, Andrew Cherlin, and Robert Moffitt. 2009. *Welfare, Children, and Families: A Three-City Study.* ICPSR04701-v7. Ann Arbor, MI: Inter-university Consortium for Political and Social Research [distributor], 2009-02-10. doi:10.3886/ICPSR04701.v7

Lareau, Annette. 2011. *Unequal Childhoods: Class, Race, and Family Life*. Berkeley: University of California Press.

CHAPTER 3: TRANSITION TO ADULTHOOD

Coles, Roberta. 2010. *The Best Kept Secret: Single Black Fathers*. Lanham, Md.: Rowman & Littlefield.
Coles, Roberta, and Charles Green, eds. 2009. *The Myth of the Missing Black Father*. New York: Columbia University Press.
Precious. Studio: Lionsgate. Release year: 2009. Run time: 1 hour 50 minutes.
Juno. Studio: 20th Century Fox. DVD release date: April 15, 2008. Run time: 96 minutes.

CHAPTER 4: INTIMATE PARTNER VIOLENCE

Brush, Lisa. 2011. *Poverty, Battered Women, Work, and U.S. Public Policy*. Oxford, UK: Oxford University Press.
Hattery, Angela J. 2008. *Intimate Partner Violence*. Lanham, Md.: Rowman & Littlefield.

CHAPTER 5: EDUCATION

Kozol, Jonathan. 1992. *Savage Inequalities*. New York: HarperPerennial.
———. 2000. *Ordinary Resurrections*. New York: HarperPerennial.
Suskind, Ronald. 1998. *A Hope in the Unseen*. New York: Doubleday.
HBO Documentary: *LaLee's Kin: The Legacy of Cotton*. Directed by Deborah Dickson, Susan Frömke, and Albert Maysles. HBO, 2001.

CHAPTER 6: ATHLETICS

Clotfelter, Charles. 2011. *Big-Time Sports in American Universities*. Cambridge, UK: Cambridge University Press.
Smith, Earl. 2009. *Race, Sport and the American Dream*. Durham, NC: Carolina Academic Press.

CHAPTER 7: POVERTY AND WEALTH

Blow, Charles. 2011, December 16. "Inconvenient Income Inequality." *New York Times* www.nytimes.com/2011/12/17/opinion/blow-inconvenient-income-inequality.html?nl=todays headlines&emc=tha212.
Hill, Anita. 2011. *Reimagining Equality: Stories of Gender, Race and Finding Home*. Boston: Beacon Press.

Murray, Charles. 2012. *Coming Apart: The State of White America.* New York: Crown Forum Press.
HBO documentary: *LaLee's Kin: The Legacy of Cotton.* Directed by Deborah Dickson, Susan Frömke, and Albert Maysles. HBO, 2001.

CHAPTER 8: INCARCERATION

Armstrong, Ken, and Maurice Possley. 1999, January 10. "Trial and Error; How Prosecutors Sacrifice Justice to Win; The Verdict: Dishonor." *Chicago Tribune.*
Hattery, Angela J., and Earl Smith. 2010. *Prisoner Reentry and Social Capital: The Long Road to Reintegration.* Lanham, Md.: Lexington Books.
Mauer, Marc, and Kate Epstein. 2012. *To Build a Better Criminal Justice System.* Washington, D.C. The Sentencing Project, www.sentencingproject.org.
Thompson-Cannino, Jennifer, Ronald Cotton, and Erin Torneo. 2009. *Picking Cotton: Our Memoir of Injustice and Redemption.* New York: St. Martin's Press.
HBO documentary: *The Trials of Darryl Hunt.* Directed by Annie Sundberg and Ricki Stern, Break-Thru Films, 2006.

CHAPTER 9: HEALTH, NUTRITION, AND CHRONIC DISEASES

Smith, Earl, and Angela Hattery. 2012. "Health, Nutrition, Access to Healthy Food and Well-being among African Americans." pp. 47–59 in A. Lemelle, ed., *Handbook of African American Health: Social and Behavioral Interventions.* New York: Springer Publications.
Collins, Catherine Fisher. 2006. *African American Women's Health and Social Issues.* Westport, CT: Greenwood Press.

CHAPTER 10: POLITICS

Gillespie, Andra. 2009. *Whose Black Politics?: Cases in Post-Racial Black Leadership.* New York: Routledge.
Zweigenhaft, Richie, and G. William Domhoff. 2006. *Diversity in the Power Elite: How It Happened, Why It Matters.* Lanham, Md.: Rowman & Littlefield.

CHAPTER 11: RECOMMENDATIONS AND CONCLUSION

Charles W. Mills. 1999. *The Racial Contract.* Ithaca, NY: Cornell University Press.
Griffin, John Howard. 1961. *Black Like Me.* New York: Houghton Mifflin.
Stockett, Kathryn. 2009. *The Help.* New York: Berkley Books.

Index

About the Authors

Angela J. Hattery (BA Carleton College, Ph.D. University of Wisconsin–Madison) is a sociologist and serves as the associate director of the Women and Gender Studies Program at George Mason University. Her research focuses on social stratification, gender, family, and race. She is the author of numerous articles, book chapters, and books, including *The Social Dynamics of Family Violence* (2012), *Prisoner Reentry and Social Capital* (2010), *Interracial Intimacies* (2009), *Interracial Relationships* (2009), *Intimate Partner Violence* (2008), *African American Families* (2007), and *Women, Work, and Family* (2001).

Earl Smith, Ph.D., is professor of sociology and the Rubin Distinguished Professor of American Ethnic Studies at Wake Forest University. He is the former director of the Wake Forest University American Ethnic Studies Program and the former chairperson of the Department of Sociology, Wake Forest University, 1997–2005. Prior to his appointment at Wake Forest University, he was the dean of Division of Social Science at Pacific Lutheran University (PLU) in Tacoma, Washington. He also served as chairperson of the Department of Sociology at PLU. He is the author of numerous articles, book chapters, and books, including *The Social Dynamics of Family Violence* (2012), *Prisoner Reentry and Social Capital* (2010), *Sport and Social Theory* (2010), *Race, Sport and the American Dream* (2007/2009), *Interracial Intimacies* (2009), *Interracial Relationships* (2009), and *African American Families* (2007).